Civic Engagement and Social Media

Civic Engagement and Social Media

Political Participation Beyond Protest

Edited by

Julie Uldam and Anne Vestergaard
Copenhagen Business School, Denmark

palgrave
macmillan

First published 2015 by
PALGRAVE MACMILLAN

Palgrave Macmillan in the UK is an imprint of Macmillan Publishers Limited,
registered in England, company number 785998, of Houndmills, Basingstoke,
Hampshire RG21 6XS.

Palgrave Macmillan in the US is a division of St Martin's Press LLC,
175 Fifth Avenue, New York, NY 10010.

Palgrave Macmillan is the global academic imprint of the above companies
and has companies and representatives throughout the world.

Palgrave® and Macmillan® are registered trademarks in the United States,
the United Kingdom, Europe and other countries.

ISBN 978–1–137–43415–9

This book is printed on paper suitable for recycling and made from fully
managed and sustained forest sources. Logging, pulping and manufacturing
processes are expected to conform to the environmental regulations of the
country of origin.

A catalogue record for this book is available from the British Library.

A catalog record for this book is available from the Library of Congress.

Typeset by MPS Limited, Chennai, India.

Contents

List of Figures and Tables

Figures

Tables

Foreword

Much controversy swirls around social media as mechanisms for civic engagement. Some critics dismiss mediated participation as 'clicktivism' or 'slacktivism'. Such attitudes are balanced at the opposite extreme by overselling the importance of digital media in politics by casually talking about Twitter or Facebook revolutions. Neither extreme helps us understand the roles of media in civic processes, as they both miss the core challenges of developing good questions, concepts, and theories. This book is an important corrective. The editors and authors of *Civic Engagement and Social Media* advance consistent themes and questions across chapters while offering a rich set of topics and cases to challenge our thinking.

The first theme that shines through many chapters is that both civic engagement and the role of media need to be grounded in changing social structures, arenas of power, and repertoires of action. It is clear that the forms, arenas, and mechanisms of engagement have expanded beyond common textbook definitions that lag behind changes in both politics and communication. For example, popular access to power and democratic representation in many societies has been disrupted as political institutions have been corrupted by business pressures and neoliberal political regimes. As noted by various authors in this book, a number of interesting forms of civic engagement have flowed from these disruptions, including direct citizen engagement with business corporations and entire industrial sectors that have evaded more conventional accountability mechanisms for corporate social responsibility (CSR) established in earlier political eras. At the same time, the capacity of citizens to organize with social media has enabled large publics to be heard and seen in public spaces around the world, including many authoritarian regimes.

In analysing these developments, the authors in this book raise a number of key questions, including whether the highly visible popular uprisings of recent years are limited by the lack of credible institutional mechanisms for directly engaging with decision-making processes. Another important question raised in various ways in this book is whether reliance on social media for engagement diminishes the organizational and ideological foundations that have typically defined protest movements and interest-advocacy in past eras. Several of the authors, beginning with the introductory chapter by Uldam and Vestergaard, suggest that these important changes on the political scene mean that much contemporary civic engagement is 'informal', by contrast with more formal engagement with sites and processes of institutional power. This is an important topic to which I will return in my conclusion. First, however, I would like to note a number of very interesting contributions that recommend this volume to scholars and students interested in this lively and rapidly changing field of study.

Among the strengths of the entire book is the rich contextualization of participation and media. Many academic fields tend to reify the subjects of study by fragmenting complex realities into concepts, variables, and measures that take on lives of their own, often without returning to ground the resulting analyses in social and political contexts. In the analyses here, actors and processes are respected as complex and holistic entities, enabling concepts and frameworks to illuminate key problems and perform the necessary work of simplification and generalization. This rich contextualization brings a focus to many under-theorized and taken-for-granted aspects of the contemporary political scene, including: the nature of civic engagement in different settings, the limits of social media networks in focussing action, the problematic aspects of commercial media platforms, and the ever-present problem of surveillance by corporations who own personal data and governments that can compel access to commercial data and develop invasive means of monitoring public communication.

I am also struck by the ways in which several of the authors push an idea that I have tried to develop in my own work: the paradigm shift in media research from thinking about communication as sending and receiving messages to understanding that social media can also act as organizational processes by providing (more or less) coherent allocation of resources, creating divisions of labour, curating and retrieving content, and responding to events and changing ecological conditions. For example, Castelló and Barberá offer a very useful framework for understanding the organizational levels of the Spanish M15 movement, along with many similarly decentred crowds. Inventive variations on these ideas of communication as organization appear in several chapters, including Anne Kaun's rich look at how the 'Occupy' meme became a 'travelling narrative' around which very different occupations became organized, and Eleftheria Lekakis' interesting look at how Greek consumers provoked novel forms of civic engagement during a media campaign against a large supermarket chain. In these and other analyses in this volume, social media become important to the story of engagement, but in richly contextualized ways that remind us that both media and engagement are embedded in different political and social experiences. The balance between the particular and the general in these studies is impressive.

Civic activism has always produced tension between citizens who promote new and challenging demands and the responses of official institutions that typically lag behind the arc of change. In many cases, official responses are not simply slow; they may be repressive. Surveillance and policing have haunted most significant movements. However, the introduction of social media has produced new forms of surveillance that shrink the bounds of privacy and challenge the very definition of democracy. The problems of surveillance and policing associated with social media are addressed by several of the authors in this volume. A compounding issue here is that progressive activists may be particularly vulnerable to policing due to their frequently shared values of transparency and inclusiveness embodied in many social media platforms. As state and business interests have become increasingly aligned and antagonistic to popular demands for putting people first, they readily yield to temptations to spy on citizens and use the information to suppress more robust forms of engagement. Indeed, the ease of assembling large, real-time databases and using them to identify particular instigators of action becomes a direct threat to the promise of responsive democratic institutions. However, the collusion between state and media businesses is also strained by the threat of consumer resistance that can impact on corporate relations with consumers, on whose trust and commercial support those corporations depend. This new social media triangle of consumers, media corporations, and governments represents an important field of civil society relations in the digital age. For example, after the revelations by Edward Snowden about the extent of collusion between media and communication corporations and the US government's National Security Agency spying on citizens around the world, both privacy groups and broad public outcry raised questions about whose interests companies should support. Some of these issues played out in legislative and judicial institutions, but other and possibly more important arenas involved direct consumer relations with giant media companies and Internet service providers. Consumer engagement prompted several media giants such as Google and Apple to introduce encryption into customer communication, setting off a new round of government pressures on the companies. These engagement cycles reveal complex and interesting political dynamics in which initiatives from citizens can result in corporate engagement processes that go beyond CSR and raise questions about the line between formal and informal engagement that may be drawn too sharply at times in this book.

However, it seems clear that the broad field of CSR does raise many questions about the nature of civic engagement and the type of politics involved. As one would expect from a project led by two scholars from the innovative Department of Intercultural Communication and Management at the Copenhagen Business School, this book takes a fresh look at CSR. It is clear that all of the authors who address CSR here understand the increasing importance of civic engagement with targets beyond government, such as businesses and trade organizations. These political arenas are fluid and challenging for activists and observers alike, as they cross national boundaries and seldom offer straightforward accountability mechanisms for monitoring and measuring political gains. These problems make the areas of CSR and broader corporate civic engagement both rich and interesting aspects of contemporary political life. De Bakker offers a very useful framework for thinking about how to assess the impact of CSR actions that are only conducted online, compared to more familiar categories of physical engagement such as boycotts or other protests that use social media to amplify their impact. Among other things, this framework reminds us that in a world increasingly shaped by digital communication, big data, surveillance, and software, many of the most important political arenas are, in fact, online. Moreover, online behaviour need not be considered lightweight compared to physical protest. For example, hacktivism has been used to shut down nuclear production facilities, create large-scale security breaches in banking and other personal databases, and release alarming information about state surveillance. These kinds of activities will surely become more the political norm as the digital age continues to define so many aspects of public and private life. Indeed de Bakker shows how both online and physical CSR activism are more importantly understood as containing splits between reformists and more radical activists who disagree on both tactics and goals in targeting corporations and holding them accountable.

Even when activists appear to be making progress with engaging targets of action, it is not clear how to evaluate and certify the gains. Uldam notes that CSR is a very slippery political field, with few of the mechanisms for accountability that have defined more conventional democratic politics. Most of the authors agree that mediated engagement must be understood as entailing more than simple protest and resistance repertoires, as the set of engagement processes now rivals more conventional or formal participation in its multitude of forms and possible outcomes. Lefkakis, for example, shows how pressures from Greek citizens displaced by severe economic collapse and government limitations moved directly to businesses such as large supermarket chains, creating something of an ongoing interaction between business and citizen consumers, and resulting in what she describes as civic engagement by business.

Every chapter raises interesting questions about the who, what, and how of engagement in these civic fields that often do not resemble the politics, practices, and processes of earlier 'textbook' citizenship aimed at formally engaging institutions within national boundaries. In the process, the book raises profound questions about the nature of politics and civic life in an era that many activists and some scholars are beginning to think of as post-democratic. The tools of engagement are now carried by citizens in the form of phones and computers, along with the proliferating software platforms that are often built for commercial rather than civic purposes. Yet, the types of engagement enabled by these networked citizens often seem 'informal' in the sense of lacking sustained engagement with institutional mechanisms that offer clear accountability and standards against which to measure the attainment of political goals. Corporations may claim to be more responsive to the demands of publics concerned about a host of political issues, but activists seldom have the access or the resources to fully monitor levels of compliance.

My sense is that this distinction between informal and formal engagement is a good one in some respects but not in others, particularly when it implies that activists may have more formal means of engagement that they are not pursuing. Indeed, many participants in corporate campaigns and protests against various economic and political injustices are raising questions about the viability of formal engagement itself. As states are captured by business and financial interests, the resulting limits on formal engagement are structural, not tactical. Real Democracy Now, the slogan of M15, comes to mind here. All of this cautions against thinking that effective formal engagement is available if only citizens would drop their phones and take up good, old-fashioned political organizing. Most civic action based on stronger and more ideologically focussed action has triggered higher levels of surveillance and more invasive policing. There are exceptions of course, as many issues remain open to formal engagement, but they tend to be social and moral concerns such as immigrant rights, gay marriage, and, in some cases, modest shifts towards greener economies. However, despite the important shifts in discourse brought about by citizens brave enough to occupy public spaces from London to Cairo to Beijing, the core problems of economic inequality and the associated imbalances of political power and representation do not yield easily to formal engagement.

In the past, such limits to formal engagement have produced reform movements and revolutions. Such things continue to occur of course, but the restructuring of civil societies as a result of neoliberal policies that have swept the globe undermines the traditional foundations for such action in many societies. Perhaps what some authors in this book term informal engagement is the new norm in societies rocked by crises of institutional legitimacy. Perhaps the informal processes described in these interesting case studies are the mechanisms for negotiating new civic orders in a changing world.

W. Lance Bennett
University of Washington, Seattle

Notes on Contributors

Jess Baines is a historical and cultural studies lecturer in the School of Design, London College of Communication. Her doctoral research at the London School of Economics and Political Science investigates the contemporary history of radical and feminist printing organizations in Britain. Previous writing on the subject has been published in *Communicative Approaches to Politics & Ethics in Europe* (Carpentier et al., 2009) and *Cultural Policy, Criticism & Management Research Journal*. She has advised V&A and ICA on exhibitions of protest posters and both organized and contributed to events on the radical histories of creative production.

David Barberá is Associate Professor in the Polytechnic University of Valencia (Spain). Dr Barberá earned his PhD in Innovation Projects from the Polytechnic University of Valencia. His academic research uses both quantitative and qualitative approaches for inquiry in several innovation domains, as innovation policy, medical innovation, or social innovation. His research has been published in high impact journals such as *Research Policy, Technology Forecasting and Social Change*, and the *Journal of Economic Geography*. He has been a visiting researcher at UC Berkeley, Stanford University, Copenhagen Business School, and Universidad Carlos III de Madrid. In the organizational realm, Dr Barberá's interests are centred on institutional entrepreneurship in artistic and social movement fields.

Bart Cammaerts is Associate Professor and Director of the PhD programme in the Department of Media and Communications at the London School of Economics and Political Science (LSE). He is the former chair of the Communication and Democracy Section of European Communication Research and Education Association (ECREA) and vice-chair of the Communication Policy and Technology section of IAMCR. His most recent books include *Mediation and Protest Movements* (edited with Alice Matoni and Patrick McCurdy, 2013) and *Media Agoras: Democracy, Diversity and Communication* (edited with Iñaki Garcia-Blanco and Sofie Van Bauwel, 2009).

Itziar Castelló is Assistant Professor of Management in the Business Department at Carlos III University of Madrid and Lecturer at the Copenhagen Business School. She holds a PhD in Management and an Executive MBA from ESADE Business School, Spain and an MSc in Economics from the College of Europe, Belgium. She has been a visiting scholar at the Haas School of Business (UC Berkeley), Bocconi University, the Cass Business School, and Stanford University. She has published in international journals such as *Research Policy, Business & Society*, the *Journal of Business Ethics*, and *Corporate Governance*. Her research interests lie in the areas of corporate social responsibility, engagement in social media, and social innovation.

Frank G.A. de Bakker is an associate professor at the Department of Organization Sciences, VU University Amsterdam, the Netherlands. His current research focusses on the intersection of institutional theory, stakeholder management and social movement theory, specifically concerning interactions between NGOs and firms: How (networks of) NGOs try to impact firms and norms on issues of corporate social responsibility is a central question in his work, increasingly focussing on the role of online media. His work has appeared in the *Academy of Management Review*, the *Journal of Management Studies, Business and Society*, the *Journal of Business Ethics, Organization Studies*, and several other journals.

Emil Husted is a PhD Fellow at the Department of Organization, Copenhagen Business School. His core research interest centers on the notion of 'political participation' in radical political movements, and how to organize and manage this kind of extra-institutional activity without compromising its democratic legitimacy. Specifically, he explores political movements, such as The Alternative in Denmark and Podemos in Spain, and their efforts to institutionalize radical politics through the parliament. Emil is furthermore Vice Chair of the *Danish Association of Media Researchers* and editorial board member of the peer-reviewed journal, *Politik*.

Anne Kaun is a visiting post-doc researcher at the Annenberg School for Communication, University of Pennsylvania and senior lecturer at Södertörn University. Her current research is concerned with the relationship between crisis and social critique, investigating historical forms of media participation that emerged in the context of the current and previous economic crises. She has published in, among others, *New Media and Society, Participations*, the *European Journal of Cultural Studies*, and *Communications*. Anne is board member of ECREA and vice-chair of ECREA's Communication and Democracy Section.

Eleftheria J. Lekakis is Lecturer in Global Communication at the School of Media, Film and Music at the University of Sussex. Prior to this, she was a research fellow at the Centre for the Study of Global Media and Democracy at Goldsmiths College, University of London and Visiting Scholar at the Annenberg School for Communication, University of Pennsylvania. She holds degrees in Political Science (University of Crete) and Media and Communications (London School of Economics, Goldsmiths College). Her research interests include consumer cultures and politics, promotional cultures, economic cultures of austerity, and crisis communication.

W. Lance Bennett is Professor of Political Science and Ruddick C. Lawrence Professor of Communication at the University of Washington, Seattle, USA, where he directs the Center for Communication and Civic Engagement (www.engagedcitizen.org). The focus of his work is on how communication processes affect citizen engagement with politics. His publications include *Civic Life Online: Learning How Digital Media Can Engage Youth* (M.I.T.), and *The Logic of Connective Action: Digital Media and the Personalization of Contentious Politics* (with Alexandra Segerberg, 2013). He has received the Ithiel de Sola Pool and Murray Edelman career awards from the American Political Science Association, and the National Communication Association has recognized him as a Distinguished Scholar for lifetime achievement in the study of human communication.

Julie Uldam is an assistant professor at Copenhagen Business School. She conducted her postdoctoral research in a collaboration between the London School of Economics (LSE) and the Free University of Brussels. Her research explores the relationship between online media and civic engagement from three avenues of enquiry: (1) challenges to political participation, (2) corporate surveillance of social movements, and (3) interactions and collaborations between civil society, government, and business. Julie's work has been published in peer-reviewed journals, including *New Media & Society*, the *International Journal of Communication*, *Policy & Internet*, *Sociology Compass*, and the *International Journal of Electronic Governance*. Julie is chair of ECREA's Communication & Democracy section and chair of the network on Social Innovation and Civic Engagement (nSICE)

Anne Vestergaard is an associate professor at the Center for Corporate Social Responsibility at Copenhagen Business School. Her research revolves around mainstream discourses of morality with a particular interest in how processes of institutional, technological, and semiotic mediation contribute to them. This interest is currently pursued in two strands of research, one concerning humanitarian communication, the other concerning CSR communication. The research investigates tensions brought about by the fading division of labour between commercial and non-commercial organizations and examines how marketized practices are impacting on the identity, image, and reputation of NGOs, as well as how a moral economy is transforming discourses in and around corporations. Vestergaard's work is published in international journals such as the *Journal of Business Ethics, Language and Politics,* and *Critical Discourse Studies.*

Introduction: Social Media and Civic Engagement

Julie Uldam and Anne Vestergaard

Social media have been praised for their potential for facilitating civic engagement. At a time when one of the most difficult problems facing democracy in the Western hemisphere is the decline in citizens' participation in politics (Dahlgren, 2009), this potential has been vested with hopes that social media can help reinvigorate extra-parliamentarian political participation – i.e. participation beyond the rights and obligations of liberal citizenship (e.g. voting) – and thus strengthen democratic accountability at national and international levels (e.g. Castells, 2013; Van Laer & Van Aelst, 2010). These accounts have highlighted new possibilities for bottom-up, self-organizing participation such as direct democracy and for bypassing mass media gatekeepers and taking action to address issues directly. At the same time, sceptics have pointed to challenges social media pose to extra-parliamentarian political participation. These accounts have highlighted the dominance of commercial interests, individualization, non-committal participation – or 'clicktivism'– and security and censorship (e.g. Dahlgren, 2013; Gladwell, 2010; Juris, 2012; Uldam, 2014).

Rather than taking any of these perspectives for granted, this book explores empirically how different practices of political participation are played out in social media, focusing particularly on extra-parliamentarian political participation. Many studies have focused on extra-parliamentarian political participation as protest or resistance, drawing on examples such as counter-summits against WTO, IMF, or UNFCCC meetings (e.g. Della Porta & Diani, 2005; Juris, 2008; Uldam & Askanius, 2011). While protest is certainly a crucial part of political participation without which politics would be 'replaced by a confrontation between non-negotiable moral values or essentialist forms of identifications' (Mouffe, 1998: 13–14), extra-parliamentarian political

1

participation also involves proposals for solutions and alternatives to contested issues, for taking extra-parliamentarian political participation beyond protest (Calhoun, 2013). In order to acknowledge these multifarious aspects of extra-parliamentarian political participation, we use the term civic engagement. Addressing the competing perspectives outlined above, Bennett et al. (2011) have pointed to differences in conceptualizations of civic engagement that lead to different evaluations of the outlook for the empowering potential of social media. Therefore, before we can begin to assess how civic engagement beyond protest fares in social media, we need to first address fundamental questions about what political participation entails, and how we can understand its potential for going 'beyond protest'. In addressing these questions, this book brings together media studies, political science, and organizational and management studies. These fields have addressed different aspects of civic engagement that together can suggest a baseline for evaluating civic engagement, including its potential for going beyond protest.

Civic engagement

At the intersection of media studies and political science, key discussions of political participation argue for an understanding that captures the efforts of civil society actors to address issues of public concern beyond the rights and obligations of liberal citizenship, such as voting (e.g. Bennett, 2003, 2012; Carpentier, 2012; Dahlgren, 2009; Fenton, 2008). In this way, we can distinguish between, on the one hand, formal participation such as voting and, on the other hand, civic engagement such as volunteering, activism, and participation in community-driven initiatives. Civic engagement, then, is understood here as engagement with political and social issues, an engagement expressed in a variety of ways that do not always adhere to traditional perceptions of parliamentarian politics. One of the most recent examples is the Occupy movement with its protest camps, which served both to protest against the influence of corporate power on parliamentarian politics (among other issues) and to enact a community-driven alternative to the current neoliberal organization of society, e.g. with free libraries, free seminars, and experiments in direct democracy. Another example is the community-driven Transition Towns project, which facilitates local, self-organized food and energy provision in a growing number of cities. Civic engagement is also expressed through creative, subversive tactics such as the actions by culture jammers the Yes Men, who, for example, impersonating WTO officials, announcing the re-founding of the WTO campaign to ensure businesses help people rather than businesses (Boyd, 2013; Cammaerts, 2007). From this perspective, political participation is not necessarily in decline, but, rather, in flux. Consequently, questions about civic engagement should not just focus on declining participation in parliamentarian politics, but also what alternative modes of participation are emerging, and how they are facilitated and constrained by social media.

Formal and informal modes of civic engagement

Adopting an inclusive conception of civic engagement to capture both antagonistic and solution-oriented aspects of extra-parliamentarian political participation, makes useful a distinction between informal and formal modes of civic engagement, or what Bohm et al. term 'resistance'. Here, formal modes of civic engagement are taken to refer to acts of contestation in institutional contexts such as trade union strikes, or formal social movement organizations and non-governmental organizations (NGOs) such as Greenpeace targeting corporate practices in a campaign (Böhm et al., 2008). In contrast, informal modes are taken to refer to resistance 'outside official politics', including 'spontaneous non-organized actions to collectively organized protest events' by non-professionals such as workplace pilferage, culture jamming, and direct action' (Böhm et al., 2008). These informal modes of resistance are characterized by decentralized, non-hierarchical (or anti-hierarchical at least) organizing (Böhm et al., 2008; Den Hond and De Bakker, 2007; Kraemer et al., 2013). This distinction is not unproblematic – even as a continuum – as the two forms of 'resistance' often overlap. It is nonetheless useful for understanding civic engagement, because it allows us to explore the ways in which civic engagement is multifarious, including community-driven initiatives, participation in extra-parliamentarian politics around issues related to e.g. global justice, anti-capitalism, the environment, and gender equality as well as more recent government discourses on civic engagement as a strategic resource for voluntary provision of social services.

In employing this distinction between formal and informal civic engagement we want to depart from Böhm and colleagues' use of the term 'resistance'. 'Resistance' invokes a politics of protest and 'anti' disposition that risks backgrounding the various ways in which acts of civic engagement offer constructive articulations of solutions and alternatives to the issues that they contest or resist. Our point is that civic engagement – whether it is located in contexts of parliamentarian or extra-parliamentarian politics – often involves a dimension that takes it beyond protest. It is this dimension, which is often overlooked in the academic literature and in the mainstream press, that this volume explores, particularly in relation to social media.

Civic engagement and the business-society nexus

The growing power of multinational corporations operating on a global arena, which often escapes the jurisdictions of individual nation states or is tied to the legal frameworks of weak (or non-) democracies, has led to a proliferation of transnational movements that monitor multinationals and hold them accountable when their practices violate human rights, civic rights, and environmental standards (Della Porta & Tarrow, 2005; Matten & Crane, 2005; Palazzo & Scherer, 2007). In this way, both formal and informal modes of civic engagement increasingly target the corporate realm, with formal social movement organizations and NGOs campaigning against corporate practices or partnering with corporations in corporate responsibility programmes, and non-professionals collectively organizing protest events against corporate practices (Böhm et al., 2008; Den Hond & De Bakker, 2007). While civic engagement, in theory as well as in practice, until recently mostly centred on government issues (King & Pearce, 2010; Tarrow, 2001), increasingly also the social, political and environmental implications of business practices are becoming a matter of civic concern. Expectations that businesses assume responsibility for the consequences of their actions beyond what is required legally – known under the popular heading of corporate social responsibility (CSR) – have fundamentally shifted the relationship between corporations and their publics. Much social movement research, in response, has turned from a government-centred to a business-centred focus, investigating social and political issues, which are outside the immediate realm of public authority (De Bakker et al., 2013). While business-centred civic engagement often involves civil society groups and activists targeting individual companies, this is done with a view towards wider institutional, field-level change (Greenwood et al., 2002; Tolbert & Zucker, 1996). Business-centred civic engagement is thus not removed from demands for reform (e.g. fair trade, labour, tax, or environmental regulation in the industry) or even visionary systemic critique calling for total change to the current political and economic organization of society (Karagianni & Cornelissen, 2006; Uldam, 2013; see Starr, 2000 for a seminal categorization). The extent to which business-centred civic engagement is grounded in demands for reform or systemic change is influenced by the ways in which it is tied to formal and informal modes of engagement. *Informal modes* of engagement take two interrelated forms: First, in a reality where reputation and brand are key assets of a company, civil society actors have the power to induce financial damage to companies by exposing ethical misconduct to the general public, including consumers, investors, shareholders and (potential) employees (Bennett, 2003). Second, exposure of misconduct potentially allows civil society actors to undermine the legitimacy of a company, causing restrictions in its room to manoeuvre in terms of state and interstate regulation as well as impairing its capacity for political influence. *Formal modes* of business-centred civic engagement typically involve civil society actors engaging with companies in various forms of partnerships, providing guidance, expert knowledge and know-how. Arguably, the increased willingness to accommodate the demands of social movements and activists as well as the increasing willingness to invite NGOs into partnerships and multi-stakeholder initiatives are intrinsically tied to the risk of exposure and its associated economic and political costs for companies. As such, the relationship between civil society and business and the potential empowerment of civil society that grows out of this relation (Matten & Crane, 2005; Palazzo & Scherer, 2010), relies on the ability of various civil society actors to access the public sphere.

Civic engagement and the public sphere

The proliferation of online political sites and debate forums has stimulated a renewed scholarly interest in notions of civic engagement, generating calls for theoretical reconsideration of political deliberation within the public sphere (see e.g. Brundidge, 2010; Dahlberg, 2001; Dahlgren, 2005, 2009; Freelon, 2010; Papacharissi, 2004). The concept of the public sphere highlights the importance of the possibility for societal actors to be seen and heard by others on issues of public concern (Calhoun, 1992). Exactly how and what role societal actors and institutions should take in doing so has spurred debate in both organizational studies and in media studies (e.g. Dahlberg, 2014; Dahlgren, 1995, 2001; Edward & Willmott, 2013; Gilbert & Rasche, 2007; Scherer & Palazzo, 2011).

In organizational and management studies, research on business-society relations has adopted a Habermasian conception of the public sphere to argue that the moral legitimacy of corporations increasingly hinges on their willingness to engage in dialogic debate with their stakeholders, allowing the better argument to win (Gilbert and Rasche, 2007;

Scherer and Palazzo, 2011). The strive for consensus formation that a Habermasian conception entails informs both stakeholder theory and the CSR literature. However, this approach to corporations' engagement with civil society has been criticized for negating radical negativity (Edward & Willmott, 2013) and for not allowing for disagreement, or 'dissensual CSR' (Whelan, 2013: 762). Edward and Willmott (2013) argue that a Habermasian conception of the public sphere risks glossing over disagreements and difference. On the basis of Scherer and Palazzo's example of the Forest Stewardship Council (FSC), they demonstrate how power differences are obscured and argue that we need to pay attention to the mutual inter-penetration of system and lifeworld (i.e. the intersection of the market arena and the arena of the dispositions and practices that constitute the preconditions for people's participation in the public sphere; see Dahlgren, 2009). Whelan (2013) argues that companies should participate in 'dissent enabling public spheres' such as broadcast panel debates in which critics also participate. This suggestion grants a voice to societal actors who may consider each other enemies with fundamentally different interests, such as Shell's interests in economic growth and Greenpeace's interests in environmental protection (these are examples highlighted by Whelan). However, the kinds of 'dissent enabling public spheres' that are envisioned here (provided by Shell or mass media gatekeepers) are often difficult to access for the critics who would provide dissensual perspectives on CSR. Small, informal activist organizations or networks are often excluded from such arenas (e.g. Banerjee, 2011; Bennett, 2014). Using the example of Greenpeace (one of the biggest – and most formally organized – civil society organizations in the UK environmental movement) understates this obstacle to participation.

In media studies, research on the potential of social media for facilitating civil society actors' access to the public sphere departs from a long-standing axiom of political theory, underwritten by the Habermasian model of deliberative democracy, that engaged conversation on matters of public concern between empowered citizens is an essential prerequisite for a vital, functioning democracy (Habermas, 1962/1989; see Lunt & Livingstone, 2013 and Mansell, 2010 for useful discussions). In this vein, scholars have pointed to the limits of the model of deliberative democracy for understanding the affective and conflictual dimensions of civic engagement, highlighting the role of consensus and rationality in obscuring power relations and privileging civic engagement based on individualization and consumption in the market-place over solidarity and proposals for alternative solutions (Dahlgren, 2009; Fenton, 2007).

Building on critiques of the Habermasian conception of the public sphere (Dahlgren, 1995; Calhoun, 1992; Fraser, 1992), Fenton and Downey (2003) suggest a distinction between dominant and counter public spheres to capture the difference between, on the one hand, 'dominant media' and, on the other hand, 'civic media', along with the time and space made available for civil society actors by dominant media (18–19). It is in counter public spheres that civil society actors can connect and organize for social change. In this respect, social movements are key players. Downey and Fenton (2003) stress the importance of struggles between the two spheres, and particularly possibilities for counter public spheres to challenge the dominant public sphere. In doing so, counter public spheres come to represent 'an alternative way of ordering society as recognized in the work of Negt and Kluge (1972)', reflecting an understanding of civic engagement as both contestation and proposals for alternatives, as practices beyond protest (Downey & Fenton, 2003: 19).

Civic engagement and social media

Following the distinction between dominant and counter public spheres, the mushrooming of social media can be seen as a vehicle for counter public spheres that can challenge the dominant public sphere and its reliance on traditional mainstream media. But with the commercialization of popular social media platforms such as Facebook and YouTube, a distinction between a dominant public sphere fostered by traditional mainstream media and counter public spheres fostered by social media would be problematic. At the same time, a lot of the information that we receive via social media platforms presents one aspect of an issue, bits of information or factoids, connecting likeminded users (within specific alternative public spheres) rather than challenging our presumptions or offering new perspectives. Therefore, we suggest that we can distinguish between a dominant public sphere that relies on traditional mainstream media and, following Gitlin (1998), multiple public sphericules that variously rely on mainstream, commercial social media and alternative social media. In doing so, we stress the importance of interaction between public sphericules and between public sphericules and the dominant public sphere (see Cammaerts, 2007).

Social media have been celebrated for their potential to provide civil society actors with the opportunity to access the dominant public sphere. Reminding ourselves of the distinction between formal and informal civic engagement, we also need to consider what kinds of civic engagement are played out in different social media platforms and the public sphericules they facilitate. Drawing on a study of video responses to the Dutch-produced anti-Islam film *Fitna*, van Zoonen et al. (2010) explore playful modes of engaging with politics, arguing that we need to look beyond politically oriented fora to find civic engagement in online media. Similarly, the ways in which civic engagement is performed on social media platforms require us to look for forms of engagement beyond formal modes of engagement and citizenship. In exploring civic engagement in social media, prominent studies have proposed alternative notions of democracy and citizenship such as 'silly citizenship' (Hartley, 2010) and 'unlocated citizenship' (van Zoonen et al., 2010) and 'actualizing citizenship–dutiful citizenship' (AC–DC) (Bennett et al., 2014, see also Couldry et al., 2007; Dahlgren, 2003). Drawing on examples of spoof election campaign videos, Hartley traces the historical trajectory of conceptions of citizenship, arguing that young people's uses of irony and satire – the playful performance of self-organized and self-represented deliberation – to represent themselves in YouTube videos should also be taken as citizens' acts of engagement. Bennett et al. (2014) identify loosely networked activism that addresses issues that reflect personal values in social media that transcends institutional or communal affinities. In this way, they share the idea that social media enable engagement with politics in ways that are self-actualizing rather than dutiful, in Bennett's terms, thus contributing to a vivid civic culture that is understood in much broader terms than suggested by Almond and Verba (1963) in their seminal study of civic culture and politics (Bennett et al., 2011; Bennett et al., 2014). While social media thus provide new platforms for expressing and acting out civic engagement beyond politically oriented fora, they have also been shown to privilege formal (reformist and institutional) modes of civic engagement over informal (radical and anti-systemic) modes (Uldam, 2013; Van Laer & Van Aelst, 2010) and individual over collective engagement (Bennett & Segerberg, 2013; Fenton & Barassi, 2011). Therefore, when we explore the potential of social media for reinvigorating civic engagement and thus strengthening democratic accountability, we need to consider (i) both business-centred and government-centred critiques and demands, (ii) their expression as both formal and informal modes of engagement, and (iii) their (possibilities for providing) access to both public sphericules and the dominant public sphere.

All three aspects of civic engagement are important to civic articulations of alternatives to the issues that they contest or resist – the dimension that takes civic engagement beyond a politics of protest and an 'anti' disposition.

Civic engagement beyond protest

We propose that the dimension of civic engagement that takes it beyond protest can be construed in three ways: (i) as sustained involvement of citizens after the protest event, (ii) as the enactment of alternatives, and (iii) as cooperation with institutional actors.

The first construal reminds us that it is after the protest that the long and difficult process of articulating – and hopefully working towards – viable alternatives begins (Uldam, 2012). Possibilities for doing so are challenged in social media as the transient characteristics of many online spaces, including social media, have been shown to facilitate the instant agency of point-and-click activism, which offers easy, non-committal modes of civic participation (Fenton, 2008). Consequently, citizens' engagement with an issue may end after a single click of a mouse as is often the case when joining a Facebook group or signing an online petition (Fenton & Barassi, 2011). This potentially impedes both sustained efforts to follow an issue to the door and the nitty-gritty of everyday organizing to campaign for wider systemic change that only a few pay attention to, let alone engage with. The second construal has to do with the purpose of protest events as enactments of alternative imaginaries. With their practices of direct democracy, consensus decision-making and community-organized social provisions such as libraries, kitchens, and teaching, protest camps from the women's anti-nuclear peace camp at Greenham Common in the early 1980s to the Occupy camps in 2012 provide significant examples of enactments of alternatives to the current neoliberal organization of society (Feigenbaum et al., 2013). Also, creative interventions such as culture jammers the Yes Men work as enactments of alternative imaginaries (Boyd, 2013). For example, at a 'Gulf Coast Leadership Summit' in 2011, the Yes Men helped organize the impersonation of a BP representative who apologized for the oil company's handling of the Deepwater oil spill in the Gulf of Mexico and pledged to provide a free healthcare plan for spill and cleanup victims in the Gulf.[1] With their possibilities for non-hierarchical organizing and debate, social media have been welcomed for their potential to enable such enactments of alternatives. However, on closer inspection the affordances of social media can also provide obstacles to direct democracy and consensus-based decision-making (Husted, this volume; Munro, 2014). The third construal refers to interrelations between formal and informal modes of civic engagement and the ways in which informal civic actors collaborate with formal civic actors to achieve social and political change that does not challenge current structures of governance. Examples of such collaborations include the involvement of NGOs in companies' corporate social responsibility (CSR) initiatives (De Bakker, this volume) as well as networks co-organized by formally organized NGOs and informal radical social movement groups such as the London Mining Network, which includes formal NGOs and social movement organizations such as the World Development Movement, War on Want and UK Tar Sands Network.

The chapters in this book explore these three ways of taking civic engagement beyond protest. The chapters are organized in two parts: The first section focuses on formal modes of civic engagement. Here, Frank De Bakker's, Itziar Castelló and David Barberá's, and Eleftheria Lekakis' chapters explore different ways in which civil society actors and institutional actors cooperate to try to connect public sphericules and take civic engagement beyond protest, and specifically the role of social media in facilitating this cooperation. The second section focuses on informal modes of civic engagement. Here, Bart Cammaerts', Julie Uldam's, Jess Baines', Anne Kaun's, and Emil Husted's chapters explore different possibilities for and constraints on civil society actors' uses of both commercial and alternative social media to sustain civic engagement after protest events have taken place and to enact alternative imaginaries.

Outline of chapters

Part I: Formal modes of civic engagement and cooperation with institutional actors

Reviewing two strands of literature on (i) the interplay between activist criticism and companies' adoption of CSR initiatives and (ii) activist tactics in social media, De Bakker argues in his chapter that reformist activists tend to pursue symbolic impact (e.g. through demonstrations or online petitions), while radical activist groups tend to pursue material impact (e.g. through occupations or hacktivism). Further, he argues that reformist activist groups are inclined to collaborate with companies to achieve incremental changes. This is not a viable option for radical activist groups, because they see their targets as an inherent part of a wider systemic problem. De Bakker grounds this proposition in institutional theory. The implications of this argument and its theoretical anchoring are that for activism to have any impact beyond protest, collaborative efforts to construct alternatives are required (reinstitutionalization, in De Bakker's framework). Here, reformist activist groups are taken to be more likely to collaborate with companies as part of

CSR programmes. Two typical examples spring to our minds. One is the collaboration between and Danone and UNICEF in which Danone pledged to provide funding for ten litres of drinking water to NGOs such as the Rainforest Foundation US and the child sponsor programme World Vision for every one litre sold of their bottled water brand Volvic (Brei & Böhm, 2014). The other is the Roundtable on Responsible Soy set up by the World Wildlife Fund to establish voluntary standards that companies such as Unilever, Waitrose, and ARLA Foods have signed up to, thus agreeing to source all their soy from certified responsible sources by 2015, albeit without any legal sanctions if they fail to do so.[2] In contrast, radical activist groups are more likely to campaign for alternatives that dismiss collaborations with companies as greenwashing and instead suggest systemic change. Such approaches can be found at the radical end of the climate justice movement where groups and networks such as Rising Tide, Frack Off, and Art Not Oil organize inventive direct action events that criticize fossil fuel companies. In recent years, we have witnessed abundant examples of how social media can facilitate (albeit not without obstacles) activists' criticism of corporate and government misconduct. However, using social media to suggest alternatives (reinstitutionalization) is trickier, especially when it comes to radical alternatives that require substantial changes – to our social imaginary and to societal structures. This aspect which takes civic engagement beyond protest still requires more research for us to better grasp the democratic potential of social media. This is the important call that De Bakker puts forward in his reflections on his overview of the activist criticism and companies' adoption of CSR initiatives and activist tactics in social media.

In her study of CSR rhetoric by Greek retailers in austerity-stricken Greece, Lekakis examines formal modes of civic engagement, showing how a range of Greek supermarkets embrace the cause of the citizen movement 'We Consume What We Produce'. In the attempt to ameliorate consumer confidence, retailers appropriated the cause by promoting the movement through posters, banners and plastic bags. In a shifting terrain of trust and legitimacy, citizens turn to the marketplace to beget support with Facebook comments. The chapter explores corporate appropriation of civic engagement, where *corporate* engagement is understood as the mobilization of corporate resources to address consumer concerns. It exposes the ways in which promotional culture manifests as corporate engagement with a society, and questions the legitimacy of CSR communication in times of crisis. By exploring how CSR communication adapts to a financial crisis context, Lekakis argues that there is a push to address consumers' financial concerns around affordability, but also to engulf manifestations of the austerity-ridden nation within the bounds of their promotional culture. National super-markets are communicating CSR by addressing consumers through an explicit narrative of national pride, solidarity, and affordability, as well as through a practical restructuring of their prices. Yet, symbolically, CSR communication remains rooted in a politics of influence. Consumers are continuously conflated with citizens in a vicious circle in which consumers appeal to supermarkets to alleviate their financial difficulties, while supermarkets feed back to this a sense of solidarity through mostly symbolic repertoires.

The chapter by Castelló and Barberá analyzes the Spanish Occupy movement, also known as 15M or the Indignados, as an example of new social movements as complex, multilayered organizations heavily supported by social media and their ability to connect heterogeneous social networks – or public sphericules. They examine the organizational characteristics of a social movement beyond online processes, They argue that the 15M is not a political group, nor an established lobby, but a network of multiple rationalities, conflictive logics, and heterogeneous actors that connect mainly through social media platforms. Although organizing change in such a heterogeneous network has been argued to be an impossible task, some of the 15M claims have successfully been translated into policy changes. The chapter investigates how organizations based on complex, multilayered networks select their organizational objectives and turn them into political matters. It investigates how organizational goals emerge, how they are selected, organized, and ultimately impact the arena of institutional politics. In this way, the M15 movement draws on both informal and formal modes of civic engagement. By working to influence institutional politics – the focus of Castelló and Barberá's chapters – the movement's formal modes of civic engagement contribute to its engagement and endurance beyond protest.

Part II: Informal modes of civic engagement, enacting alternatives and sustaining involvement

In his chapter, Cammaerts draws on the concept of mediation (Martín-Barbero, 1993; Silverstone, 2002) and Foucault's notion of the technologies of the Self to suggest a theoretical framework for studying the affordances that social media provide for protest movements. On the basis of examples of informal modes of engagement such as the Arab Spring and the Occupy Movement, Cammaerts argues that we can think of

(i) dissemination and mobilization in terms of disclosure, (ii) organization and coordination in terms of examination, and (iii) recording and archiving in terms of remembrance. From this vantage point, especially the dimensions of examination and remembrance, in particular, constitute possibilities for protest movements to go beyond protest. Using social media to organize and coordinate protest activities (the mediation logic of examination) entails possibilities for supporting the enactment of alternatives. Using social media to record and archive protest activities (the mediation logic of remembrance) could help sustain activists' involvement after an event has taken place – when the nitty-gritty of everyday organizing to campaign for wider systemic change returns. However, Cammaerts also discusses the ways in which all three technologies of self-mediation are constrained by the political economy of the Internet and particularly social media: At the level of disclosure these relate to reach, impeding possibilities for reaching wider publics. At the level of examination, state surveillance and repression as central constraints are highlighted, impeding possibilities for organizing. At the level of remembrance, the corporate ownership of popular social media platforms is a constraint to freedom of expression, as companies can take down activists' material either responding to government pressure or because it contradicts their commercial interests, impeding possibilities for activists to circulate material from their protest events. Approaching these affordances and constraints from the perspective of technologies of self-mediation, Cammaerts argues, enables us to probe the disciplining effects of state and corporate power (and surveillance) on civic protest as well as activists' attempts to sidestep and subvert state and corporate control in social media.

Challenges of surveillance and repression in social media are also explored in Uldam's chapter. Focusing on surveillance conducted by multinational companies, Uldam illustrates how companies' monitoring – and sometimes silencing – of their critics can impede the potential of social media for facilitating informal modes of civic engagement. She does so on the basis of files held by BP on individual members of the climate justice movement in the UK who criticize BP's CSR communication as greenwashing. The files indicate that oil companies' monitoring of activists is underpinned by an intention to anticipate and contain their criticism in order to protect the construction of a CSR brand. The circulation of criticism to the dominant public sphere would break the illusion that oil companies' CSR initiatives provide a win-win situation by rendering visible antagonism and conflicting interests over the ethico-political values of CSR. Uldam argues that such constraints to civic engagement are connected to the wider power structures in which social media are embedded, providing possibilities for corporate actors to counter criticism and contain it within a public sphericule mainly inhabited by left-wing social movements. Specifically in relation to criticism of oil companies' CSR initiatives, Uldam argues that this impedes opportunities for taking informal civic engagement beyond protest: While activists would consider cooperating with oil companies as hegemonic co-optation, impediments to freely questioning the win-win discourse of CSR enables CSR initiatives to appear as post-political, making (the enactment of) alternatives seem obsolete.

Anne Kaun's chapter studies the status of Occupy Wall Street after encampments have disappeared and activists' ideas in various ways develop along different trajectories, focusing on how the idea of Occupy changed as it travelled to other localities. Drawing on a multi-site narrative analysis, the chapter discusses how the global and local scales of the Occupy movement were appropriated by Swedish and Latvian activists. The chapter argues that the protest network metaphor overemphasizes the technological aspects of civic engagement and social media and downplays the contextual considerations of how global narratives and practices are appropriated and recontextualized. Rather than one strongly interlinked network based on social media, the Occupy movement as an informal mode of civic engagement should be understood as a travelling narrative characterized by reinterpretations negotiating the global and the local. The chapter discusses recontextualization in activist discourse as well as recontextualization by news media in both countries. It demonstrates, for instance, that in Latvia the term 'Occupy' was itself a barrier for the local appropriation of the movement because of how this term is laden with the heavy significance of Soviet and German occupations. It demonstrates also that while activists' stories emphasized the local specifics of a global cause, mainstream news reports focused entirely on the global scope. This mitigated the importance of the movement in the local context and questioned the appropriateness of the global cause in terms of the political and economic realities in Sweden and Latvia. In this way, while the network metaphor emphasizes the global connectedness and contributes to an understanding in terms of visibility versus non-visibility, centre versus periphery, multi-site narrative analysis contributes to an understanding of the actual negotiation process between the local and the global.

The forms of civic engagement that Baines discusses in her chapter on community-driven printshops in the UK in the 1960s, 70s, and 80s can also be construed as enactments of alternatives. By providing participants with community-driven, collectivist facilities, the printshops served as alternatives to commercial print media. With roots in social movements such as the peace movement and their focus on bottom-up organizing, the printshops that Baines examines are mainly characterized by informal modes of civic engagement, working to empower local civil society by facilitating their visibility and by teaching them printing skills. In this way, the case of community printshops shows how media and user-generated content production precede online social media and the hopes for their participatory and empowering potential (as did the telegraph, the radio, and the portable video recorder). Similarly, many of the challenges to the realization of this potential mirror, for example, the challenges of reach and regulation associated with social media. However, some challenges differ. For example, in contrast to the individualistic values that underpin the raison d'être of social media platforms such as Facebook (Cammaerts, this volume), Baines shows how the printshops were driven by collective values and practices, and can thus be seen as what Downing (2001, 2008) has termed social movement media and radical media, similarly to online platforms such as IndyMedia (Sullivan et al., 2011). It was these collective values and practices that significantly influenced the potential of community printshops to foster civic engagement beyond protest: co-ownership of equipment and co-running of printing helped provide an alternative outlet for critiquing the established system as well as enact an alternative to that system.

In his chapter on Occupy Wall Street, Husted explores the challenges to civic engagement brought about by a move from an offline protest setting to social media platforms. With its popular mobilization and cluster of claims 'to be represented, to be considered in decisions, to participate, in short to be the public' (Calhoun, 2013: p. 29), the Occupy Wall Street movement can also be seen as an example of informal civic engagement. Within this realm it sought to take civic engagement beyond protest in two ways: With its community-driven libraries and direct democracy decision-making, the movement's occupation of Zucotti Park can be construed as an enactment of alternatives to the current system. At the same time, its move from an offline protest camp to social media platforms can be construed as an attempt to sustain the involvement of citizens after the protest event. However, it is this move, Husted argues, that introduces a hierarchical structure into the Occupy Wall Street movement, as members turn from 'creators' to 'amplifiers' and merely affirm content posted by the administrators of the Occupy Wall Street Facebook page rather than participating by posting content themselves. This transition contrasts with the performative role of the protest camp as an enactment of direct democracy decision-making processes. Husted also argues that, paradoxically, the increase in populism coincides with the end of the camp and Occupy Wall Street's transition into an online movement, with an even wider range of issues being addressed on the movement's Facebook page. In this light, the affordances of Facebook also have the potential to provide possibilities for the enactment of alternatives.

The chapters in this collection illustrate how social media provide both opportunities and constraints for civic engagement in the global North. While formal modes of civic engagement, and especially discourses of corporate citizenship and civic engagement based on individualization and consumption in the marketplace, are facilitated by social media, informal modes of civic engagement tend to encounter more obstacles. In this respect, the market-driven logics that underpin social media tend to privilege individualized, promotional and surveillance practices. This impedes the potential of social media to provide opportunities for informal modes of civic engagement to move beyond protest. However, all is not bleak. Different practices and different forms of organization of civic engagement negotiate with and subvert the constraining affordances and logics of social media, leaving open possibilities for connectivity and interaction between public sphericules and the dominant public sphere and for invigorated civic engagement.

Notes

1. http://louisianajusticeinstitute.blogspot.dk/2011/04/gulf-coast-activists-and-yes-men.html.
2. http://www.responsiblesoy.org/.

References

Almond, G. A. & Verba, S. (1963). *The Civic Culture: Political Attitudes and Democracy in Five Nations*. London: Sage.

Askanius, T., & Uldam, J. (2011). Online social media for radical politics: climate change activism on YouTube. *International Journal of Electronic Governance, 4*(1), 69–84.

Banerjee, S. B. (2011). Embedding sustainability across the organization: A critical perspective. *Academy of Management Learning & Education, 10*(4), 719–731.

Bennett, W. (2003). Communicating global activism. *Information, Communication & Society, 6*(2), 143–168.

Bennett, W. L. (2012). The personalization of politics political identity, social media, and changing patterns of participation. *The Annals of the American Academy of Political and Social Science, 644*(1), 20–39.

Bennett, W. L., & Segerberg, A. (2013). *The Logic of Connective Action: Digital Media and the Personalization of Contentious Politics.* Cambridge: Cambridge University Press.

Bennett, W. L., Segerberg, A., & Walker, S. (2014). Organization in the crowd: Peer production in large-scale networked protests. *Information, Communication & Society, 17*(2), 232–260.

Bennett, W. L., Wells, C., & Freelon, D. (2011). Communicating civic engagement: Contrasting models of citizenship in the youth web sphere. *Journal of Communication, 61*(5), 835–856.

Böhm, S., Spicer, A., & Fleming, P. (2008). Infra-political dimensions of resistance to international business: A Neo-Gramscian approach. *Scandinavian Journal of Management, 24*(3), 169–182.

Boyd, A. (2013). Don't Wait for the Revolution – Live it, Yes Magazine (July 2013), accessed October 2014 http://www.yesmagazine.org/issues/love-and-the-apocalypse/don-t-wait-for-the-revolution-live-it-andrew-boyd

Brei, V., & Böhm, S. (2013). '1L= 10L for Africa': Corporate social responsibility and the transformation of bottled water into a 'consumer activist' commodity. *Discourse & Society, 25*(1): 3–31.

Brundidge, J. (2010). Encountering 'difference' in the contemporary public sphere: The contribution of the Internet to the heterogeneity of political discussion networks. *Journal of Communication, 60*(4), 680–700.

Calhoun, C. (2013). Occupy Wall Street in perspective. *The British Journal of Sociology, 64*(1), 26–38.

Calhoun, C. J. (ed.). (1992). *Habermas and the public sphere.* Cambridge, MA: MIT Press.

Cammaerts, B. (2007). Jamming the political: Beyond counter-hegemonic practices. *Continuum, 21*(1), 71–90.

Carpentier, N. (2012). Discursive Structures in the Network Society. *Javnost-The Public, 19*(4), 25–40.

Castells, M. (2013). *Networks of Outrage and Hope: Social Movements in the Internet Age.* Malden, MA: Polity Press.

Couldry, N., Livingstone, S. M., & Markham, T. (2007). *Media Consumption and Public Engagement: Beyond the Presumption of Attention.* Basingstoke: Palgrave Macmillan.

Dahlberg, L. (2001). The Internet and democratic discourse: Exploring the prospects of online deliberative forums extending the public sphere. *Information, Communication & Society, 4*(4), 615–633.

Dahlberg, L. (2014). The Habermasian public sphere and exclusion: An engagement with poststructuralist-influenced critics. *Communication Theory, 24*(1), 21–41.

Dahlgren, P. (1995). *Television and the Public Sphere: Citizenship, Democracy and the Media.* London: Sage.

Dahlgren, P. (2001) 'The Public Sphere and the Net: Structure, Space and Communication', In L.W. Bennett and R.M. Entman (eds) *Mediated Politics: Communication in the Future of Democracy*, pp. 33–55. Cambridge: Cambridge University Press.

Dahlgren, P. 2003. "Reconfiguring Civic Culture in the New Media Milieu." In J. Corner, and D. Pels (eds) *Media and the Restyling of Politics*, pp. 33–55. London: Sage.

Dahlgren, P. (2005). The Internet, public spheres, and political communication: Dispersion and deliberation. *Political communication, 22*(2), 147–162.

Dahlgren, P. (2009). *Media and Political Engagement.* Cambridge: Cambridge University Press.

Dahlgren, P. (2013). *The Political Web: Participation, Media, and Alternative Democracy.* Basingstoke: Palgrave Macmillan.

De Bakker, F. G., den Hond, F., King, B., & Weber, K. (2013). Social movements, civil society and corporations: Taking stock and looking ahead. *Organization Studies, 34*(5–6), 573–593.

Della Porta, D., & Tarrow, S. (2005). Transnational processes and social activism: An introduction. *Transnational protest and global activism, 1.*

Den Hond, F., & De Bakker, F. G. (2007). Ideologically motivated activism: How activist groups influence corporate social change activities. *Academy of Management Review, 32*(3), 901–924.

Downey, J., & Fenton, N. (2003). New media, counter publicity and the public sphere. *New Media & Society, 5*(2), 185–202.

Downing, J. (2008). Social movement theories and alternative media: An evaluation and critique. *Communication, Culture & Critique, 1*(1), 40–50.

Downing, J. D. H. (2000). *Radical media: Rebellious communication and social movements.* Thousand Oaks, CA: Sage Publications.

Edward, P., & Willmott, H. (2013). Discourse and normative business ethics. In C. Luetge (ed.) *Handbook of the Philosophical Foundations of Business Ethics,* (pp. 549–580). Dortrecht: Springer.

Feigenbaum, A., Frenzel, F., & McCurdy, P. (2013) *Protest Camps.* London: Zed Books.

Fenton, N. (2007). Contesting global capital, new media, solidarity. In: Cammaerts, B., & Carpentier, N. (eds). (2007). *Reclaiming the media: Communication rights and democratic media roles.* Intellect Books.

Fenton, N. (2008). Mediating hope: New media, politics and resistance. *International Journal of Cultural Studies, 11*(2), 230–248.

Fenton, N., & Barassi, V. (2011). Alternative media and social networking sites: The politics of individuation and political participation. *The Communication Review, 14*(3), 179–196.

Fenton, N., & Downey, J. (2003). Counter public spheres and global modernity. *JAVNOST-LJUBLJANA-, 10*(1), 15–32.

Fraser, N. (1992) 'Rethinking the Public Sphere – a Contribution to the Critique of Actually Existing Democracy', in C. Calhoun (ed.), *Habermas and the Public Sphere,* pp. 109–41. Cambridge, MA: MIT Press.

Freelon, D. G. (2010). Analyzing online political discussion using three models of democratic communication. *New Media & Society, 12*(7), 1172–1190

Gilbert, D. U., & Rasche, A. (2007). Discourse ethics and social accountability: The ethics of SA 8000. *Business Ethics Quarterly,* 187–216.

Gitlin, T. (1998). Public sphere or public sphericules? In: T. Liebes, & J. Curran (eds), *Media Ritual and Identity* (pp. 168–174). London: Routledge.

Gladwell, M. (2010). Why the revolution will not be tweeted. *The New Yorker,* http://www.newyorker.com/magazine/2010/10/04/small-change-3.

Greenwood, R., Suddaby, R., & Hinings, C. R. (2002). Theorizing change: The role of professional associations in the transformation of institutionalized fields. *Academy of Management Journal, 45*(1), 58–80.

Habermas, J. (1962). Strukturwandel der Offentlicheit (Darmstadt and Neuwied); English translation: The Structural Transformation of the Public Sphere, trans. T. Burger (Cambridge: Polity Press, 1992).

Habermas, Jürgen (1987) [1981]. Theory of Communicative Action Volume Two: Liveworld and System: A Critique of Functionalist Reason. Translated by Thomas A. McCarthy. Boston, MA: Beacon Press.

Hartley, J. (2010). Silly citizenship. *Critical Discourse Studies, 7*(4), 233–248.

Juris, J. S. (2008). *Networking futures: The movements against corporate globalization.* Duke University Press.

Juris, J. S. (2012). Reflections on #Occupy Everywhere: Social media, public space, and emerging logics of aggregation. *American Ethnologist, 39*(2), 259–279.

Karagianni, K. S., & Cornelissen, J. (2006). Anti-corporate movements and public relations. *Public Relations Review, 32*(2), 168–170.

King, B. G., & Pearce, N. A. (2010). The contentiousness of markets: Politics, social movements, and institutional change in markets. *Annual review of sociology, 36,* 249–267.

Kraemer, R., Whiteman G., & Banerjee, B. (2013) Conflict and astroturfing in Niyamgiri: The importance of national advocacy networks in anti-corporate social movements, *Organization Studies, 34,* 823.

Lunt, P., & Livingstone, S. (2013). Media studies' fascination with the concept of the public sphere: Critical reflections and emerging debates. *Media, Culture & Society,* 35(1), 87–96.

Mansell, R. (2010) Commentary – mediating the public sphere: Democratic deliberation, communication gaps, and the personalization of politics. In Charles T. Salmon (ed.) *Communication Yearbook 34* (pp. 259–274). Oxford: Routledge.

Martin-Barbero, J. (1993) *Communication, Culture and Hegemony,* London: Sage.

Matten, D., & Crane, A. (2005). Corporate citizenship: Toward an extended theoretical conceptualization. *Academy of Management review, 30*(1), 166–179.

Mouffe, Chantal (1998) 'The radical centre. A politics without adversary', *Soundings,* 9, Summer: 11–23.

Munro, I. (2014). Organizational Ethics and Foucault's 'Art of Living': Lessons from Social Movement Organizations. *Organization Studies, 35*(8): 1127–1148.

Palazzo, G., & Scherer, A. G. (2008). Corporate social responsibility, democracy, and the politicization of the corporation. *Academy of Management Review, 33*(3), 773–775.

Papacharissi, Z. (2004). Democracy online: Civility, politeness, and the democratic potential of online political discussion groups. *New Media & Society, 6*(2), 259–283.

Scherer, A. G., & Palazzo, G. (2007). Toward a political conception of corporate responsibility: Business and society seen from a Habermasian perspective. *Academy of Management Review, 32*(4), 1096–1120.

Scherer, A. G., & Palazzo, G. (2011). The new political role of business in a globalized world: A review of a new perspective on CSR and its implications for the firm, governance, and democracy. *Journal of Management Studies, 48*(4), 899–931.

Silverstone, R. (2002). Complicity and collusion in the mediation of everyday life. *New Literary History, 33*(4), 761–780.

Starr, A. (2000). *Naming the Enemy: Anti-Corporate Movements Confront Globalization.* London: Zed Books.

Sullivan, S., Spicer, A. & Bohm, S. (2011) Becoming global (un)civil society: counter-hegemonic struggle and the Indymedia network. *Globalizations, 8*(5), 703–717.

Tarrow, S. (2001). Transnational politics: Contention and institutions in international politics. *Annual Review of Political Science, 4*(1), 1–20.

Tolbert, P. S., & Zucker, L. G. (1996). The institutionalization of institutional theory. In: S. R. Clegg, C. Hardy, & W. R. Nord (eds), *Handbook of Organization Studies* (pp. 175–190), London: Sage.Uldam, J. (2012). After the Protest: Online Social Media and Political Engagement. The 62nd ICA Annual Conference. Phoenix, 2012.

Uldam, J. (2013). Activism and the online mediation opportunity structure: Attempts to impact global climate change policies? *Policy & Internet, 5*(1), 56–75

Uldam, J. (2014). Corporate management of visibility and the fantasy of the post-political: Social media and surveillance, *New Media and Society*, doi: 10.1177/1461444814541526.

Van Laer, J., & Van Aelst, P. (2010). Internet and social movement action repertoires: Opportunities and limitations. *Information, Communication & Society, 13*(8), 1146–1171.

Van Zoonen, L., Vis, F., & Mihelj, S. (2010). Performing citizenship on YouTube: Activism, satire and online debate around the anti-Islam video Fitna. *Critical Discourse Studies, 7*(4), 249–262.

Whelan, G. (2013). The political perspective of corporate social responsibility: A critical research agenda. *Business Ethics Quarterly, 22*(4), 709–737.

Part I
Formal Modes of Civic Engagement and Cooperation with Institutional Actors

1
Online Activism, CSR and Institutional Change

Frank G.A. de Bakker

Introduction

Business has many influences on society and increasingly society aims to have more, and more direct, influence on business as well. A steady stream of research speaks to these business-society interactions, including the widespread attention to stakeholders and the way they influence, and are influenced by, business organizations (cf. Sharma & Henriques, 2005), or to questions of whether corporations could be regarded as 'corporate citizens' and what that would entail (Matten & Crane, 2005). With the apparent retreat of states from many markets, research increasingly highlights issues of governance and private politics (Baron, 2003), looking at how corporate behaviour could and should be governed and who should be involved in doing so.

Often these studies speak to the notion of corporate social responsibility (CSR), briefly summarized as 'actions that appear to further some social good, beyond the interests of the firm and that which is required by law' (McWilliams & Siegel, 2001: 117). The way CSR is being shaped in practice can be seen as a process in which firms and a variety of other actors are involved, for instance in defining what responsibility exactly entails, and how it should be implemented, monitored, or sanctioned. How are norms and standards of CSR developed or changed? Such questions also speak to institutional theory, which 'is perhaps the dominant approach to understanding organizations' (Greenwood et al., 2008: 2). More and more attention is now being devoted to how institutions change, or are changed, for instance focusing on issues of institutional work (Lawrence & Suddaby, 2006) and institutional complexity (Greenwood et al., 2011; Pache & Santos, 2010) that discuss the often complicated processes through which different actors try to influence institutions. Many studies have examined how these actors have operated in these attempts. Of the many actors involved in institutional change processes, in this chapter I highlight the role of activist non-governmental organizations (den Hond & de Bakker, 2007; Yaziji & Doh, 2009) and their use of online and social media in such processes (cf. Castelló et al., 2013; Fieseler et al, 2010; van den Broek et al., 2012; Van Laer & Van Aelst, 2010). As Snow (2004: 536) noted, 'activists promote particular ways of understanding the world'. They use a variety of tactics to engage in this promotion; with the rise of the Internet a wide range of new tactics has become available for activists. The Worldwide Web offers different modes of communication and allows for a greater speed in communication (Garrett, 2006). As 'online media provide activist groups with potentially powerful tools of open, web-based communications' (de Bakker & Hellsten, 2013: 809), the impact of the Internet on movements and activists has increasingly been documented in different fields such as media and communication studies (cf. Bennett, 2003; Bimber et al., 2005) and social movement studies (cf. Castells, 2012; Van Laer, 2010). This chapter focuses on how online media and their use by activists can be linked to processes of institutional change. I briefly examine several tactics activists can use to instigate institutional change on issues of CSR and then highlight the potential of the Internet, and especially online media, to execute these tactics. In doing so, I build on a growing stream of research that examines activism and the rise of social media, for instance through studies on ways to trace protest campaigns through Twitter (Gerbaudo, 2012), or on how online technologies such as social media have changed the activist landscape (Uldam, 2013). Such literature offers useful insights for examining how activists try to establish institutional change, as well as some empirical examples. In the next section I will first discuss how activists aim for institutional change on issues of CSR and how they use a variety of tactics in doing so. Then I will briefly highlight some prominent characteristics of online activism and online media tactics. Combining these perspectives then leads to a new typology to analyze how online activism could be used to change norms in CSR. The chapter ends with a discussion of the applicability of this typology and of the applicability of online tactics in general, followed by some concluding remarks.

Activists, CSR, and institutional change

The debate on CSR goes way back (Bowen, 1953; Carroll, 1999) but responsibilities of business are still being debated heavily, both in scholarly discussions and in the popular management press (cf. Crane et al., 2014). Over the last decades, CSR has become a topic that firms cannot neglect. Firms need to find new ways of coping with a variety of different stakeholder demands as noted in the abundant literature on stakeholder management (cf. Rasche & Esser, 2006; Sharma & Henriques, 2005). CSR is then usually defined in broad terms, for example as encompassing 'the economic, legal, ethical and discretionary expectations that society has of organizations at a given point in time' (Carroll, 1979: 500). Such broad definitions are open to various interpretations and therefore create room to manoeuvre for firms, who can select the interpretation that best suits their needs and their profiles to demonstrate to a wider audience how they act in some socially responsible manner. Although a range of studies have appeared on CSR, ranging from prescriptive studies to theory-building contributions (for reviews see Aguinis & Glavas, 2012; de Bakker et al., 2005), the interpretation of the concept remains contested and is often criticized, for instance as 'greenwashing' or 'window dressing' (Ramus & Montiel, 2005). Different actors are all providing their own takes on the definition of the concept and its implementation.

In this chapter I focus on how one specific category of actors aims to influence how CSR is defined: I look at activist groups. This term obviously links to a range of concepts such as non-governmental organizations (NGOs), civil society organizations, or secondary stakeholders, and in a broader sense to social movement organizations. Yet, I here opt for the term 'activist groups' to emphasize their intention to establish change. Building on earlier work (den Hond & de Bakker, 2007), I argue that activist groups aim for institutional change. They want to influence the way CSR is conceptualized and framed and therefore try to gather support and legitimacy for *their* interpretations of CSR (van Huijstee & Glasbergen, 2010). By formulating claims on what firms should or should not do in order to be acting responsibly, and by bringing these claims to the attention of a wide range of stakeholders through various tactics, activist groups seek to influence corporate policies and practices on issues of CSR (Spar & La Mure, 2003), and seek to influence norms in CSR, both within companies and within society at large.

Such activist tactics usually are not intended to create change at just one particular (target) firm but to have an impact on a range of firms or industries. For instance, building on Jensen (2003), den Hond and de Bakker (2007) pointed at the well-known controversy between Greenpeace and Shell over the Brent Spar oil rig in 1995. Greenpeace clearly indicated that their protest was aimed at preventing the sinking off old oil rigs into the deep sea becoming a standard practice: Shell's plans provided a useful case for Greenpeace to highlight their position and to try to influence the common opinion on such disposal practices. By using a range of tactics that included consumer boycotts and direct action, Greenpeace succeeded in making Shell revisit its plans: 'deepwater disposal' was no longer a viable option internationally and a moratorium on such disposal was debated politically (Jørgensen, 2012), even though the scientific evidence Greenpeace put forward to substantiate their claims was contested. According to De Jong (2005), Greenpeace did not have the scientific credentials but still succeeded in mobilizing many different groups through its tactics, supported by the poor environmental awareness on the side of the firm and policy-makers. Greenpeace thus succeeded in influencing the norms on these deepwater disposal practices and the definition of responsible corporate behaviour in this context.

Such efforts by activists can be regarded as attempts to establish institutional change, trying to shape or maintain certain 'field frames' (Lounsbury et al., 2003) or 'norm systems' (den Hond & de Bakker, 2007). Field frames 'provide order and stability in an organizational field, since they comprise the technical, legal, or market standards that define the normal modes of operation' (den Hond & de Bakker, 2007: 904). These frames indicate what is seen as 'normal' in a particular field; once established such frames are fairly stable and considerable effort has to be made to alter them. A growing stream of research therefore focuses on how activists and other social movement organizations play a role in changing field frames, building on a combination of social movement studies and institutional theory (cf. Davis et al., 2005; de Bakker et al., 2013; Rao et al., 2000). After all, such activists aim to establish change in existing field frames, changing what is considered as the normal mode of operation, in order to make the dominant frames fit better with their own interests and ideologies. Nevertheless, as Schneiberg and Lounsbury (2008: 665) note, 'our knowledge of how movements create favourable political contexts for the diffusion and translation of alternatives is relatively undeveloped'.

To change field frames, existing dominant frames first need to be called into question first, and activists then need to ensure that alternative field frames are developed and accepted (den Hond & de Bakker, 2007; Lounsbury et al., 2003). Activists will thus need to work on discussing the legitimacy of both these frames, first providing arguments to convince field members of the need to abandon an existing frame. They will engage in tactics aimed at deinstitutionalization. If they succeed, room is created for new frames to emerge and at that stage activists will start to deploy tactics aimed at winning field members over to their proposed alternative frame. Such attempts at reinstitutionalization could involve a range of changes in norms, standards, or operating procedures. Depending on their ideological position, different activist groups will select different tactics and call upon different forms of legitimacy when doing so (den Hond & de Bakker, 2007; Zald, 2000). More radical activist groups 'offer a more comprehensive version of the problem and more drastic change as a solution' (Zald & McCarthy, 1980: 8) whereas their more moderate or reformist counterparts 'believe that although companies are part of the problem, they can also be part of the solution' (den Hond & de Bakker, 2007: 903) and thus aim for more incremental changes within fields. These ideological positions also influence the choice of potential targets: during deinstitutionalization, reformist activists will target firms lagging behind to drag them along with their peers, while radical activists will focus on proactive firms in order to push the bar even higher, demonstrating to the field that even more change is feasible. During reinstitutionalization, reformist activists groups will be inclined to work with proactive firms to establish a new field frame. Radical activist groups will focus on changing the economic order without much collaboration with firms at all as they don't see current firms as capable of demonstrating sufficient change (den Hond & de Bakker, 2007). Yet, in all these activities both types of activists can use a broad range of tactics, from more collaborative to more disruptive ones; in doing so the processes of deinstitutionalization and reinstitutionalization do not necessarily unfold as in discrete stages. These processes will often run simultaneously, or at least with overlaps, using a variety of tactics that could reinforce one another.

To discuss tactics activist groups have at their disposal, den Hond and de Bakker (2007) then build on the work of della Porta and Diani (1999) and distinguish two different logics through which activist tactics' effectiveness can be understood: the logic of damage/gain which raises (or lowers) the cost of continuing some contested practices, and the logic of numbers which concerns the number of supporters or participants required to make a tactic work[1]. The logic of damage can be divided into symbolic and material damage/gain, depending on whether the tactics aim to influence meanings and discourses (symbolic) or to have a direct influence on the firm's resources and assets (material) (den Hond & de Bakker, 2007). These influences can either be harmful (damage) or beneficial (gain). Based on these logics, den Hond and de Bakker (2007) propose a typology of tactics, arguing that activists are likely to start their attempts for institutional change by using tactics that only require limited resources: low dependence on participatory forms of action and a focus on a symbolic impact. Examples of such tactics are shareholder activism and street theatre. Even a small number of dedicated activists can then have an impact. Whenever conflict endures and/or escalates, different activist groups will resort to different tactics, depending on their ideological positions and on whether they aim for deinstitutionalization of disavowed practices and field frames or for the (re-)institutionalization of a new frame or practice. More reformist activists will try to mobilize larger numbers of protesters through tactics aimed at a symbolic impact, such as demonstrations and petitions, while more radical activists will opt for tactics aimed at a material impact without involving large numbers of participants.

In their typology, den Hond and de Bakker (2007) discussed a range of tactics, including some that are increasingly being used in online environments, such as petitions or 'hacktivism'. Examining the potential of the Internet and online media for activists to influence processes of institutional change in more detail could still provide a useful extension of current thinking about activists' tactics to influence norms in CSR. In the next section I will examine the link between activist tactics, online media, and institutional change regarding CSR.

Activist tactics, online media, and CSR

The Internet and the rise of online media have opened up new areas for research on social movements and their tactics. These developments have offered a whole new range of tools for activists to organize their campaigns and to mobilize support for their claims. New terms such as 'cyberactivism' (McCaughey & Ayers, 2003) or 'tweetjacking' (Lyon & Montgomery, 2013) have gained prominence and the potential of online activism for activists and social movement organizations is clear. The opportunity to communicate directly with one's audiences, 'bypassing the mechanisms and commercial bias of the mainstream media' (Kavada, 2005: 209), is often mentioned as an important feature of social media for activists, together with the 'speed, reach, and effectiveness of communication and mobilization efforts' (Obar et al., 2012: 5). Over the last decade, attention to social movements and social media has indeed burgeoned. This attention comes from media studies and communication science (Bennett, 2003; Cammaerts, 2012; Nielsen, 2009) and social movement studies (cf. Earl & Kimport, 2009; Van Laer, 2010; Van Laer & Van Aelst, 2010), but also from many other disciplines (Castells, 2012; Clark & Themudo, 2006).

At the same time, the potential of the Internet and online media to communicate on CSR in general has also received a good deal of attention, including studies of blogging or CSR reporting (Capriotti, 2011; Fieseler et al., 2010). Yet, far less attention has been paid to how activists could use these media and the Internet to influence what is understood by CSR. A lot can be learned here from studies that focus on activists' efforts in other domains. What are the tactical options available through these information and communication technologies? How could tactics be related to institutional change and what are the specifics of social media-related tactics? In this section, I first provide a short overview of some studies of online activism. I will then discuss a few characteristics of these different online activities that go beyond merely their technological characteristics and finally relate these activities to processes of institutional change on CSR, providing a typology of tactics activists use online in these efforts for change.

Online activism

Over the past decade, in analyses of what is now termed Web 1.0, website functions have often been discussed and studied. Nearly a decade ago, comparing the websites of civil society organizations, Kavada (2005: 218) noted that 'the internet is used more as an extension of the offline media rather than as an autonomous medium with its own strategy and techniques' (Kavada, 2005: 218). Shumate and Dewitt (2008) pointed at functions of activists' websites: to promote cyberactivism, to inform its audiences, and to link to other organizations. Analysing website content then is one way to examine activists' objectives and tactics: which causes are promoted, what kind of information is shared with whom, how are supporters mobilized and which other organizations are linked to? Jun (2011), for instance, studied how 'climate change organizations' were building and maintaining relationships with media, donors, volunteers, and communities through their websites and social networks.

An alternative way to analyse activists' online activities through their websites is by considering the hyperlink structure of their websites. Such hyperlink analyses inform us of the way they present themselves online (de Bakker & Hellsten, 2013; De Maeyer, 2013). De Maeyer (2013) notes that in social sciences hyperlinks are usually seen as indicators of other phenomena. Hyperlinks are considered to contain information about the relationship between those persons or organizations linked and can help us in understanding the broader context of activists' claims. To understand how interpretations of norms travel across a network, examining such hyperlink networks could provide a useful indicator (de Bakker, 2012). As de Bakker and Hellsten (2013) show, hyperlink analysis can reveal information about the tactics activists apply to achieve institutional change on CSR issues; some websites, such as BankWatch or BayerWatch, are mainly aimed at revealing information about a particular industry or firm, whereas others are focused on calls for action or support. Here the three types of activists' websites Vegh (2003) suggested are instructive: (1) awareness/advocacy; (2) organization/ mobilization; and (3) action/reaction. This distinction provides an insight in the different functions activists' websites can serve, and focuses on the direction of the initiative: 'whether one sends out information or receives it, calls for action or is called upon, or initiates an action or reacts to one' (Vegh, 2003: 72). This distinction can help in pinpointing the main objectives of a website, while hyperlink analyses can assist in pinpointing the structure of such a website, even though these functions may be blurred at times, for instance when information provision is supplemented with calls for action, as often is the case in online media (cf. van den Broek et al., 2012). Next to hyperlink analysis, a lot of work has also been done on 'how companies communicate their ethical stance on their Web sites' (Pollach, 2003: 277; see also e.g. Capriotti, 2011). Yet, these studies of Web 1.0 by definition focus on only one side of the communication.

Moving into the more interactive realm, Web 2.0 offers a wide array of applications that **are now often studied**. Many different types of applications have become available to activists, from weblogs to micro-blogging services, content-sharing sites, and social media platforms. For instance, the importance of microblogging service Twitter for activists has attracted a lot of attention over the last few years, both in the scholarly literature and in the popular press (cf. Castells, 2012; Gerbaudo, 2012; Juris, 2012), emphasizing its role in 'the fast, viral diffusion of images and ideas' (Castells, 2012: 2). Many of these studies have examined how Twitter has been used to inform and mobilize (potential) activists, and the importance of social media in the formation of social networks has often been discussed, with regard, also, to other social media applications such as YouTube and Flickr (cf. Poell & Borra, 2012). These different social media applications have certain characteristics in common. Lyon and Montgomery (2013) point at the non-hierarchical nature of social media that usually do not have gate-keepers, allow for a rapid and public response, are available at low cost of for free, focus on relationships and trust, and allow for interactions and conversations. They also mention the ad hoc and shifting networks that such information flows in social media often are based on (Lyon & Montgomery, 2013). The literature now is replete with examples of how activist groups and many others have used social media. They range from studies on cyber-protest against the World Bank (Vegh, 2003) to work that looks at how social media were used in the Occupy movement (Juris, 2012) or during processes of mobilization (Walgrave et al., 2011). According to Cammaerts (2012: 118), 'there is a need to theorize and encompass the various ways in which media and communication are enabling and constraining for activists and activism in the current ultra-saturated media and communication environment'. Expectations of Web 2.0 and its interactive nature have been high, as it could potentially involve a wide audience in an active manner. Or, as Obar et al. (2012: 2) phrased it: 'proponents of social media's democratizing function laud its ability to empower and connect individuals as well as groups'. How could this ability be used by activists in their tactics to establish institutional change on issues of CSR? In the next section I suggest a new typology to help address this type of question.

Towards a new typology

As noted, in aiming for institutional change on issues of CSR, activists are expected to work on the deinstitutionalization of disavowed practices and field frames and/or on the reinstitutionalization of new frames or practices. They have a range of different tactics at their disposal but whether they use these will also depend on their ideological positions. The many studies on social media, and the increasing number of studies considering their application by activists, provide several insights into the options social media offer for activists aiming for institutional change. Building on a combination of insights, I propose a framework to highlight how activists can turn to social media to work towards institutional change on issues of CSR. This framework builds on a combination of perspectives recently put forward in the literature, combining insights from social movement studies and media studies with institutional theory. Van Laer and Van Aelst (2010) offer a typology of the digital media repertoire of activists while Cammaerts (2012) suggests ideas on protest logics and mediation opportunity structure to examine different situations in which these different media repertoires could be applied. Both these frameworks are discussed in relation to the insights den Hond and de Bakker (2007) offer to examine how activists' online tactics can influence these processes of institutional change. This leads to a new typology for characterizing different online tactics activists deploy during processes of institutional change. As processes of institutional change often require a range of tactics in a longer running strategy, such a typology can be helpful in identifying different stages in a continuing conflict.

Van Laer and Van Aelst (2010) propose a fairly elaborate typology to analyze the 'digitalized action repertoire' along two dimensions: Internet-supported versus Internet-based and low versus high thresholds. Internet-supported tactics include the traditional tools available to activists, such as demonstrations or consumer activism that can be supported through the Internet, whereas Internet-based tactics only exist because of the Internet. Online petitioning, hacktivism, and email-bombing are some examples of the latter. As Van Laer and Van Aelst (2010) also look at the thresholds for participation, their typology nicely complements the one den Hond and de Bakker (2007) proposed to examine activists' tactics for institutional change. The distinction between reformist and radical ideological activists is important in understanding whether certain tactics are considered to be appropriate; the threshold for more radically informed tactics will be higher. Yet, the need to involve larger numbers of people to make a tactic work will also raise the threshold. As noted, den Hond and de Bakker (2007) therefore suggested that most activists will depart from a 'tactical starting position' that involves only a limited amount of people and aims for making a symbolic impact – an argument often noted in social movement theory where thresholds for participation have often been studied (cf. Klandermans, 1984).

The typology Van Laer and Van Aelst (2010) suggest connects to the increasing attention given to media opportunity structures (Cammaerts, 2012; Sampedro, 1997; Uldam, 2013). In social movement studies, 'the key recognition in the political opportunity perspective is that activists' prospects for advancing particular claims, mobilizing supporters, and affecting influence are context-dependent' (Meyer, 2004: 126). This means that a lot of attention in this approach focuses on the conditions under which activists operate, for instance understanding their mobilization potential, their choice of causes (and tactics), their willingness to enter into alliances, and their options to affect 'mainstream institutional politics and policy' (Meyer, 2004: 126). A huge stream of research has developed to distinguish between different types of opportunity structures. In an effort to link some of these ideas to media studies, Cammaerts (2012) suggests examining a 'mediation opportunity structure'. As he notes, this 'mediation opportunity structure [...] allows us to differentiate between different media actors with different forms of organization, adopting various formats and different ideological frames' (Cammaerts, 2012: 119). Starting from this perspective, he then distinguishes three areas in which mediation opportunity structures can play out and relates these to different logics of action that drive activists' tactics and strategies.

First there are the media representations: how are activists portrayed in the mainstream media and how does this strengthen or harm their positions and their ability 'to bring about broader social change' (Andrews & Caren, 2010: 841)? What kind of tactics, and what kind of ideological positions are able to 'make it into the media'? A lot of work has been done in this direction; Andrews and Caren (2010: 856), for instance, found that 'news media report more extensively on organizations that are geographically proximate, have greater organizational capacity, mobilize people through demonstrations or organizations, and use conventional tactics to target the state and media'. The second area is self-mediation, in which activists take the initiative, in becoming part of the media themselves. As Cammaerts (2012: 125) notes, 'the Internet provides them with extensive mediation opportunities to inform independently, to debate internally, to link up directly with those interested in their cause in a cost-efficient way, potentially across the time-space continuum'. Likewise, Hands (2011) speaks of the digital author as a producer of (mass) media. There are many examples around, including the well-known case of Indymedia.org, a platform 'of over sixty autonomously operated and linked Web sites' (Kidd, 2003: 49). Finally, Cammaerts (2012) points at 'resistance through technology', noting that the Internet is not only a platform but can also be a means of protest tactics. This connects well to the typology provided in Table 1.1 where quite a few of the tactics are indeed enabled through the Internet. One example is provided by Lyon and Montgomery (2013), who discuss the notion of 'tweetjacking' and indicate how activists captured 'hashtags' from tweets from McDonalds to use them for their own objectives of informing and influencing the general audience about issues relating to CSR such as labour conditions or animal welfare.

Cammaerts (2012) then links these three domains to different protest logics. Whereas den Hond and de Bakker (2007) argued for viewing the logic of witnessing as a logic that aimed to strengthen both other logics (logic of numbers and logic of damage/gain), Cammaerts (2012), like della Porta and Diani (1999), opts to see bearing witness as an independent protest logic. He offers an overview of how these three logics can play out in the three areas of the mediation opportunity structure he suggests, addressing both opportunities and constraints. For instance, an opportunity in self-mediation could be to make resistance real and

Table 1.1 Typology of activist groups' online tactics for institutional change and their type of objective and impact

	Internet-supported tactics	Internet-based tactics
Low number of participants/Symbolic impact	Call for donations	Protest website Culture jamming
High number of participants/Symbolic impact	Demonstration Transnational meeting	Online petition
High number of participants/Material impact	Sit-in Occupation Consumer impact (boycott or *buycott*)	Email bomb/virtual sit-in Crowd-funding
Low number of participants/ Material impact	Sabotage Destruction of property Obstruction of work	Hacktivism Culture jamming

Source: Based on den Hond and de Bakker (2007) and Van Laer and Van Aelst (2010).

credible, whereas a constraint in media representation could be a lack of media interest.

Although they stem from different theoretical backgrounds, both these approaches speak to the typology den Hond and de Bakker (2007) provided. Combining these different views leads to a more nuanced overview of four different categories of tactic, each of which can in turn be distinguished in Internet-supported and Internet-based tactics as shown in Table 1.1. This illustrative typology specifically focuses on online tactics; the distinction Van Laer and Van Aelst (2012) suggested between low and high threshold is now included in the categories of tactics reformist and radical activists are more likely to select. The typology allows us to characterize (combinations of) tactics and their objectives in terms of institutional change, for instance on issues of CSR but also in other domains. Which online tactics could be expected to be used by which type of activists in different situations? Deinstitutionalization calls for other tactics than reinstitutionalization and the ideological stance will also influence the choice of tactics as it influences what is seen as 'problem' and as 'solution' (den Hond & de Bakker, 2007). In the discussion, I will return to some of the tactics listed in the typology (Table 1.1).

In addition, Cammaerts' (2012) framework offers further insights into the contexts in which different tactics can be situated; different areas of the mediation opportunity structure provide room for different tactics. His overview can hence contribute to the application of the general model den Hond and de Bakker (2007) offered, although it does not speak directly to the link between tactics and institutional change. It is the combination of tactics, working in different areas of the mediation opportunity structure (and other opportunity structures as well, as Cammaerts (2012) also notes), ideological positions and of course the responses of other actors (notably firms, in the case of CSR) to these tactics that determine their influence on processes of institutional change. Den Hond and de Bakker (2007) suggested a series of propositions to indicate how activists with different ideological positions would turn to different tactics in an effort to stimulate deinstitutionalization or reinstitutionalization on issues of CSR. Cammaerts' (2012) framework provides more details about the context in which this would happen.

Discussion and conclusion

In the previous section I have combined perspectives from different streams of theory to develop a typology of online media tactics that could be deployed in activists' efforts for institutional change. In this section I will first briefly discuss the potential applicability of this typology and then turn to some potential pitfalls related to online media in general. After all, despite the many enthusiastic stories and case studies, several issues for debate have also been raised in the literature. Here I will highlight three such issues: reach, capabilities, and networks, and then end the chapter with some concluding remarks.

The typology developed here is essentially a device to categorize different online tactics, the way they relate to one another and the way they can influence processes of institutional change. The typology is not meant to deliver a complete overview of tactics but rather to sketch out examples of tactics along two axes: the type of online tactic, and its objective and desired impact. As den Hond and de Bakker (2007) noted, one could expect most activists to start from a similar starting-point, using tactics aimed at a symbolic impact and relying on only limited numbers of participants. After all, these tactics often are easier to start and less resource-intensive. In the typology I listed, calls for donations, culture jamming, and protest websites are some examples of these initial tactics: the Internet-supported tactics, such as (online) calls for donations, are essentially the online versions of tactics already available to activists offline, whereas Internet-based tactics extend the tactical repertoire by adding a new type of tactic, based on the Internet.

Protest websites are a clear example here, aimed at either distributing information, calling for action, allowing visitors to react (cf. Vegh, 2003), or combining these functions. Earlier on in this chapter several examples of such websites have been identified. The third tactic, culture jamming, which 'seeks to undermine the marketing rhetoric of multinational corporations, specifically through such practices as media hoaxing, corporate sabotage, billboard "liberation", and trademark infringement' (Harold, 2004: 90), might be somewhat in-between both categories as this tactic initially was deployed offline but seems to be increasingly Internet-based. Using (modified versions of) corporate logos, as Greenpeace did in its viral video on Nestlé's chocolate bar Kitkat (cf. Champoux et al., 2012) is one example here: the Internet-based tactics allowed for a quick transmission of Greenpeace's CSR message to source palm oil only from certified producers, while Nestlé's handling of the issue on its corporate Facebook page mainly resulted in further support for Greenpeace's claims.

In the other three categories similar distinctions also apply: the Internet-supported tactics are mainly the online extensions of offline tactics (such as the coordination of demonstrations, or calls for boycotts), whereas the Internet-based expand the tactical repertoire with novel tools (such as online petitioning, or hacktivism). From identifying these tactics online, the activists who use them, and the claims involved, an analysis can be made of the process of (desired) institutional change. After all, while debate over a specific field frame endures, activists can call on other tactics following the initial starting-point (den Hond & de Bakker, 2007). Depending on their ideological position they will make different choices, with the more radical activists aiming more directly for tactics with a material impact. They don't see their targets as part of the solution and hence will choose to be more confrontational, whereas more reformist activist groups will try to exert pressure through tactics aimed at having a symbolic impact first. Later on, in processes of reinstitutionalization, these reformist activists will try to work with firms to 'win them over' for their alternative field frame, whereas more radical activists will try to demonstrate the viability of a field frame that does not include business-as-usual. Here, for instance, crowd-funding for all sorts of alternative solutions can be found, as this can allow radical solutions to develop, next to the regular order.

The typology serves to structure online tactics and to provide a way to think about the implications of tactics for institutional change but it cannot be seen as independent from offline tactics (cf. den Hond & de Bakker, 2007; Taylor & Van Dyke, 2004). Often combinations of tactics are deployed, while several controversies can well occur simultaneously. In controversies over CSR raising consumer awareness, exerting pressure on producers and legislators and coordinating activities with allies all are likely to take place, sometimes at the same time. The typology does not offer a temporal dimension, although the different objectives and impacts suggest a certain pattern through the tactical repertoire, depending on the ideological position and the objective of deinstitutionalization or reinstitutionalization. More theorizing, and more empirical work, on how such processes unfold remains necessary. Nevertheless, through the typology and the discussion in this chapter, I aim to highlight some of the peculiarities of online tactics and how they could play a role in processes of institutional change. This adds to the tools on offer to understand how activists try to change field frames, norms, and standards, for instance on issues of CSR.

That being said, there are some more general considerations on social media that need to be kept in mind. First the actual *reach* of social media has been called into question. Are organizations really able to reach their target audience? As Van Laer (2010) found in a comparative study of online and offline protest participation, there were notable differences between the two. He suggested that these were signs of a 'democratic divide', with online activists being, for instance, 'significantly younger, better educated' and having 'more general interest in politics and previous protest experience' (Van Laer, 2010: 360). Van Laer (2010: 361) argued that the Internet attracts a particular kind of activist and that the reach beyond these 'superactivists' 'has thus far gone unrealized'. In addition there are discussions on what protest participation in an online environment actually means. Terms like 'clicktivism', 'clickstream activism', or 'slacktivism' have been coined in this respect (Karpf, 2010), denoting acts that only have a limited real life impact and that allegedly mainly work to 'enhance the feel-good factor for the participants' (Christensen, 2011). Christensen (2011) nevertheless found little evidence that Internet activism would indeed be slacktivism, while Karpf (2010: 29) emphasizes how e-petitions should be seen 'as an individual tactic within a broader strategic mobilization efforts'.

Secondly, there is the issue of capabilities. Some studies point at concerns about the required capabilities to handle social media. For instance, Obar et al. (2012) found that some of the organizations they studied discussed a generational/digital literacy gap that prevented them from using social media productively. Although this might be an issue that is relatively easy to overcome, for the time being it can certainly hamper an effective use of online media. This becomes all the more problematic when potential adversaries *do* master these capabilities, as is often the case in activism targeting (large) corporations. Furthermore, and closely linked to the activist organizations' capabilities, there is the ability to deal with diffuse responses, as organizations cannot always speak with one single voice (Obar et al., 2012). Yet, this can also be seen as one of the advantages of social media as it allows for a variety of voices to be heard and thus to weigh in on the debate. In discussing debates on CSR and the process of corporate legitimization and responsible business, Castelló et al. (2013) call for more polyphony, combining different voices, allowing contributors to the debate to hold on to their own identities and ideas and to bring them into the discussion.

The final issue for debate in social media that I discuss here involves networks. Bennett and Segerberg (2012) proposed taking a different look at social movements and social media, noting that a long-accepted driver of activism, collective action, would no longer suffice for understanding the processes going on in recent acts of activism. They noted that:

> younger citizens are moving away from parties, broad reform movements, and ideologies. Individuals are relating differently to organized politics, and many organizations are finding they must engage people differently: they are developing relationships to publics as affiliates rather than members, and offering them personal options in ways to engage and express themselves. This includes greater choice over contributing content, and introduces micro-organizational resources in terms of personal networks, content creation, and technology development skills. (Bennett & Segerberg, 2012: 760–761)

Whereas collective action focused on collective identity, the logic of connective action is based 'on personalized content sharing across media networks' (Bennett & Segerberg, 2012: 739), as the authors illustrate with several cases of recent 'digitally networked action' (DNA). As they note, some of these 'DNA networks turn out to be surprisingly nimble, demonstrating intriguing flexibility across various conditions, issues, and scale'. The emphasis that has often been placed on 'traditional' social networks to stimulate collective action (Castells, 2012) seems to work differently in online activism. Several authors have emphasized these differences (cf. Cammaerts, 2012; Gerbaudo, 2012; Hands, 2011; Van Laer & Van Aelst, 2010), also pointing to activists' need to express themselves (Hands, 2011; Valenzuela, 2013). More work on social networks is hence needed, to understand, also, how networks of activists strive for institutional change on issues of CSR (de Bakker, 2012). Yet, regardless of the temporary or more permanent organizational form of activist organizations, examining their tactical repertoire and the conditions under which these tactics could be applied fruitfully by activists remains relevant.

To conclude, in this chapter I have aimed to sketch out how social media could play a role in activists' efforts to influence how CSR is seen, that is, to establish institutional change on a contested concept. They use a rich repertoire of tactics to support their claims; depending on their ideological position they will consider different tactics to reach their objectives. Social media offer many new possibilities to exert influence, both through Internet-supported and Internet-based tactics; these online tactics allow them to address other audiences and can help in spreading their causes swiftly. They can also contribute to processes of institutional change because the interactive character of social media enables them to include a variety of voices and thus add to processes of deinstitutionalization, calling existing field frames into question, or to processes of reinstitutionalization, lending support to alternative field frames. In this way these tactics can contribute to changing the standards and norms within an industry, or within an organizational field, for instance on issues of CSR, as argued in this chapter. After all, examining activists' efforts in this area ties in with recent calls for more research into social media and its legitimation of the role of corporations in society (Castelló et al., 2013). A good understanding of the development of CSR within a particular field requires an insight in activists' tactics and the responses they receive, and online tactics need to be factored into such analysis. The typology I have offered here aims to contribute to these objectives by presenting an alternative representation of online tactics, geared towards processes of institutional change.

Note

1. A third logic della Porta and Diani (1999) suggest was not incorporated in the framework of den Hond and de Bakker (2007: 909). In this logic of witnessing, 'protesters show their dedication and commitment to the cause they support by deliberately running personal or financial risk'. Den Hond and de Bakker argued that this logic was mainly used to strengthen the vehemence of activists' protest and would therefore be used in combination with one of the other two logics. Cammaerts (2012: 121) recently suggested using all three logics in analysing mediation, noting that they are not mutually exclusive and that the logic of bearing witness involves 'public performance and civic disobedience'. His approach will be discussed further on in this chapter.

References

Aguinis, H. & Glavas, A. (2012). What we know and don't know about corporate social responsibility: A review and research agenda. *Journal of Management*, *38*(4): 932–968.

Andrews, K. T. & Caren, N. (2010). Making the news: movement organizations, media attention, and the public agenda. *American Sociological Review*, *75*(6): 841–866.

Baron, D. P. (2003). Private politics. *Journal of Economics & Management Strategy*, *12*(1): 31–66.

Bennett, W. L. (2003). Communicating global activism. Strengths and vulnerabilities of networked politics. *Information, Communication and Society*, *6*(2): 143–168.

Bennett, W. L. & Segerberg, A. (2012). The logic of connective action. *Information, Communication & Society*, *15*(5): 739–768.

Bimber, B., Flanagin, A. J. & Stohl, C. (2005). Reconceptualizing collective action in the contemporary media environment. *Communication Theory*, *15*(4): 365–388.

Bowen, H. R. (1953). *Social Responsibilities of the Businessman*. New York, NY: Harper.

Cammaerts, B. (2012). Protest logics and the mediation opportunity structure. *European Journal of Communication*, *27*: 117–134.

Capriotti, P. (2011). Communicating corporate social responsibility through the internet and social media. In Ø. Ihlen, J. L. Bartlett & S. May (eds), *The Handbook of Communication and Corporate Social Responsibility*. Boston, MA: John Wiley-Blackwell.

Carroll, A. B. (1979). A three-dimensional conceptual model of corporate performance. *Academy of Management Review*, *4*(4): 497–505.

Carroll, A. B. (1999). Corporate social responsibility. Evolution of a definitional construct. *Business & Society*, *38*: 268–295.

Castelló, I., Morsing, M. & Schultz, F. (2013). Communicative dynamics and the polyphony of corporate social responsibility in the network society. *Journal of Business Ethics*, *118*(4): 683–694.

Castells, M. (2012). *Networks of Outrage and Hope. Social Movements in the Internet Age*. Cambridge: Polity Press.

Champoux, V., Durgee, J. & McGlynn, L. (2012). Corporate Facebook pages: when 'fans' attack. *Journal of Business Strategy*, *33*(2): 22–30.

Christensen, H. S. (2011). Political activities on the Internet: Slacktivism or political participation by other means? *First Monday*, *16*(2).

Clark, J. D. & Themudo, N. S. (2006). Linking the web and the street: Internet-based 'dotcauses' and the 'anti-globalization' movement. *World Development*, *34*(1): 50–74.

Crane, A., Palazzo, G., Spence, L. J & Matten, D. (2014). Contesting the value of 'Creating Shared Value'. *California Management Review*, *56*(2): 130–153.

Davis, G. F., McAdam, D., Scott, W. R. & Zald, M. N. (eds). (2005). *Social Movements and Organization Theory*. New York, NY: Cambridge University Press.

de Bakker, F. G. A. (2012). Exploring networks of activism on corporate social responsibility: Suggestions for a research agenda. *Creativity & Innovation Management*, *21*(2): 212–223.

de Bakker, F. G. A., den Hond, F., King, B. & Weber, K. (2013). Social movements, civil society and corporations: Taking stock and looking ahead. *Organization Studies, 34*(5–6).

de Bakker, F. G. A., Groenewegen, P. & den Hond, F. (2005). A bibliometric analysis of 30 years of research and theory on corporate social responsibility and corporate social performance. *Business & Society, 44*(3): 283–317.

de Bakker, F. G. A. & Hellsten, I. (2013). Capturing online presence: Hyperlinks and semantic networks in activist group websites on corporate social responsibility. *Journal of Business Ethics, 118*(4): 807–823.

de Jong, W. (2005). The Power and Limits of media-based international oppositional politics – A case study: The Brent Spar conflict. In W. de Jong, M. Shaw & N. Stammers (eds), *Global Activism, Global Media* (pp. 110–124). London: Pluto Press.

De Maeyer, J. (2013). Towards a hyperlinked society: A critical review of link studies. *New Media & Society, 15*(5): 737–751.

della Porta, D. & Diani, M. (1999). *Social Movements. An Introduction.* Oxford: Blackwell.

den Hond, F. & de Bakker, F. G. A. (2007). Ideologically motivated activism: How activist groups influence corporate social change activities. *Academy of Management Review, 32*(3): 901–924.

Earl, J. & Kimport, K. (2009). Movement societies and digital protest: Fan activism and other nonpolitical protest online. *Sociological Theory, 27*(3): 220–243.

Fieseler, C., Fleck, M. & Meckel, M. (2010). Corporate social responsibility in the blogosphere. *Journal of Business Ethics, 91*: 599–614.

Garrett, R. K. (2006). Protest in an information society: A literature review on social movements and new ICTs. *Information, Communication & Society, 9*(2): 202–224.

Gerbaudo, P. (2012). *Tweets and the Streets. Social Media and Contemporary Activism.* London: Pluto Press.

Greenwood, R., Oliver, C., Sahlin, K. & Suddaby, R. (2008). Introduction. *The Sage Handbook of Organizational Institutionalism* (pp. 1–46). Thousand Oaks, CA: Sage,

Greenwood, R., Raynard, M., Kodeih, F., Micelotta, E. R. & Lounsbury, M. (2011). Institutional complexity and organizational responses. *The Academy of Management Annals, 5*(1): 317–371.

Hands, J. (2011). *@ is for Activism. Dissent, Resistance and Rebellion in a Digital Culture.* London: Pluto Press.

Harold, C. (2004). Pranking rhetoric: 'Culture jamming' as media activism. *Critical Studies in Media Communication, 21*(3): 189–211.

Jensen, H. R. (2003). Staging political consumption: A discourse analysis of the Brent Spar conflict as recast by the Danish mass media. *Journal of Retailing and Consumer Services, 10*(2): 71–80.

Jun, J. (2011). How climate change organizations utilize websites for public relations. *Public Relations Review, 37*(3): 245–249.

Juris, J. (2012). Reflections on #Occupy Everywhere: Social media, public space, and emerging logics of aggregation. *American Ethnologist, 39*(2): 259–279.

Jørgensen, D. (2012). Rigs-to-reefs is more than rigs and reefs. *Frontiers in Ecology and the Environment, 10*(4): 178–179.

Karpf, D. (2010). Online political mobilization from the advocacy group's perspective: Looking beyond clicktivism. *Policy and Internet, 2*(4): Article 2.

Kavada, A. (2005). Civil society organisations and the Internet: The case of Amnesty International, Oxfam and the World Development Movement. In W. de Jong, M. Shaw & N. Stammers (eds), *Global Activism, Global Media* (pp. 208–222). London: Pluto Press.

Kidd, D. (2003). Indymedia.org: A new communication commons. In M. McCaughey & M. D. Ayers (eds), *Cyberactivism. Online Activism in Theory and Practice* (pp. 47–94). New York, NY: Routledge.

Klandermans, B. (1984). Mobilization and participation: Social-psychological expansisons of resource mobilization theory. *American Sociological Review, 49*: 583–600.

Lawrence, T. B. & Suddaby, R. (2006). Institutions and institutional work. In R. S. Clegg, C. Hardy, T. B. Lawrence & W. R. Nord (eds), *Handbook of Organization Studies* (pp. 215–254). London, UK: Sage.

Lounsbury, M., Ventresca, M. & Hirsch, P. M. (2003). Social movements, field frames and industry emergence: A cultural-political perspective on US recycling. *Socio-Economic Review, 1*: 71–104.

Lyon, T. P. & Montgomery, A. W. (2013). Tweetjacked: The impact of social media on corporate greenwash. *Journal of Business Ethics*, 118(4): 747–757.

Matten, D. & Crane, A. (2005). Corporate citizenship: Toward an extended theoretical conceptualization. *Academy of Management Review*, 30(1): 166–179.

McCaughey, M. & Ayers, M. D. (eds) (2003). *Cyberactivism. Online Activism in Theory and Practice*. New York, NY: Routledge.

McWilliams, A. & Siegel, D. (2001). Corporate social responsibility: A theory of the firm perspective. *Academy of Management Review*, 26(1): 117–127.

Meyer, D. S. (2004). Protest and political opportunities. *Annual Review of Sociology, 30*: 125–145.

Nielsen, R. K. (2009). The labors of internet-assisted activism: Overcommunication, miscommunication, and communicative overload. *Journal of Information Technology & Politics*, 6(3–4): 267–280.

Obar, J., Zube, P. & Lampe, C. (2012). Advocacy 2.0: An analysis of how advocacy groups in the United States perceive and use social media as tools for facilitating civic engagement and collective action. *Journal of Information Policy*, 2: 1–25.

Pache, A.-C. & Santos, F. (2010). When worlds collide: The internal dynamics of organizational responses to conflicting institutional demands. *Academy of Management Review*, 35(3): 455–476.

Poell, T. & Borra, E. (2012). Twitter, YouTube, and Flickr as platforms of alternative journalism: The social media account of the 2010 Toronto G20 protests. *Journalism*, 13(6): 695–713.

Pollach, I. (2003). Communicating corporate ethics on the world wide web: a discourse analysis of selected company web sites. *Business & Society*, 42(2): 277–287.

Ramus, C. A. & Montiel, I. (2005) When are corporate environmental policies a form of greenwashing? *Business & Society*, 44(4): 377–414.

Rao, H., Morrill, C. & Zald, M. N. (2000). Power plays: Social movements and collective action create new organizational forms. In B. M. Staw & R. I. Sutton (eds), *Research in Organizational Behaviour*, (Vol. 22: pp. 239–282). New York, NY: Elsevier.

Rasche, A. & Esser, D. E. (2006). From stakeholder management to stakeholder alignment. *Journal of Business Ethics*, 65: 251–267.

Sampedro, V. (1997). The media politics of social protest. *Mobilization, 2*(2): 185–205.

Schneiberg, M. & Lounsbury, M. (2008). Social movements and institutional analysis. In R. Greenwood, C. Oliver, K. Sahlin & R. Suddaby (eds), *The SAGE Handbook of Organizational Institutionalism* (pp. 650–672). Thousand Oaks, CA: Sage.

Sharma, S. & Henriques, I. (2005). Stakeholder influences on sustainability practices in the Canadian forest products industry. *Strategic Management Journal, 26*(2): 159–180.

Shumate, M. & Dewitt, L. (2008). The north/south divide in NGO hyperlink networks. *Journal of Computer-Mediated Communication, 13*(2): 405–428.

Snow, D. A. (2004). Framing processes, ideology, and discursive fields. In D. A. Snow, S. A. Soule & H. Kriesi (eds), *Blackwell Companion to Social Movements* (pp. 380–412). Oxford: Blackwell.

Spar, D. L. & La Mure, L. T. (2003). The power of activism: Assessing the impact of NGOs on global business. *California Management Review, 45*(3): 78–101.

Taylor, V. & van Dyke, N. (2004). 'Get up, stand up': Tactical repertoires of social movements. In D. A. Snow, S. A. Soule & H. Kriesi (eds), *Blackwell Companion to Social Movements* (pp. 262–293). Oxford: Blackwell.

Uldam, J. (2013). Activism and the online mediation opportunity structure: Attempts to impact global climate change policies? *Policy and Internet, 5*(2): 57–75.

Valenzuela, S. (2013). Unpacking the use of social media for protest behavior: The roles of information, opinion expression, and activism. *American Behavioral Scientist, 57*(7): 920–942.

van den Broek, T., Ehrenhard, M. L., Langley, D. J. & Groen, A. J. (2012). Dotcauses for sustainability: Combining activism and entrepreneurship. *Journal of Public Affairs, 12*(3): 214–223.

van Huijstee, M. & Glasbergen, P. (2010). NGOs moving business: An analysis of contrasting strategies. *Business & Society, 49*(4): 591–618.

Van Laer, J. (2010). Activists 'online' and 'offline': Internet as an information channel for protest demonstrations. *Mobilization, 15*(3): 405–421.

Van Laer, J. & Van Aelst, P. (2010). Internet and social movement action repertoires: Opportunities and limitations. *Information, Communication & Society, 13*(8): 1146–1171.

Vegh, S. (2003). Classifying forms of online activism. The case of cyberprotest against the World Bank. In M. McCaughey & M. D. Ayers (eds), *Cyberactivism. Online Activism in Theory and Practice* (pp. 71–95). New York, NY: Routledge.

Walgrave, S., Bennett, W. L., Van Laer, J. & Breunig, C. (2011). Multiple engagements and network bridging in contentious politics: Digital media use of protest participants. *Mobilization, 16*(3): 325–349.

Yaziji, M. & Doh, J. P. (2009). *NGOs and Corporations: Conflict and Collaboration*. Cambridge: Cambridge University Press.

Zald, M. N. (2000). Ideologically structured action: an enlarged agenda for social movement research. *Mobilization, 5*: 1–16.

Zald, M. N. & McCarthy, J. D. (1980). Social movement industries: competition and cooperation among movement organizations. In L. Kriesberg (ed.), *Research in Social Movements, Conflicts and Change* (Vol. 3: pp. 1–20). Greenwich, CT: JAI Press.

2
Why Some Political Opportunities Succeed and Others Fail: Bridging Organizational Levels in the Case of Spanish Occupy

Itziar Castelló and David Barberá

Introduction and theory claims

The 'Occupy' protests provide numerous examples of new social movement organizations based on a complex, multilayered ecosystem heavily supported by social media and its ability to connect heterogeneous social networks. Studies of these type of organizations have stressed not only the importance of new media tools as a mobilization channels but also the influence of the Free Culture Movement on the genealogy, in terms of its composition, agenda, framing, and organizational logic (Fuster-Morell, 2012). Studies of the Occupy movements' activities have shown the importance of the online tools for new forms of mass mobilizations, for example (Borge-Holthoefer et al., 2011). Mobilizations become different in their nature: they are faster, can connect previously unlinked people, and are spontaneous (Bennett, 2003). However, few studies have looked into organizational characteristics beyond the online processes and their effect on mobilization. This article investigates how new forms of organizations characterized by being complex and multilayered networks select their organizational objectives and turn them into political matters. We ask how these organizational goals emerge, how they are selected, organized and ultimately impact the political arena.

We take the example of the 15M[1] movement (also called Spanish Occupy or the *Indignados* (indignated)). The 15M movement has become part of the Spanish political arena. Supported by 80% of the Spanish population,[2] 15M is a political force, an organization that conveys protest and leads political initiatives. It is not a political group, nor an established lobby, but a network of multiple rationalities, conflictive logics, and very heterogeneous actors in ongoing struggle and contestation that connects physically but mainly through social media networks. Radical leftish, anarchist, squatters, animal rights activists, pensioners, university students and professors, lawyers, the unemployed ... people with very different interests have been swelling the ranks of 15M. Many claimed that organizing change in such a heterogeneous group of people would be an impossible task. However, some of the 15M claims, such the 'non-recourse loan clause', have successfully materialized in policy changes. Others, such as 'Electoral Act reform', have died in oblivion.

Social movement scholars argue that movement activists do not choose their goals at random; it's the political contexts which stress certain grievances around which movements organize (Meyer, 2004). This political context has been described often in the theories of political opportunity structure (Meyer, 2004). Tarrow broadly defines political opportunity as 'consistent – but not necessarily formal or permanent – dimensions of the political struggle that encourage people to engage in contentious politics' (Tarrow, 1994: 19).

Political sociology and social movement theorists identify which political aspects affect the development of social movements, and how, and therefore which political structures have been considered to present an opportunity for action. As reviewed in Meyer (2004), they have considered changes in public policy (Costain, 1992; Meyer, 1993), international alliances and the constraints on state policy (Meyer, 2003), state capacity (Amenta et al., 1994; Kitschelt, 1986), the geographic scope and repressive capacity of governments (Boudreau, 1996) or the activities of countermovement opponents (Andrews, 2002; Fetner, 2001; Meyer & Staggenborg, 1996; Rohlinger, 2002), potential activists' perceptions of political opportunity (Gamson & Meyer, 1996; Kurzman, 1996), strategic outcomes (della-Porta et al., 1998; Jenkins & Eckert, 1986), different repertoires (Tarrow, 1994; Tilly, 1995), and even the prospects for personal affiliations (Goodwin, 1997).

Political opportunities have been analyzed through the underlying structures existing in the political fields that activists tactically appropriated in pursuit of particular claims at a particular time (Tilly, 1978). However, even authors like Tarrow argue that this is misleading, as most opportunities need to be perceived, and are situational and not related only to the circumstances surrounding a political landscape (Meyer, 2004). As argued by Meyer (2004), political research has often neglected the importance of the embedded agency in the creation of political opportunities.

We conceptualize political opportunity from an agentic perspective, to go beyond external forces of mobilization and look at dynamic processes of change of organizations in an institutional context (Lounsbury et al., 2003; Zietsma & Lawrence, 2010). We recognize in 15M a multilayered organization (Schneiberg & Soule, 2005) that mainly organizes online. Online organization fosters a loose, decentralized character, facilitating conflict and multiple, tolerant identities (Bennett & Segerberg, 2012).

We look at how an organization creates new paths or reproduces taken-for-granted practices to produce change, in the process of building arguments around a political opportunity. We analyze the political opportunity through its process of dynamic structuration (Phillips et al., 2000; Rosenkopf & Nerkar, 2001) and cohesion of the different organizational levels. Decisive in this approach is understanding how activists use a combination of different objects to disturb taken-for-granted assumptions, highlight injustice, and legitimate claims for reform (Kostova & Zaheer, 1999; Phillips et al., 2004; Suddaby & Greenwood, 2005), and how they do it in a new online environment that requires a different language, organization structure, and control of social engagement (Castelló et al., 2013; Castelló et al., 2013a).

The analysis of political opportunities and agency allows for researching the characteristics of successful initiatives and the processes of achieving success. With the case of 15M, we compare two political opportunities that emerged at approximately the same time: the first succeeded, while the second failed in being 'appropriated' and developed by 15M and ultimately implemented in national level politics. With this approach we look at the characteristics of failed and successful political opportunities and how they interact with complex mobilization processes mainly organized online. We measure successful mobilizations as those leading to policy reform (Meyer, 2004) or a change in law or 'soft law' (formal recommendations from the government, in this case to the banks, to modify their policies).

Methodology, data collection, and analysis

We approach the study of the role of political opportunities within the 'cycle of protest' proposed by Tarrow (1994) and look at the formation of an organization in a longitudinal manner. This study relies on the tradition of interpretative longitudinal case studies and, in particular, on those research projects which focus on deep longitudinal micro-level analyses of single exceptional cases (e.g. Etzion & Ferraro, 2010; Maguire & Hardy, 2009).

Data gathering covers a period spanning from May 2011 to December 2012 during which the authors engaged in several methods of data collection and analysis. The data collection addressed the study of the change process over time and triangulates (Jick, 1979) the information with multiple sources of evidence (Flick, 1998; Merriam, 1998; Patton, 2002). The different sources of data collection contained the following mix of qualitative methods:

First, participant observation: Both authors participated in the 15M movement, mainly in the Valencia occupations from the 16 May 2011 to 20 October 2011. More than 198 hours of participant observation were transcribed in 37 pages of ethnographic notes. We had informal non-recorded conversations with at least 180 activists, participated in more than 30 meetings and undertook other activist participation in campaigns, etc. One author also led a commission in the Valencia encampment for two months and was an active member of the neighbourhood group Zaidia in Valencia for about 18 months. We also visited the Sol encampment in Madrid and the Barcelona encampments and communicated often with their activists.

Second, netnography: Netnography is an ethnographic research method adapted to the study of online communities (Kozinets, 2002) in social media. In our netnographic research we first took a participant observation approach and became part of the network of activists. We also systematically collected data from social media platforms such as Facebook, Twitter, and open source, collaborative social media networks. We traced patterns of behaviour amongst the online communities at the squares' encampments, working groups, commissions, and neighbourhood groups.

Third, interviews: We performed 15 semi-structured interviews with selected members of 15M that were considered to have an active, key role in the movement, mainly in the Valencia encampment, but also in the Sol encampment. We took a snowball sampling approach to select those people that could provide information about the influences and change processes in the organization. We also performed 14 semi-structured interviews with activists from Madrid Sol in which we specifically asked about the differences between the non-recourse loan clause and the Electoral Law political claims.

Fourth, other material and archival data: We collected 22 press and academic articles specifically about 15M from major journals in Spain and academic journals. We also collected 23 posters and brochures. Twenty one pictures were taken by the authors.

The objective of the different sources of data collection was to be able, first, to understand the complexity and multiple layers of the organization. Second, to triangulate the data ensuring the accuracy of our conclusions and the formation of our theoretical claims (Gioia & Pitre, 1990; Lewis & Grimes, 1999).

The data analysis comprised four stages: In a first stage, based on the archival data and the participant observation data we identified the main organizational activities and field, configuring events such occupations, demonstrations, key meetings, and festivals. We also collected and classified symbols that were associated with the organizational activities and field-configuring events. We collected the symbols mainly through participant observation and netnographic data. In a second stage we classified them as relating to a micro, meso, or macro level of analysis. In a third stage, through our participant observation data, we identified the main political opportunities. We then traced collective agency by analyzing conversations, interviews, ethnographic notes and other articles to qualify and quantify the impacts of each political opportunity and its agency in the 15M organization (stage four).

Spanish Occupy: Emergence and selection of the political opportunities

On 15 May 2011 a crowd of about 20,000[3] people gathered at Puerta del Sol (Sol) (Madrid's central square) claiming 'They (politicians) do not represent us'. The demonstration filled up the square for few hours and ended with the usual rough encounter with the police and some detentions. Late at night, once the police left the square, a number of people lingered around and toyed with the idea of spending the night at the square. Precedents of square occupation were fresh in people's minds since the so called 'Arab Spring' had been taking place only few months before, filling the Spanish news. A tweet went out marking the decision: 'We have just encamped at Sol in Madrid. We are not leaving until we reach an agreement #acampadasol (occupy sol)'. Some 30–40 people spent the night in the open air until police evicted them at around five in the morning. Most people left the square saying that they would be coming back the next day.

The following day, people in Sol Square began to get together and organize a camp for spending the night. From the very start, campers showed an acute consciousness of the various dimensions of their public actions, such as planting a tent as a symbol of occupation and nominating a spokesperson who would manage press and police relations. During the night the tent and campers were evicted by the police again. However, early next morning the encampment had been set up again.

The third day, mainly through the Twitter hastag #acampadasol, campers called for an assembly that thousands of people attended (an estimated 300,000),[4] unprecedented for a spontaneous mobilization. After the initial spark in Madrid, the occupation of public spaces was quickly replicated across the country, even among Spanish communities abroad; more than 180 'occupy' communities were registered on hundreds of Facebook pages and blogs. David Bravo and Javier de la Cueva, two digital and intellectual property lawyers, drafted and made available on the Internet the legal proviso for rightful public demonstrations on 18 May 2011 (and thereafter), which campers were encouraged to submit to their respective local government delegations. Popular assemblies were organized every afternoon at 8pm, gathering thousands of people who devoted two or three hours per day to debating different political claims. For almost a month, squares such as Sol, Plaza Catalunya in Barcelona, and Plaza del Ayuntamiento in Valencia became hubs of vibrant political and cultural activity. Estimates put the number of participants in the movement during the first weeks of the encampments at between six and eight million.[5]

Activists, activities, and political claims

The initial mobilizations had been organized by an online forum 'Democracia Real Ya!' (Real Democracy Now!, DRY). The DRY group called for street protests at various public squares in Spain, demanding better political instruments and a more healthy democracy. Local elections were taking place a week later (22 May) and the economic crisis and numerous corruption scandals were at the centre of the political debates. DRY coordinated a platform of social movements which included the distributed collective Anonymous, Juventud en Acción (Youth in Action) or No Les Votes (Do Not Vote For Them). These groups were active parts of the Free Culture and Digital Commons Movement (FCM) and as such had mastered the techniques of online networking. DRY and the rest of the groups had been coordinating their protest for months before 15 May. Their claims were diverse and their space of action was very much online but they felt they needed more visible action, showing mobilized muscle in the streets, and therefore called for the 15M demonstration.

Had it not been for the Sol occupation and the support it received in the few days after, the DRY mobilization would have remained just another demonstration taking place in Madrid during those days. However, the square occupations and the organized online activity gave a special character to the protests, giving birth to a new social movement.

During the initial days, a specific target of the protest was difficult to discern. A simple walk around the encampments in central squares such as Sol gave an understanding of the diversity of the topics discussed and the heterogeneity of the groups gathered in the squares. Animal rights and women's rights activists shared spaces with people concerned with unemployment or the rise of the neoliberal policies imposed by the International Monetary Fund and the European Union. Ecologists and their urban orchards cohabitated with political activists demanding change in electoral law. The common claims were a call to occupy the squares, and online debates as spaces of self-made political action. Civic participation as a democratic principle was prioritized over ideologies or a single political claim. Activists claimed that the goal of the movement was not just to ask for economic and political justice and accountability but also to create horizontal links between individuals in similar conditions and thus strengthen Spaniards' sense of citizenship.

Only few days after the first occupations, the need to find a common claim emerged. The effort of the different groups in the occupations was diverted to coordinate a list of ten very concrete political claims that a representative of the 15M organization would present to the central government of Spain. The main activity of the occupations and online activity began to revolve around creating a list of top ten top political claims. Commissions and working groups were created around main areas of expertise such as economy, politics, banking, and housing issues. Commissions convened people interested in each of the topics, who would discuss multiple online proposals and would gather every afternoon at 6pm to define their priority claims. For example, the economic commission discussed potential measures to avoid corruption, regulate the banking industry, or impose a financial tax on speculative transactions. Hundred of proposals were discussed and lists and rankings of top ten political priorities circulated around the different encampments and online forums. On 22 May, Sol, which was the most influential square encampment in Spain, posted on their website and circulated amongst the rest of the occupations in Spain a list of ten main claims that people called the 'Sol Decalogue'. The political commissions in the different encampments led the distribution of the Sol Decalogue, which became the baseline of debates in all Spanish encampments.

The Sol Decalogue's top four political claims were the following: (i) The reform of the Electoral Law Act, since it was claimed that the current law favoured the two main political parties and damaged smaller parties. (ii) The internal reform of political parties, demanding open lists. (iii) The creation of a public bank that would be in charge of providing loans to small and medium-sized business. (4) A change in the mortgage law to allow for the full cancellation of a mortgage in cases of insolvency.

Despite the strong initial mobilization capacity of the Sol Decalogue, the aim of creating a coordinated, single, and common list was aborted only few days later. Accusations of manipulation by politicized groups such as DRY were loudly rumoured at the peripheral encampments such as Barcelona and Valencia. Rumours of the Decalogue being manipulated were also loud within the different Sol commissions. These rumours and the complexity of mainly an online communication between the platforms led to the rejection of the Sol Decalogue.

A complex dispute on ownership of and independency between political parties in relationship with any political claim was constantly collapsing the debate at the square assemblies and online forums. In the encampments, the transmission of information happened through informal networks created during the days of the occupation and the constant feed of tweets and posts in the web pages created by each commission. The absence of a centralized source of information promoted a constant rotation of news and rumours. The encampments; activists firmly rejected any sign of political influence from other political parties. The tension increased when some political leaders, mainly from political parties such as Izquierda Unida (IU) and Union Progreso y Democracia (UPyD) were pointed out as the main drivers of the political action in the encampments. As argued by one activist from Valencia: 'The political commission has a very manipulated dynamic. The guy with the long hair is the one having the microphone and selecting who talks. He is also answering to everybody. I know this guy, he is a guitar professor of a friend of mine, he is from UPyD' (Activist EN). The rejection of political intrusion was even formalized in a 'rule' in the encampments. Sol voted in one assembly that all political symbols would be forbidden in the square. People wearing small pins, flags, or banners were asked not to enter in the encampments. They were encouraged to participate in the movement but with the condition of removal of any political identification. This policy was soon adopted in several of the main squares, such as Valencia and Barcelona.

The movement was unable to find a list of concrete political claims that unified it and provided it with a concrete political voice that could be presented in formalized political institutions. The fear of political influence and manipulation of political parties was very present, reinforcing the push for very open fora of debate and leading to meetings in the camps that often lasted for three to four hours and had few executable outcomes. The online forums were unable to provide a clear priority to the different political opportunities in debate. The debates were increasingly fragmented and polarized towards certain political positions of those who dominated the online forums. However, even if, quantitatively, most of the activity was happening on the online forums, the legitimacy of these forums to actually set rules of action was challenged. Decisions had to be taken mostly in the commissions, offline, increasing the complexity of the exchanges.

The formation of a multilayer organization

The defeat in the creation of a political programme and the increasing pressure of eviction from the central squares from institutional forces such the police and health and safety departments pushed the encampments to work at preparing the transition of the movement towards decentralization in 'los barrios' (the neighbourhoods) and further online connectivity. The movement started to understand the need for the creation of a stable organizational logic that could support a multitude of political claims and interests and would maintain some physical presence but would mainly operate online.

Commissions started to change the focus of their debates to prepare a transition that would ensure the maintenance of the network and the activities of the 15M. At the encampments a call was made to help 'make the neighbourhood visible once again' (Activist A). Political claims such as the change in the electoral law, banking regulation, or financial sector taxation started to be replaced with a willingness to reinvent the municipalist tradition very present in the '60s and '70s in Spain during the transition to democracy.

During May and half of June the encampments were still the central meeting points of 15M. However, on 12 June, the Sol encampment decided to cease the occupation of the square. The rest of the encampments around the country followed a few days after. For several months an information contact point was kept in the central squares. General assemblies were also taking place once a month. The central squares' organizational structure was maintained in the websites and online forums but lacked concrete physical space. Some of the commissions and working groups kept up their activities, discussing proposals and organizing workshops and gatherings, but mainly the central squares' assemblies were devoted to the coordination of different initiatives led by new the neighbourhoods groups.

The de-centralization process lead to two new type of organization: the neighbourhood groups and the issue-specific platforms. The neighbourhood groups replicated the organizational structure of the central square encampments, with a variety of commissions being created in accordance with the residents' needs and interests. Meetings started to be held every one to two weeks, and reported back to the central squares' assemblies, where online discussions were at the same time still very present. Neighbourhood activities ranged from the creation of local orchards and time-banks, to the occupation of local banks, etc. Despite the variety of activities, most of the neighbourhoods maintained the 15M identifying symbols and organizational principles. Their names evoked their belonging to the more general movement (e.g. 15M Zaidía, 15M Russafa) and their principles of behaviour and relationships were constantly related to the general rules defined at the central squares assemblies. Inclusive participation was encouraged, and voting formats, rules, and signs were maintained; online platforms were also created and online debates dominated the neighbourhood activities. Even if they were constituted as independent organizational units, belonging to the broader 15M movement was important to reinforce their legitimacy.

Issue-specific platforms such as the PAH (Platform of People Affected by Mortgages (Hipoteca)) were developed in parallel. They often related to the neighbourhood assemblies, to gather support such as signatures for the popular legislative initiative (in Spanish the ILP) or Change.org petitions, or for concrete activities such bank occupations. However, they kept a distinct structure and a very specific agenda. Issue-specific platforms acted often as bricoleur agents, configuring their own initiatives while borrowing at the same time the symbolic and network structure from the 15M. They developed their own symbols (e.g. the 'stop desahucios' symbol) while maintaining the reference to the 15M in their narratives. This bricolage provided them with the legitimacy of the 15M movement and also with an important network, already aware of established principles of behaviour which they could leverage. Activists in the neighbourhoods worked on the activities organized by the issue-specific platforms. For example, during the two months that the PAH was collecting signatures most of the neighbourhood organizations had a PAH representative person in charge of the signature collection in each of the neighbourhood gatherings. Activists associated the success of these initiatives to the 15M; as argued by one activist: 'one of the most important initiatives of the 15M is related to the non-recourse loan clause' (Activist G).

We argue the 15M became an organization with a complex and multilayered structure with three main levels: First, a macro-level brand, labelled as the '15M movement' by the activists, but also by the media, politicians, and other members of society. The 15M brand was associated with a larger network of international contestation events such as Occupy Wall Street or the Spring Revolution in Arabic countries. It shared a common narrative that related to being a non-violent citizen based in an inclusive movement willing to enhance citizenship participation in the political arena. The 15M brand acted as legitimizing object that was appropriated by several issue-specific initiatives as well as the neighbourhood groups. It was a 'floating signifier' (Laclau, 1989) with no one specific political aim beyond the willingness to increase civic engagement to enhance democratic accountability in Spain and around the globe. The 15M brand constituted a first macro level of the organization since it created an overarching structure of signification in which different sub-structures were recognized.

Second, a meso level represented by the central squares' encampments such as Sol. Central squares organizational units convened activities such as the general assemblies, commissions, working group, music concerts, poetry jams, etc. The square had the function of evoking a common physical space for the organization, even after the movement abandoned the stable encampments. It was represented by symbols that related to the physical place. The squares as places of sociability developed their own rules of communication and organization (e.g. voting signs, rules in the assembly, rules for space distribution, rules for de-politization of the place). It also represented the multiplicity of the movement, embracing all different activities and political claims, which was replicated in the multiple online forums that were supporting the square activities.

Third, the micro level, in which the issue specific platforms and the neighbourhood groups developed. At the micro level, actions were concrete and actionable but unified by the common identity of the 15M. The common narratives were forged around the very specific needs of the citizens (e.g. a house to live in, an orchard to grow vegetables, a time-bank to exchange English lessons for babysitting). This level sometimes borrowed from the meso level specific resources such as central square assemblies and online platforms.

The characteristics of political opportunities in a multilayered organization

The 15M was able to create a network of civic engagement. It was recognized as a new and different political force in Spain. Demonstrations were convened under the claims of the 15M, occupations eventually happened, and the 15M spirit was represented in citizen actions such as demonstrations to stop evictions of families who could not pay their mortgage.

Several political claims emerged during the initial days of the 15M, however only few succeeded. The successful claims did not reduce the heterogeneity of the movement but fuelled its mobilization capacity and created symbolic cohesion. But from the whole range of political claims discussed in the working groups, general assemblies, and neighbourhood platforms, few were able to bridge the different levels of the organization and gain popular but also political recognition.

We analyze the characteristics of two political claims present in the first Decalogue of the Sol encampment on 22 May. Both claims were present from the first days in the encampments; both represented in the first demonstration; both had support from several groups inside the organization and were heavily discussed in the assemblies. However, the first, the 'non-recourse loan clause', succeeded, and concrete political action was taken. It was discussed at the Spanish parliament and presented as government recommendation and ultimately changed in January 2013. The second, the change in the Electoral Law Act, failed and disappeared from the political debate.

We study the role of political opportunities in the movement's attempt develop civic engagement by bridging the different organizational levels. Political opportunities set the political agenda and the resolution of that agenda, defining new frames (Kurzman, 1996).

The non-recourse loan clause and its bridging functions

The non-recourse loan clause (datio in solutum) is a claim to change the mortgage law which currently obliges mortgage payers to be 100% liable for the mortgage even if the loan-to-value ratio is positive. The claim for changing the mortgage law was not new to Spanish civil society, nor exclusive to 15M. Since 2010, the PAH (Platform for People Affected by the Mortgages (Hipotecas)), an organization demanding the change of the Spanish mortgage law to non-recourse loans had been working with law associations, trade unions, and the media to present alternatives to the mortgage law. Their claims were presented in the local press, especially in Barcelona, where the PAH had its most active hub. The PAH exercised successful lobby pressure which lead to the presentation of a petition for creating a study commission in the national parliament in June 2010. The proposal for the creation of a study commission was accepted but the law was not changed due to the opposition of the main Spanish political parties PSOE (Partido Socialista Obrero Español) and PP (Partido Popular). During 2011 evictions increased dramatically,[6] giving media visibility to the issue.

PAH supporters participated very actively in 15M. They created working groups in the main city encampments and supported the discussion with logos and slogans. Their claims appeared on the Sol Decalogue. Indeed, we argue that from May 2011 the PAH acted as a de facto issue-specific platform within the 15M movement. PAH understood their claims were well received by 15M and decided to collect citizen endorsement to present a Popular Legislative Initiative (ILP in Spanish), a political procedure to present a new Bill to Parliament based on citizen endorsement. The 15M neighbourhood organizations took charge of the collection of citizen endorsements. Collecting endorsements involved the printing of gadgets, t-shirts, and stickers combining the 'Stop' symbol used by the PAH with those use by 15M. Furthermore, 15M neighbourhood groups often participated in stopping the actual house evictions. Activists would simply gather in the doorway of the family being evicted, peacefully obstructing the work of the police, who were forced to postpone the eviction giving some time to the families to re-negotiate the loan with the banks. 15M was representing the common citizen and their interventions to stop the evictions were giving further meaning to the movement. As argued by one activist, people easily related to the issue: 'This person evicted could be me or my mother' (Activist D). The 15M presence in the evictions provided them with visibility in the media, increasing popular awareness of the problem. In July 2011 the ILP had gathered 1,402,854 signatures, with more than 600 focal points for signature collection,[7] and was presented to Parliament. Parliament did not pass the PAH Bill, but the ILP lead to the creation of a study commission in Parliament, a series of suggestions from the government to the banks to renegotiate the loans to avoid evictions, and eventually to a new Mortgage Law in January 2013.

The non-recourse loan clause claim contained elements that bridged all movement levels of action. It was commonly associated to the 15M movement. 15M played an important role in the visibility of the issue (as confirmed by most of our informants in the interviews). It was also present in the discussion of the squares at meso level and became one of the main claims in the Sol Decalogue. The non-recourse loan clause was an instrument which bridged the relationship between 15M and neighbourhood groups that took on the ILP and the stopping of people's evictions as one of their main activities. The non-recourse loan clause claim gave concrete political meaning to the 15M organization. It was a political claim that was easily embraced by the 15M participants since it appealed to a very basic sense of justice and redistribution. As argued by an activist: 'The non-recourse loan clause is tangible and affects all of us in a very physical way' (Activist A). Finally, the non-recourse loan clause, although supported by some of the left political parties such as IU (Izquierda Unida) and ERC (Esquerra Republicana de Cataluña), was not perceived as a political claim but as a 'people's' claim. The claim was lead by an issue-specific platform not previously associated with any official political party.

The change in the Electoral Law Act and its inability to settle at the micro level

The Electoral Law Act[8] claim was for a better distribution of the seats in national voting for Parliament representatives. It demanded that the seats in Parliament attributed to each political party should be proportional to the number of votes (since the current law favours the big national parties (PP and PSOE)). It was argued that the current Electoral Law prevented minority voices from accessing Parliament. The change in the Electoral Law Act was considered a main claim of 15M. It was at the basis of the DRY demonstrations for greater democracy and better political representation.

Similarly to the non-recourse loan clause claim, the change in the Electoral Law was very present in the Spanish political arena before 15M. Groups such as DRY pushed it hard in the political debates, convening special Internet forums. It was also an important claim of some of the small national political parties such as IU and UPyD.

15M intensely embraced the change in Electoral Law, demand it be included in the Sol Decalogue. Some of the encampment commissions, such the short-term political commission, made the change in Electoral Law its focal cause. They argued it was the basis of the Spanish political reshuffle that could ensure their representation in the national parliament.

Although the change of Electoral Law claim was well supported in the demonstrations and encampments at the meso level, it never reached the activities of the micro level groups at the neighbourhoods. DRY also acted as an issue-specific platform (as PAH did). They launched a citizen endorsement campaign at the Internet platform Change.org. Change.org had been very successful supporting some claims in the past and the online space was considered natural for groups such as DRY and the Free Cultural Digital Commons Movement also supporting this initiative. However, the Change.org petition was closed with only 12,733 petitions. The initial efforts in consolidating the political claim did not materialize in an opportunity that could be leveraged by the neighbourhood organizations: 'The change in Electoral Law was important but did not resonate with our activities in the neighbourhood, it was too far from people' (Activist A). Consequently, the change in the Electoral Law, although considered an important democratic claim by many of the 15M groups, did not go through in the Spanish political arena. It was not able to create a recognizable object of action that could be enacted in the everyday life. Although it appealed to fundamental democratic claims, people did not feel it was an authentic claim of 15M, but rather a political claim from existing political parties.

Discussion: Political opportunities and their boundary-spanning functions

Our study examines agency in multilevel-type organizations. We define the 15M movement as a three-level or layer organization: (i) macro: the global brand (the Occupy movement); (ii) meso: the city assemblies that act as coordinating committees (brokering between different groups of activists); (iii) micro: the neighbourhood groups and the issue-specific platforms (which implement actions with different repertoires). We observe that the 15M is an exemplary case of complex, multilayered organization enabled by new technologies of the Internet and social media tools. We argue that such a multilayered and heterogeneous organization requires new forms of meaning-creation to reduce uncertainty and dispersion in mobilization.

We studied the role of political opportunities, bridging elements between the different organizational levels. We defined successful political opportunities as being able to bridge the different levels of the organization.

Boundary political opportunities set the political agenda and the resolution of that agenda, defining new prognostic frames that enabled people in 15M to take action and further mobilize constituents.

We finally argue that the identification of several boundary political opportunities has proven necessary for the survival of the 15M, since it provides meaning to activists and society. However, the approach to social movements and their related organizations that we propose celebrates the heterogeneity of actors, multiple logics, and plural spaces of communication. We argue that, contrary to other social movements, 15M was not created around a concrete political opportunity, but enacted the agentic appropriation of several opportunities. Such a perspective concentrates less on the contagion of unitary practices or a singular rationality, but rather on multiple forms of rationality and multiple forms of communication that inform the decision-making of activists in the process of civic engagement and provide foundations for ongoing research on the understanding of new forms of organizations that are mainly based on online communications, and their models of civic engagement through struggle and contestation.

The Occupy movement and 15M are examples of the importance of conceptualizing a social movement as a multilayered, fragmented, and contested organization (Lounsbury, 2007; Schneiberg & Soule, 2005; Washington & Ventresca, 2004), as an ontological starting point. It directs analytical attention to how political opportunities are perceived at multiple organizational levels. The multiple level approach creates possibilities for understanding how social movements couple agency and mobilization with the characteristics of political opportunities that shape the capacity of movements to produce change (Lounsbury et al., 2003; Schneiberg & Lounsbury, 2008). It also gives meaning to more holistic perspectives on social movements and encompasses the possibility of analysis of online and offline activities.

Acknowledgements

The authors would like to acknowledge the support of the Entrepreneurship Platform at Copenhagen Business School, the Danish Ministry of Science and Technology, and the Strategic Research Council and the Universidad Carlos III de Madrid and its mobility programme. The authors would also like to express their gratitude for the valuable comments of participants of the workshop 'Social Media and Civic Engagement: Contesting the Mainstream', organized by the nSICE network, and to the editors of this book.

Notes

1. The name of the movement represents the day of the first demonstration, on 15 May 2011 in Madrid.
2. RTVE: 'Entre 6 y 8,5 millones de personas han participado de alguna forma en el 15-M' (accessed online 7 August 2011).
3. *El País* (Editorial section); 'Indignados en la calle', 17 May 2011 (accessed online 17 May 2011).
4. RTVE. 'Entre 6 y 8,5 millones de personas han participado de alguna forma en el 15-M' (accessed online 7 August 2011).
5. RTVE. «Entre 6 y 8,5 millones de personas han participado de alguna forma en el 15-M». (Web access 7 August/8/2011).

6. 350,000 people had been evicted since 2008 (http://suite101.net/article/unas-350000-familias--desahuciadas-en-espana-tras-la-crisis-a69973).
7. http://afectadosporlahipoteca.com/campana-dacion-en-pago/.
8. Ley Orgánica 5/1985, de 19 de junio, del Régimen Electoral General. Also known as the 'Ley D'Hont'. More information in http://www.publico.es/30838/las-verdades-y-mentiras-de-la-ley-electoral.

References

Amenta, E., Dunleavy, K. & Bernstein, M. (1994). Stolen thunder? Huey Long's 'Share our Wealth,' political mediation, and the second New Deal. *American Sociological Review*, 59: 678–702.

Andrews, K. T. (2002). Movement-countermovement dynamics and the emergence of new institutions: The case of 'White Flight' schools in Mississippi. *Social Forces*, 80: 911–936.

Bennett, W. L. (2003). *New Media Power: The Internet and Global Activism*. Oxford: Rowman & Littlefield.

Bennett, W. L. & Segerberg, A. (2012). The logic of connective action: Digital media and the personalization of contentious politics. *Information, Communication & Society*, 15(5): 739–768.

Borge-Holthoefer, J., Rivero, A., Garcia, I., Cauhe, E., Ferrer, A. & Francos, I., et al. (2011). Structural and dynamical patterns on online social networks: The Spanish May 15th movement as a case study. *PLoS ONE*, 6(8): doi: 10.1371/journal.pone.0023883

Boudreau, V. (1996). Northern theory, southern protest: Opportunity structure analysis in cross-national perspective. *Mobilization*, 1: 175–189.

Castelló, I., Etter, M. & Nielsen, F. A. (2013). *Legitimacy Building in the Networked Society and the Locus of Control*. Paper presented at the Academy of Management Annual Conference, Orlando, Miami.

Castelló, I., Morsing, M. & Schultz, F. (2013a). Communicative dynamics and the polyphony of corporate social responsibility in the network society. *Journal of Business Ethics*, 118(4): 683–694. doi: 10.1007/s10551-013-1954-1

Costain, A. N. (1992). *Inviting Women's Rebellion: A Political Process Interpretation of the Women's Movement*. Baltimore, MD: Johns Hopkins University Press.

della-Porta, D., Fillieule, O. & Reiter, H. (1998). Policing protest in France and Italy: From intimidation to cooperation? In D. S. Meyer & S. Tarrow (eds), *The Social Movement Society: Contentious Politics for a New Century*. Lanham, MD: Rowman & Littlefield.

Etzion, D. & Ferraro, F. (2010). The role of analogy in the institutionalization of sustainability reporting. *Organization Science*, 21(5): 1092–1107.

Fetner, T. (2001). Working Anita Bryant: The impact of Christian antigay activism on lesbian and gay movement claims. *Social Problems*, 48: 411–428.

Flick, U. (1998). *An Introduction to Qualitative Research*. London: Sage Publications Ltd.

Fuster-Morell, M. F. (2012). The Free Culture and 15M movements in Spain: Composition, social networks and synergies. *Social Movement Studies*, 11(3–4): 86–392.

Gamson, W. A. & Meyer, D. S. (1996). Framing political opportunity. In D. McAdam, J. D. McCarthy & M. N. Zald (eds), *Comparative Perspectives on Social Movements* (pp. 275–290). Cambridge, UK: Cambridge University Press.

Gioia, D. & Pitre, E. (1990). Multiparadigm perspectives on theory building. *Academy of Management Review*, 15: 584–602.

Goodwin, J. (1997). The libidinal constitutions of a high-risk social movement: Affectual ties and solidarity in the Huk Rebellion. *American Sociological Review*, 63: 53–69.

Jenkins, J. C. & Eckert, C. (1986). Elite patronage and the channeling of social protest. *American Sociological Review*, 51: 812–829.

Jick, T. (1979). Mixing qualitative and quantitative methods. Triangulation in action. *Administrative Science Quarterly*, 24: 602–611.

Kitschelt, H. P. (1986). Political opportunity structures and political protest: Anti-nuclear movements in four democracies. *British Journal of Political Science*, 16: 57–85.

Kostova, T. & Zaheer, S. (1999). Organizational legitimacy under conditions of complexity: The case of multinational enterprise. *Academy of Management Review*, 24: 64–81.

Kozinets, R. (2002). The field behind the screen: Using netnography for marketing research in online communities. *Journal of Marketing Research*, 39: 61–72.

Kurzman, C. (1996). Structural opportunity and perceived opportunity in social movement theory: The Iranian Revolution of 1979. *American Sociological Review*, 61: 153–178.

Laclau, E. (1989). Politics and the limits of modernity. *Social Text*, 21: 63–82.

Lewis, M. & Grimes, A. (1999). Metatriangulation: Building theory from multiple paradigms. *Academy of Management Review*, 24(4): 672–690.

Lounsbury, M. (2007). A Tale of Two Cities: Competing logics and practice variation in the professionalizing of mutual funds. *Academy of Management Journal*, 50: 289–307.

Lounsbury, M., Ventresca, M. J. & Hirsch, P. M. (2003). Social movements, field frames and industry emergence: A cultural-political perspective on US recycling. *Socio-Economic Review*, 1: 71–104.

Maguire, S. & Hardy, C. (2009). Discourse and deinstitutionalization: The decline of DDT. *Academy of Management Journal*, 52: 148–178.

Merriam, S. B. (1998). *Qualitative Research and Case Study Applications in Education*. San Francisco: John Wiley & Sons Inc.

Meyer, D. S. (1993). Peace protest and policy: Explaining the rise and decline of antinuclear movements in postwar America. *Policy Studies Journal*, 21: 35–51.

Meyer, D. S. (2003). Political opportunity and nested institutions. *Social Movement Studies*, 2: 17–35.

Meyer, D. S. (2004). Protest and political opportunities. *Annual Review of Sociology*, 30: 125–145.

Meyer, D. S. & Staggenborg, S. (1996). Movements, countermovements, and the structure of political opportunity. *American Journal of Sociology*, 101: 1628–1660.

Patton, M. Q. (2002). *Qualitative Research & Evaluation Methods*. Thousand Oaks, California: Sage Publications, Inc.

Phillips, N., Lawrence, T. B. & Hardy, C. (2000). Inter-organizational collaboration and the dynamics of institutional fields. *Journal of Management Studies*, 37: 23–43.

Phillips, N., Lawrence, T. B. & Hardy, C. (2004). Discourse and institutions. *Academy of Management Review*, 29: 635–652.

Rohlinger, D. A. (2002). Framing the abortion debate: Organizational resources, media strategies, and movement-countermovement dynamics. *Sociology Quarterly*, 43: 479–507.

Rosenkopf, L. & Nerkar, A. (2001). Beyond local search: Boundary-spanning, exploration, and impact in the optical disk industry. *Strategic Management Journal*, 22: 287–306.

Schneiberg, M. & Lounsbury, M. (2008). Social movements and institutional analysis. In R. Greenwood, C. Oliver, K. Sahlin & R. Suddaby (eds), *The SAGE Handbook of Organizational Institutionalism*. London, UK: Sage Publications Ltd.

Schneiberg, M. & Soule, S. A. (2005). Institutionalization as a contested, multilevel process: The case of rate regulation in American fire insurance. In G. F. Davis, D. McAdam, W. R. Scott & M. N. Zald (eds), *Social Movements and Organization Theory*. Cambridge, UK: Cambridge University Press.

Suddaby, R. & Greenwood, R. (2005). Rhetorical strategies of legitimacy. *Administrative Science Quarterly*, 50: 35–67.

Tarrow, S. (1994). *Power in Movement: Collective Action, Social Movements and Politics.* Cambridge University Press.

Tilly, C. (1978). *From Mobilization to Revolution.* Reading, MA: Addison-Wesley.

Tilly, C. (1995). *Popular Contention in Great Britain 1758–1834.* Cambridge, MA and London: Harvard University Press.

Washington, M. & Ventresca, M. J. (2004). How organizations change: The role of institutional support mechanisms in the incorporation of higher education visibility strategies, 1874–1995. *Organization Science*, 15: 82–96.

Zietsma, C. & Lawrence, T. B. (2010). Institutional work in the transformation of an organizational field: The interplay of boundary work and practice work. *Administrative Science Quarterly*, 55: 189–221.

3
Responsible Retailing in the Greek Crisis? Corporate Engagement, CSR Communication, and Social Media

Eleftheria J. Lekakis

Introducing responsible retailing

In June 2012, in the midst of much uncertainty in the political and business world of austerity-stricken Greece, seven supermarkets decided to embrace the cause of supporting Greek products as foregrounded by the citizen movement 'We Consume What We Produce'.[1] The retailers took to the cause by promoting the movement through posters, banners, and plastic bags – one of the promotional strategies with which corporate entities (retailers) engaged in order to ameliorate consumer confidence. In a shifting terrain of trust and legitimacy, citizens turned to the marketplace for support; in a comment to the Facebook site of a supermarket, a citizen exclaims: 'Do whatever you can with your offers, because these sold-out politicians plan to exterminate us. Make your offers real offers, in order to provide us with the possibility of survival. Thank you'. As wages, pensions, and employment were continuously slashed, the human fabric of sustenance and economic subsistence became explicitly entwined and torn throughout. The traumatic reconfigurations of the Greek political system and culture directly impacted the market, causing an adaptation of corporate social responsibility (CSR) communication to the crisis setting. CSR communication is understood here as a type of global communication which defines and describes the ways in which Multinational Corporations (MNCs), but also national and local businesses attempt to communicate their responsibility towards their location and context. In this vein, this chapter explores a top-down approach to institutional engagement, by focusing on corporate engagement with consumers in dire financial straits. Hence, this chapter questions how supermarkets communicated responsibility and corporate engagement in the Greek crisis, following on from a broader question about the responsibility of business towards society which has occupied the social sciences more broadly since the 1970s.

What follows is an outline of corporate engagement with the crisis within an unstable context for both institutions and society. The difference between corporate engagement and civic engagement is that civic engagement refers to the mobilization of civic resources to address civic concerns, while corporate engagement refers to the mobilization of corporate resources to address consumer concerns. This chapter differs from the preceding ones in that it exposes the ways in which promotional culture manifests as corporate engagement with a society, and questions the legitimacy of CSR communication in times of crisis. By exploring CSR communication in a financial crisis context, I argue that there is a push to address consumers' financial concerns around affordability, but also to engulf manifestations of the nation within the bounds of their promotional culture. In what follows, I will elaborate on the Greek retail sector and outline the rhetorical and structural demonstrations of responsibility from supermarkets towards financially crippled consumers. Through the examination of four national supermarkets, a systematic analysis of their CSR reports and particularly their social media use, I posit that the demonstration of responsible retailing in crisis ranges from practical to symbolic restructuring of market strategy to remain relevant in an uncertain terrain. Understanding how national supermarkets adopt CSR practices is an extension of the exploration of responsible retailing through the study of responsibility towards the consumer body in crisis. In austerity-stricken Greece, there is an abundance of corporate social responsibility strategies in retail. National supermarkets are communicating CSR by addressing consumers through an explicit narrative of national pride, solidarity, and affordability, as well as through a practical restructuring of their prices. This introduction is followed by a theorization of corporate and crisis communication, a methodological section, the analyses of official (directed towards other institutions) and unofficial (directed towards consumers) CSR communication, a discussion of CSR practices in the social base of nations through ritualistic adaptation, as well as a rhetoric of national responsibility for business and citizens alike, and a conclusion which revisits the main argument.

Theory: crisis communication in the Greek retail sector

As political formations have been shifting their ideologies and allegiances and the civic body has continuously resisted the austerity measures which pull the noose tighter around its neck, Greece is undeniably closer to tension than ever since the post-junta democracy (cf. Rogers & Vasilopoulou, 2012). The rise of responsible retailing is connected to the significance of retail in the Greek economy and the negotiations of its perception among consumers. Do supermarkets have more responsibility than other members of the business world? In brief, yes, for internal purposes of survival and for external purposes as demonstrations of responsibility to the civic body for which they continue to be the main platforms for daily consumption. Robinson (2010) posits that changes in supermarket behaviour are evident when consumer trust is at stake. The crisis has created a complicated matrix of consumer saving and spending. The national retail sector has sought different solutions to overcome this through various CSR strategies analyzed below. As the main arteries of food distribution, supermarkets are faced with the difficulties of both commercial survival and remaining relevant within a trampled consumer economy.[2] Organized retail sales through supermarkets continue to capture the consumer needs of the population. Basic household goods are bought in supermarkets, creating a direct link between everyday consumption and sustenance of the national economy throughout the crisis. Furthermore, market research on the expectations that citizens have from responsible companies and from themselves as consumers shows that the values of ethical market behaviour (product reliability, environmental sustainability, social responsibility, affordability, and fair employee treatment) significantly increased during the period before and after the beginning of the crisis.[3] Yet, the economic crisis has severely impacted consumer spending in the Greek economy.

Crises are impromptu events which harm the equilibrium of a given situation and can spread swiftly, affecting all layers of societal organization. Sellnow and Seeger (2013) offer a theoretical framework which extends beyond strategic business communication; their take on crisis communication outlines how a corporate crisis develops, how it can be detected, where it can lead, how it can be responded to, how it is mediated, what its influence is, how risk can be managed, and what the ethics vested in crisis communication are. Based on this, corporate engagement through CSR communication will be analyzed in terms of its communication and attempted influence. Responsible retailing is thus indirectly aligned to crisis communication on a meta level. Instead of understanding how retailers are trying to manage their image and business in the context of the Greek crisis, this chapter discusses crisis communication as the way in which the financial crisis absorbs corporate communication and creates relationships which aim to extend beyond consumer concerns. Typically, crisis communication is described as 'the ongoing process of creating shared meaning among and between groups, communities, individuals and agencies, within the ecological context of a crisis, for the purpose of preparing for and reducing, limiting and responding to threats and harm' (Sellnow and Seeger, 2013: 13). CSR communication in crisis, then, can refer to two modalities of business communication. The first is influence, which is related to persuasion, public relations, and promotional cultures. The parameter of influence is perhaps the most strategic element to be identified in crisis communication. Yet, as the authors argue, 'rhetoric alone is neither moral or immoral. Rather, the application of rhetoric to a crisis situation reveals the communicator's morality' (ibid.: 163). Similarly, Argenti (1996) constructs various aspects of corporate communication such as image and identity, corporate advertising, media relations, financial communication, employee relations, corporate philanthropy, government relations, and crisis communication. The second parameter is ethics. While this work does not engage with the philosophical extensions of ethical markets, it is important to reflect on what 'responsible communication' (Seeger, 1997) means as the combination of accountability and responsibility of corporate actors in a post-crisis situation. Influence remains a strong element of crisis communication, and, as will be demonstrated later, this is reflected in the ways in which responsible retailing is communicated in Greece.

This chapter conceptualizes the changing landscape of CSR communication within the Greek retail sector with respect to its stance on societal responsibility. For marketing scholars, the effects of the financial crisis in CSR performance are seen as potentially detrimental, although 'the global financial crisis provides great opportunities for companies such as corporate brands, employees' satisfaction, economic performance and increased productivity' (Giannarakis & Theotokas, 2011: 4). Yet, the extent to which CSR remains a topic of concern is burdened by the telos of corporate survival. Predictably, household expenditure has dropped dramatically in the wake of the financial crisis (cf. Barda & Sardianou, 2010). So, while responsible retailing has typically been concerned with the balance between consumer interest and producer protection (cf. Robinson, 2010) or the wellbeing of the consumers (cf. Colls & Evans, 2008), responsible retailing here refers to responsibility towards the national context in which it operates.

The question of the relationship between corporate social responsibility and the financial crisis is typically framed as one accepting that CSR is 'the tool to accomplish a harmonic coexistence between local community, enterprises and the public' (Metaxas & Tsavdaridou, 2012: 3). Yet, CSR communication intersects with promotional culture (Wernick, 1991). This is the basis of the critique of corporate engagement offered in this piece. Responsible retailing is not merely a question of local adaptation where business can grow with respect to local customs and conditions, but also of societal responsibility which considers the living standards of consumers. In order to remain relevant and profitable, retailers are communicating recognition of financial difficulties by responding with a rhetorical extension and practical implementation of CSR policies. This chapter highlights the rhetorical turns in responsible retailing in Greece, post-financial crisis and allows for a problematization of notions of responsibility and the nation in crisis.

Methodology: social media and retailers in Greece

The supermarket sector has been hit as a consequence of the financial blows on the Greek population. Several supermarkets were hit harder than others. Two instances particularly indicate this. Firstly, the Greek-owned supermarket *Atlantic* closed down in August 2011, firing 800 employees and holding a debt of over €200 million.[4] Secondly, Carrefour Marinopoulos, the biggest Greek supermarket chain, has been restructured heavily since its 1995 formation as an equal joint venture between the Greek (Marinopoulos) Group and the French (Carrefour) Group. During the election turmoil in early 2012, its French counterpart pulled out of the venture, leaving the Marinopoulos group to tackle management alone. By 2013, the double strike of Eurozone bailouts through austerity measures had been directly followed by a considerable decline in consumer spending.[5] In this context, retailers shifted their communication strategies towards social media. Rather than employing traditional marketing strategies, retailers tried particularly to engage with the social base of the population through the popular platform of Facebook.

In order to scrutinize responsible retailing in the Greek context, I employ a hybrid methodological approach inclusive of case studies of four retailers, a systematic analysis of their CSR reports, and, crucially, their social media communication. The case studies are chosen based on, primarily, the criterion of financial sustainability since 2005 and, secondly, that of the regularity of Facebook use. The choice of exploring this particular social media platform is based on the importance of interactivity in social responsibility issues (Capriotti & Moreno, 2006) and the popularity of Facebook in Greece.[6] Financial sustainability is defined as the business-as-usual model and discerned through data available in the 2005 and 2012 Panorama of Greek supermarkets. These are yearly editions of an independent business publishing company (Boussias Communications) delving into CSR communication in Greece. Moreover, most successful retailers in Greece increasingly use Facebook daily to improve their visibility. Furthermore, the increase of retailers' use of social media occurred in a post-crisis context; Alfa-Beta Vassilopoulos employed Facebook as a communication tool in September 2011.

The Greek supermarket landscape features a specific range of players (Table 3.1), the majority of whom are domestically owned:

Amongst the top five supermarkets in terms of financial sustainability, four are Greek-owned and one is Belgian-owned, while three are national and two are regional (operating in the capital, Athens). The top three supermarkets whose annual sales in 2011 exceeded one billion

Table 3.1 Top ten retailers in Greece circa (2005–2011)

Name	Ownership	Revenue (2005) (in thousands of Euros)*	Revenue (2011) (in thousands of Euros)**
Carrefour-Marinopoulos	Greek	1.775.167	1.832.940
Alfa-Beta Vassilopoulos	Belgian	908.001	1.537.544
Lidl Hellas	German	(est.) ***	(est.) ****
Sklavenitis (regional)	Greek	806.619	1.260.864
Veropoulos	Greek	732.396	702.768
Masoutis (regional)	Greek	463.976	702.183
Atlantic	Greek	576.726	(defunct, 2011)
My Market	Greek	499.828	681.911
Galaxias	Greek	349.898	432.852
Arvanitidis (regional)	Greek	N/A	222.274

Notes:
*With the exception of Lidl Hellas, these are drawn from the Panorama of Greek Supermarkets 2006.
**With the exception of Lidl Hellas, these are drawn from the Panorama of Greek Supermarkets 2012.
***Lidl, as their German competitor Aldi, do not publish financial reports. This is an estimation of Lidl Hellas' average 2008 revenue being between 1.000.000.000-1.300.000.000 according to the Greek market research company K&B Analysis Ltd [http://www.x-hellenica.gr/PressCenter/Articles/2140.aspx, 18 January 2014] and the newspaper *To Vima* [http://www.tovima.gr/finance/finance-business/article/?aid=293360, 18 January 2014].
****This is an estimation of Lidl Hellas' 2008 revenue being approximately 1.200.000.000 during this period according to the forecasting of the newspaper *To Vima* [http://www.tovima.gr/finance/finance-business/article/?aid=293360, 18 January 2014].

Euros include two national supermarkets, the Greek-owned Carrefour Marinopoulos, and the Belgian-owned Alfa-Beta Vassilopoulos (AB Vassilopoulos), as well as the Athens-based Sklavenitis. In terms of social media use, the top two supermarkets are non-Greek owned and capture over 1,000 'fans' on Facebook (Table 3.2).

In order to select case studies, revenue was defined as the strongest parameter (70% weight in decision-making) and social media use as the second strongest parameter (30%). The rationale was to examine the dominant repertoires of CSR through which dominant economic players attempt to engage with consumers. By giving decreasing values of ten, starting at 100 and descending in both these lists, and proportionately calculating for averages, the top four supermarkets were Alfa-Beta Vassilopoulos, Carrefour Marinopoulos, Lidl Hellas, and Veropoulos. They are discussed below as Supermarket A, Supermarket B, Supermarket C, and Supermarket D.

The selected case studies represent different types of supermarkets in the retail sector of the Greek market. Supermarket A is a competitive foreign-owned supermarket: Alfa-Beta Vassilopoulos' history features a company which was founded as a grocery store in 1939 owned by the Vassilopoulos brothers and has expanded as part of the Belgian Delhaize group since 1992. Their motto is 'and the bird's milk', a saying originating from the ancient Athenian comic playwright Aristophanes. As of 2013, it owned 216 stores across the country and employed approximately 9,500 workers. Supermarket B is a strong Greek newcomer in the retail sector whose organizational structure changed dramatically during the crisis: Marinopoulos was and is now again a purely Greek

Table 3.2 Retailers in Greece and social media communication

Name	Date of FB Entry	Likes*	Talking about this*
Alfa-Beta Vassilopoulos	01.09.2011	140,777	6,129
Lidl Hellas	17.05.2012	124,516	1,946
My Market	10.09.2012	73,326	10,651
Carrefour Marinopoulos	29.05.2012	38,786	2,095
Veropoulos	11.01.2012	20,104	474
Galaxias	15.11.2009	1,795	62
Masoutis *(regional)*	09.10.2012	1,166	98
Sklavenitis *(regional)*	29.03.2011	874	16
Arvanitidis *(regional)*	N/A	N/A	N/A
Atlantic	N/A	67	N/A

Note: *As of 4 April 2013

business, originally set up in 1939 and becoming a joint-venture of the French Carrefour group and the Greek Carrefour group in 1995, rebranding to Carrefour Marinopoulos. This joint venture lasted until 2012 when the French group withdrew, in light of the financial fiasco.[7] The remaining Greek counterpart operates with the motto 'every day something positive' and controls in total 644 stores on a national scale which carry subsidiaries under various names,[8] while employing approximately 13,000 people. Supermarket C is a financially sustainable foreign-owned discounter which has been operating its subsidiary in the national market since 1998: Lidl is part of the major German holding company Schwarz Gruppe and releases no official financial or operational data. According to a Facebook comment by Lidl Hellas:

> Lidl Hellas was founded in Greece and has created over 4,000 Greek, and not German, jobs. It cooperates with 1,500 Greek producers and service providers, thus securing the employment and wages of 50,000 Greek people. A big percentage of our turnover comes from Greek products, while we cater for promotion of Greek products in 24 countries of our company's operations in a European scale, a fact which significantly supports the export performance of Greece. (16 November 2013)

As a major platform for considerably discounted products, Lidl Hellas has seen relatively positive growth both pre- and post-crisis. Finally, Supermarket D is a struggling Greek-owned national retailer: Veropoulos was founded in 1973 and is part of SPAR, the Dutch international retail chain. As of 2013, it employed roughly 6,500 people across 233 stores in Greece.[9] Since its inception, and until 2012, Veropoulos had been addressing the generic housewife through the slogan 'she's happy, she's returning from Veropoulos'. In 2012, the slogan was changed to 'υπεύΦΘΗΝΑ', a combination of the words 'υπεύθυνα' (responsibly) and 'φθηνά' (affordably), to highlight its CSR for affordability. In analysing the communication strategies of these four market actors, this chapter captures the changing dynamics of the interrelation of corporate communication, promotion, and national adaptation.

A hybrid approach was undertaken to analysing primary data on the CSR communication of retailers in the Greek market. This approach employed computer-assisted qualitative analysis software, and specifically Discover Text, a web-based system for collecting, coding and analysing text. This analytic network draws big data into a three-step system of human evaluation. For purposes of clarity, big data are hereby defined as the publicly available types of communication which are predominantly posted on social media and part of both one-to-many and many-to-many communication. The cloud computing platform can be useful in drawing and managing data and metadata from selected social media (Facebook, Twitter, YouTube). This is a paid service, which I employed and used myself through a trial version for the purposes of the research presented here. The communication practices of retailers can be identified explicitly in their CSR reports and implicitly in their daily exchanges with customers through the physical spaces of their aisles and the posters and banners that decorate them, as well as, increasingly, the virtual spaces of social media where retailers have planted their presence. While the importance of news media has been underscored (Carroll, 2010), the growing embedding of social media in organizational communication necessitates an exploration of CSR communication in developing digital contexts. Here, this is informed in part by the content analysis of approximately 2,000 Facebook feeds for each case study (2,130 from Alfa-Beta Vassilopoulos, 2,300 from Carrefour Marinopoulos, and 2,230 from Lidl Hellas), with the exception of Veropoulos (454 feeds).[10] The results of this analysis are the rhetorical dimensions of the categories identified, as illustrated in the example below (Figure 3.1).

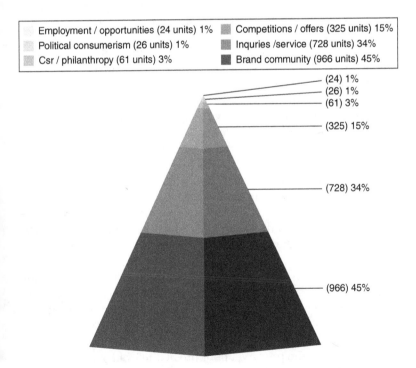

Figure 3.1 Facebook feeds at Supermarket A
Source: Object created and coded by author through Discover Text.

Figure 3.1 represents the Facebook feeds of Supermarket A, which were produced through Discover Text. This is the final result, which visualizes the frequency of categories after a process of data-gathering according to the codes I have created and attributed to each feed. This study aims to contribute to a diverse body of work ranging from CSR communication to economic cultures and cultural politics in austerity by looking at both the explicit and implicit declarations of responsibility beyond the provision of produce of appropriate quality and affordable price. Moreover, pricing represents an added responsibility in the specific context of Greece where affordability has become a national issue (see later section on CSR and social media).

Analysis of responsible retailing: CSR communication through official reports

An analysis of the selected supermarket data illuminates consistencies and discrepancies between corporate retailers. Discrepancies are met in the frequency of reporting on their CSR communication. Half of them have produced relevant official reports. Carrefour Marinopoulos is the most prolific communicator of its CSR policies and practices, yet its reporting has been minimal. Both of its official reports were published after the beginning of the crisis (2009, 2011). Alfa-Beta Vassilopoulos published one report in 2011. Then, Lidl Hellas and Veropoulos utilize their website to publicize their responsible image and operations. Lidl Hellas features a news-based approach: the policies are presented and ensued by a series of news bits related to their policies.[11] Veropoulos employs CSR communication as image promotion, by outlining different fundamental strands of the company's corporate philosophy.[12] Therefore, the financial crisis has evoked a type of responsible retailing based on the rise of CSR reporting. Consistencies can then be identified in the framing of CSR communication across the case studies. The prominence of the 'triple bottom line' reverberates in the rhetoric of retailers in Greece. The Alfa-Beta Vassilopoulos 'Corporate Responsibility Actions Report' states that:

> We commit ourselves to approaching the concept of the 'triple bottom line' that our overall performance, as a company, must be calculated on the basis of our combined effort towards Economic Development, Environmental Protection and Social Capital. (2011: 22)

When it comes to the primary aim of product reliability, the company employs various tools and programmes such as the HACCP system for food safety[13] or their 'agro-security' programme. When it comes to people and CSR, Alfa-Beta Vassilopoulos promotes the wellbeing, educational, and personal development of their employees, as well as a programme of corporate values. The particular values are not mentioned in the second official report, which broadly states that 'an aim of the programme is to instil the corporate values and vision of AB, in particular working behaviour' (Alfa-Beta Vassilopoulos Corporate Responsibility Actions, 2011: 10). In terms of local communities, AB demonstrates philanthropic behaviour, delivering up to €329,618 in 2011, supporting the Pan-Hellenic campaign of the Athens Cathedral and the Skai TV station, and other voluntary initiatives. Finally, environmental responsibility is advocated through a variety of initiatives such as collaboration with WWF Hellas for sustainable fishing, initiatives for the tackling of climate change,[14] the spreading of a network of 'green' stores, and the presence of recycling centres.

Similar announcements are made in the Carrefour Sustainable and Responsible Development Report (for 2010). The structure and content of the report are based on the 'Sustainability Reporting Guidelines' (version G3.1, 2011) of the Global Reporting Initiative (GRI). Its principles are informed by the UN Global Compact. Incongruously, the statement from the former CEO, which emphasizes the relevance of the crisis and the adaptability of CSR communication, states:

> 2010 was an important year for Carrefour Marinopoulos, as despite the peak of the global financial crisis and the bleak conditions in the national market, we systematically continued to materialise our strategic plan, thus investing in our developmental vision. In this type of report, published for the second years, we present all the areas of action in which we are focusing as a Group. With awareness of the conditions in which we are operating, we owe responsible actions and diffusion of responsible practices as much to our collaborators as to our customers. Our nonnegotiable aim remains the responsible function which we have adopted throughout our history and the steady orientation towards the values and priorities of the Group. We will continue to respond to the increasing consumer needs in the most efficient way, by utilising new opportunities created within the business environment.

This statement demonstrates the fragility of CSR communication; despite the motto 'for a better way of life, on a daily basis', the Carrefour Group pulled out of the Greek market. The main CSR model of governance for this supermarket group is defined as 'supporting the rhythmic function and development of local communities and the country', thereby focusing more on the 'profit' and 'people', though not necessarily in a specific order. Companies have specific and direct communication strategies for their local communities and consumer bases. The supermarket utilizes various tools and CSR communication, such as call centres, satisfaction surveys, and events organization, to reach its various social partners.

Lidl Hellas also shares the triple bottom line vision. For the company, society, products, partners, and the environment shape the basis of their CSR model in terms of principles, governance, and conduct. Here, responsible behaviour is demonstrated predominantly through social projects (i.e. education, health, nutrition), product reliability (i.e. safety, quality), personal development (i.e. education and growth), and environmentally responsible conduct (i.e. tackling climate change). The rhetoric in CSR communication, for Lidl Hellas, is predominantly grounded in image communication, where the company states its principles and updates its website visitors for projects conducted through its partners such as the 'Open Embrace' NGO. This is a social project where the company organized a visit to a children's hospital to provide support through the positive iconography of clowns. Similar social projects conducted by Lidl do not mention the crisis situation in Greece. The company is accustomed to a traditional CSR model, as part of the evolution of philanthropy towards local community welfare. It demonstrates the manifestation of 'philanthrocapitalism' as the acceptance that 'markets and morals are not distinct phenomena, but rather commensurate goods' (McGoey, 2012: 186). Philanthrocapitalism, for its proponents, is synonymous with the new modalities of business for the for-profits, in which altruism is an inherent element (Bishop & Green, 2008). Similarly, but to a lesser extent, Veropoulos is the least vocal CSR communicator. The website promotes the image and profile of the company, by featuring their point of presence, facilities, members, and own brand label products. These are descriptive points of intent and action, focusing on details of ownership and operations. Beyond the profile of the company, the website offers information on price policy and product reliability when it comes to demonstrating social responsibility on behalf of the retailer.[15] In responsible retailing, there are fundamental differences to be identified between structural and rhetorical extensions of CSR communication. This is primarily because of the strategic decision-making in addressing businesses and consumers. The following section expands on this in terms of the broadening of corporate engagement with consumers and society at large through social media.

Analysis of responsible retailing: CSR communication and social media

Responsible retailing manifests as promotional communication intended to build and boost brand image, personality, and consumer engagement and extend the information and reportage of CSR. Six categories arose in the analysis of CSR communication through social media (Table 3.3).

'Inquiries/services' are practically extensions of customer service relations between a company and its customers. Included in this type of communication are responses to questions about offers, product availability, returns, competitions and announcements. Most of the supermarkets respond consistently to all service-related inquiries and post both inspiring and interrogating statements and questions. Similarly, 'brand community' refers to the image communication of retailers. 'Competitions/offers' include specific daily, weekly, or monthly opportunities for winning products and selected discounts. The category of 'CSR/philanthropy' refers to the retailers' communication of their philanthropic work. Next, 'Political consumerism' is the use of the market space for political claim-making (Lekakis, 2013; Stolle et al., 2005). Finally, the category of 'employment/opportunities' refers to information which is relevant to possibilities of labour for the retailer. Three categories are more relevant to responsible retailing: CSR communication as *responsible image, responsible community relations* and *responsible national relations*.

Responsible image communication typically manifests as promotional communication in the creation of brand images and consumer engagement. In particular, brand communities in social media are mobilized through different tactics: 'fill-in-the-blank' posts, memes, curating content, and showcasing employees or fans. Alfa-Beta Vassilopoulos is the most engaged retailer on all corporate communication fronts. It delivers constant reminders of the exciting

Table 3.3 Greek retailers' CSR communication through social media

CSR Communication	Percentage
Responsibility towards customer (inquiries/services)	42.25
Responsibility towards fan base (brand community)	31.75
Responsibility towards affordability (competitions/offers)	20.25
Responsibility as philanthropy	3.50
Responsibility towards the nation (political consumerism)	1.00
Responsibility towards society (employment opportunities)	0.75

competitions and fresh offers, much like a close friend with an astute interest in its customers. It responds consistently to all service-related enquiries and posts both inspiring and interrogating statements and questions; for example, Alpha-Beta Vassilopoulos posted: 'It smells like honeysuckle and jasmine ... it smells like the open air cinema. Whoever missed it, LIKE this!' (22 June 2012). Through this strategy, the company encourages consumer engagement by making itself a platform for communication with its fans within Facebook. Similar tools are used by other retailers. Yet, this 'fill-in-the-blank' approach does not often succeed in engaging fans. Instead, CRS sees more consumer engagement through its responsibility to entertain. This denotes the highly promotional performance of responsible retailing, which displays a light-hearted, market-driven rhetoric to protect its financial sustainability. Both cases, however, including Carrefour Marinopoulos, appeal to the imagination of their users, thus echoing the permeation of labour in the digital experience (cf. Scholz, 2012).

Additionally, content curation is a particular type of brand display, as it does this through the marketing mechanism of local adaptation. The nation itself becomes the background for this type of corporation communication. The 'Greek table' here becomes the display for the products available for purchase and in such a way demonstrates the adaptation of the retailer to the nation through a sensuous embedding of the colours, imagery, and aesthetic symbolism associated with it. Greek retailers in particular, such as Alpha-Beta Vassilopoulos, use such imagery to demonstrate ritualistic adaptation, whereby corporate engagement with its stakeholders is mediated by national rituals, such as the 'Greek table', laid in a blue tablecloth and covered with national dishes. Retailers communicate responsibility in terms of affordability in price, solidarity with the Greek cause, and national belonging. Supermarkets have incrementally increased consumer participation schemes in light of their declining affordability for Greek consumers, such as many structural initiatives to ameliorate consumer spending. The most direct communication related to the financial crisis has been implemented by Alfa-Beta Vassilopoulos. The supermarket restored prices to their pre-crisis (2008) equivalent value in a tactical attempt to appeal to the austerity-stricken consumer body. A proliferation of similar initiatives has also occurred, as this was followed by a 2009 restoration of prices across the board of supermarkets, according to research published by the Research Institute of Consumer Goods Retailing.[16] These initiatives, because of their large scale, are more closely related to market restructuring than to responsible retailing. CSR, therefore, is more closely related to corporate image (Argenti, 1996) than the manifestation of responsibility.

Price adjustment has reverberated throughout all of retailers. This communicative initiative can, however, be interpreted in a critical light. Oftentimes, it is a reaction to consumers' comments rather than corporate engagement with the Greek crisis. A number of consumers have used retailers' Facebook pages to demand a price decrease; in the following exchange of comments, a citizen was successful in engaging the retailer:

Dimitris:

I have been a customer of Alfa-Beta Vassilopoulos for 45 Years!!! What I expect from you is a real decrease in your prices and not merely a superficial effort!

Alpha-Beta Vassilopoulos:

Good morning Dimitris! Our company is very sensitive to the price issue and is investing great efforts every day, while systematically following the evolution of production cost and product availability from our providers. We would also like to assure you of our efforts to offer quality products in competitive prices and add value to our customers' purchases. (9 May 2012)

With respect to the aforementioned Price Restoration initiative, another citizen (May) struck a troubling chord by making three points: (a) people had more access to money in 2008, whereas now they do not, (b) between 2008 and 2012 the retailer's prices went up while there was inflation, and (c) prices need to fall to their pre-2000 equivalent, otherwise Greeks are not going to be able to go to the supermarket. The same retailer responded by summarizing their contemporary CSR communication of responsibility towards Greece:

Dear May, in response to your valid questions, the financial crisis is a phenomenon that impacts on us all, not just citizens but companies, who are also called to pay for urgent contributions and remain profitable in this difficult financial juncture. As a company we would like to publicize that we have in no way decreased salaries, but on the contrary last year we offered a small rise to over 10,000 of our employees. The specific initiative of 'Price Restoration' took place explicitly because we are aware of this and want to actively support the Greek consumer in these difficult moments. Precisely for this reason, we are not enforcing this just for the next fortnight, as we usually do with offers. This specific initiative is exclusively funded by Alfa-Beta, with a full sense of responsibility towards its customers. Of course, we recognize that some people might disregard this. However, it has been our principle, in our 74-year-long history, never to lie or promise more than we can do. (26 May 2012)

This type of civic-corporate interaction through social media needs further exploration, in illustrating the power dynamics of market governance and communication. What remains emphatic in this quote is the address of consumers as citizens, demonstrating the enunciation of responsibility not merely towards society as a configuration of consumers (through the restructuring of their prices), but also as citizens (through responsibility in hiring and employability).

The category of CSR communication of responsible retailing to the nation is directly related to the financial crisis, the subsequent crisis of political legitimacy, and the civic crisis which has ensued. An example of how CSR communication and political consumerism intersect can be seen in the increased emphasis on ethnicity within the promotion of 'Greek products' (consumer goods of national origin, production, and distribution). There is a cohesive address of consumers as a collective, who are often implicitly addressed in terms of mutual solidarity – support us, so that the economy regenerates. The propagation of the Greek flag as an element of the branded goods that circulate in supermarkets, but also kiosks and mini-markets, is becoming mainstreamed in the collective Greek consumer subconscious (Lekakis, 2014). This corresponds to a global phenomenon of banal nationalism, whereby nationalism is constructed in symbolic repertoires of superficial connections with the emblems of states (Billig, 1995).

Such calls collectively address consumers in Greece and seek to consider the financial hits which detonate the crisis. Yet, the type of corporate engagement arising here operates in a historical and political vacuum frame, suggesting that the financial crisis can be tackled with by consumers, thus overlooking the further crises which are part and parcel of the national economic decline (political crisis with partisanship and polarization co-existing with apathy and disengagement, or, significantly, social crisis with exclusion and aggression towards settled or in transit immigrant parts of the population). In this manner, the integration of patriotic elements in promotional culture is consistent with a type of economic nationalism where a nation is constructed by the consumer practices of its citizen subjects (cf. Crane, 1998; Gerth, 2011). The way in which some of these initiatives are communicated is also directly relevant to the promotion of national ownership. Veropoulos and Marinopoulos both emphasize the national roots of their business historical activity in Greece:

> One of the oldest Greek businesses, we are next to you to bring to you the best quality products at the most affordable prices. (Veropoulos, 24 January 2012)

Proximity to and even kinship with the nation is, therefore, a minor but monumental element of responsible retailing. In order to build on the trust demonstrated towards specific corporate actors, supermarkets correlate their image, performance, and identity with the Greek nation, in a manner that does not question its present state of distrust, disorganization, and disillusionment.

Discussion

Three key points arise. Firstly, CSR communication is predominantly an issue of influence and a continuation of promotional culture. What can loosely be identified as responsible retailing can manifest in many different ways in a crisis context, ranging from practical to symbolic restructuring of engagement with the consumer body. Structurally, supermarkets have engaged in initiatives to enhance consumer spending through welfare tactics. The interlacing of market and state initiatives to endure the crisis signifies a changing landscape for CSR communication, as business adapts to a transformative context in order to survive and provide for an austerity-stricken population. For instance, the unemployment card issued by the government body Manpower Employment Organization ensures additional discounts in national supermarkets such as Carrefour Marinopoulos, but also locally owned and operated stores. Yet, symbolically, CSR communication remains rooted in a politics of influence. The way in which Sellnow and Seeger (2013) account for rhetoric speaks to the retailers' morality; after all, as mentioned above, retailers have been hit hard by the crisis and their demonstration of philanthropy and promotional communication addresses the consumer base mainly for purposes of service, strengthening the brand community and providing information on offers, mainly through ritualistic adaptation. This brings us to the second point.

Secondly, corporate engagement with an austerity-stricken state and society reinforces the idea of the adaptability of neoliberal capitalism to the crisis. Instead of exploring alternatives to neoliberal trade models and an emerging grassroots social economy (cf. Chatzidakis et al., 2012; Nasioulas, 2012; Rakopoulos, 2014), supermarkets continue to normalize the same type of consumer-driven concerns. This calls for further problematization of the role of consumption in a crisis context. So-called responsible retailing can also occur indirectly, through the promotion of local and national folklore, customs, and rituals, and mainstream religious beliefs. Consumers are continuously conflated with citizens in a vicious circle in which consumers appeal to supermarkets to alleviate their financial downturn, while supermarkets feed back into this a sense of solidarity through mostly symbolic repertoires. The exploration of the relationship between austerity, consumption, and promotional cultures in crisis merits further exploration.

Finally, retailers engage with the nation in crisis in a normative manner. This means that they enfold the ideas, rituals, and connotations of the nation in their promotional communication, thus encouraging a particular type of political consumerism to which ethnicity and belonging are central. In other words, they call for a type of 'ethnocentric consumption'. Retailers communicate their strongest associations with the nation (i.e. ownership, performance, philanthropy) in an attempt to gain further legitimacy for supporting the national cause. This type of CSR communication is relevant to the mining of economic nationalism (Gerth, 2012). The promotion of the nation becomes an integral part of CSR communication, occurring directly through underscoring the levels of national production, distribution, and consumption as an individual, collective, and community-based response to the crisis.

Conclusion: rhetorical turns in CSR communication in a crisis context

Crisis communication is the unravelling of a sophisticated part of corporate communication, as Argenti (1996) included in his definition of the field. Yet, there is a lot to explore in CSR communication in a crisis context. In Greece, responsible retailing emerges in an engaged manner, publicizing CSR reports in official articulations and simultaneously promoting that information in an informal manner through social media, in an attempt to engage with a crisis-stricken consumer body for the purpose of their financial sustainability. Responding to crisis has become a prerequisite for business organizations, not merely for their own survival, but also for the survival of their reputation. When the financial crisis hit Greece, retailers responded tactically in terms of their financial stability, but also in terms of safeguarding their reputation in a changing terrain. CSR communication defines the responsibility of corporate entities towards multiple stakeholders. As the Greek triple crisis of economy, politics, and society developed, a matrix of communicating responsible retailing towards consumers, communities, and the nation was created. The particular rhetorical traits of that communication pertaining to responsibility included practical (affordability), symbolic (community), and qualitative (adapting to the nation) parameters. In particular, the ties of the majority of retailers examined here (with the exception of Lidl Hellas) bound them to the citizens' movement 'Προτιμώ Ελληνικά' (translation: 'I prefer Greek')[17] which surfaced in October 2010, a few months after the signing of the first Memorandum. The main motto of the movement is 'we consume what we produce', **encouraging the Greek consuming population to spend** their money within the Green economy and thus support companies in order to preserve employment in them (Lekakis, 2014). For the societal responsibility of business, this means that the goal of CSR communication is more closely defined as engagement with a post-crisis, austerity-stricken nation. Social media provide platforms where the personalization of politics (cf. Bennett & Segerberg, 2012) can also engage consumers in a nationalist economy, as is evident in the proliferation of groups which are linked to campaigns for Greek political consumerism on Facebook; such groups typically demonstrate intensified nation-branding, which is often neutral with respect to national politics.

Marketing strategies have thus been significantly changed to adapt to and address the crisis. Greek citizens are often implicitly addressed in terms of mutual solidarity, in a 'support us, so that the economy regenerates' narrative. By attempting to connect personal micro-acts of consumption with a broader macro-economic responsibility to the nation in crisis, supermarkets align their interests with the interests of their consumers. Secondly, there is an increasing rhetoric of affordability through constant product promotions. This relates to an increased practice in Greek retailing within and beyond supermarkets which includes the proliferation of special schemes for participation. These schemes are both structural and rhetorical and are presented as genuine opportunities for citizens which expand beyond economic exchanges. Finally, adapting to the nation can also be identified as a strategy in responsible retailing. This corporate attempt to associate with an economic, political, social, or cultural structure or phenomenon, in order to draw from its authenticity, outlines a phenomenon where economic actors seek to become further integrated with the imagined and actual components of a nation. This is currently evident in the propagation of the Greek flag as an element of branded goods, while the nation continues to feature prominently in the market-driven narratives of supermarkets. This is also illustrated in various campaigns for supporting Greek products and companies, as mentioned above. The financial crisis fuels corporate engagement with the societal basis of the austerity-ridden state, yet the model of corporate governance which emerges is a homogenous and depoliticized one, which ignores the fundamental tensions and issues that occupy the Greek nation beyond its economy.

Notes

1. Retailers who heeded this call were: Alfa-Beta Vassilopoulos, a subsidiary of the Belgian Delhaize S.A. (a corporation of stores in the US, Belgium, Romania, Indonesia, Luxembourg, and Greece) and its Cretan branch of Chalkiadakis, as well as the Greek chains Sklavenitis, My Market, Veropoulos, Thanopoulos, and Galaxias. This was met by a further embracing of the cause by other supermarkets, including the Greek Carrefour-Marinopoulos, and Proton.
2. According to the Hellenic Statistical Association, groupings of the retail sector include (a) supermarkets, (b) department stores, (c) food, beverages, and tobacco, d) automotive fuel-lubricants, (e) pharmaceuticals and cosmetics, (f) clothing and footwear, (g) furniture, electrical goods, household goods, (h) books, stationery, and other articles, and (i) sales not in stores.
3. This research charted the opinions of a representative national sample (1,001 Greek citizens) in 2009 through structured questionnaires and compared this with the same data from 2005. Available: http://www.scribd.com/doc/18022365/CSR-2009-Food-Sector [28 February 2014].
4. http://greece.greekreporter.com/2011/08/03/atlantic-supermarket-chain-bankrupted-800-employees-are-fired/ [23 January 2014].
5. In the European Union, Greece currently holds fourth place in terms of the fall of consumer spending after the three Baltic states (Estonia, Latvia, and Lithuania), according to Eurostat data for consumer expenditure between 2008 and 2011. http://epp.eurostat.ec.europa.eu/statistics_explained/index.php/Household_consumption_expenditure_-_national_accounts [25 March 2013].
6. According to MRB Hellas, in the period 2008–2010, the population of social networks in Greece rose by 350%. http://owni.eu/2011/06/09/greece-social-networks-in-times-of-crisis/ [28 January 2014].
7. http://www.reuters.com/article/2012/06/15/idUS46695+15-Jun-2012+BW20120615 [29 January 2014].
8. These are 35 stores named Carrefour, 266 named Carrefour Marinopoulos, 250 Carrefour Express, 98 Smile, and 93 OK stores.
9. 92 of these stores are in the capital of Athens, 89 in the periphery, and 38 in Crete under the name Chalkiadakis.
10. This was prevented by technical issues.

11. http://www.lidl.gr/cps/rde/xchg/SID-A64BBB52-519447FD/lidl_gr/hs.xsl/ 9219.htm [30 January 2014].
12. https://www.veropoulos.gr/eshop/index_group.asp? [30 January 2014].
13. HACCP, or the Hazard Analysis Critical Control Point System is a process control system for purposes of food hazard identification and prevention. HACCP was first implemented by the Pillsbury Company and has received endorsement from the National Academy of Sciences, the National Advisory Committee for Microbiological Criteria for Foods, and the Codex Alimentarius. http://haccpalliance.org/alliance/haccpqa.html [31 May 2013].
14. This is implemented through the monthly registering of energy consumption. In 2011, AB Vassilopoulos' energy consumption was estimated to be 770 kWh/m^2.
15. https://www.veropoulos.gr/eshop/index_group.asp? [29 January 2014].
16. http://news247.gr/eidiseis/oikonomia/agora/h_krish_erikse_tis_times_twn_ proiontwn_sta_souper_market.2191104.html [5 February 2014].
17. http://protimoellinika.gr

References

Alfa-Beta Vassilopoulos (2011) 'Corporate Responsibility Actions Report'. Available: http://www.ab.gr/assets/pdf-files/2011_csr_ab.pdf
Argenti, P. A. (1996). Corporate communication as a discipline: Toward a definition. *Management Communication Quarterly*, 10(1): 73–97.
Barda, C. & Sardianou, E. (2010). Analysing consumers' 'activism' in response to rising prices. *International Journal of Consumer Studies*, 34: 133–139.
Bennett, W. L. & Segerberg, A. (2012). The logic of connective action. *Information, Communication & Society*, 15(1): 739–768.
Billig, M. (1995). *Banal Nationalism*. London: Sage.
Bishop, M. & Green, M. (2008). *Philanthrocapitalism: How the Rich Can Save the World*. London: Bloomsbury Press.
Capriotti, P. & Moreno, A. (2006). Corporate citizenship and public relations: The importance and interactivity of social responsibility issues on corporate websites. *Public Relations Review*, 33: 84–91.
Carroll, C. (ed.) (2010). *Corporate Reputation and the News Media*. London: Routledge.
Chatzidakis, A., Maclaran, P. & Bradshaw, A. (2012). Heterotopian space and the utopics of ethical and green consumption. *Journal of Marketing Management*, 28(3–4): 494–515.
Colls, R. & Evans, B. (2008). Embodying responsibility: Children's health and supermarket initiatives. *Environment and Planning A*, 40(3): 615–631.
Crane, G. T. (1998). Economic nationalism: Bringing the nation back in. *Millenium – Journal of International Studies*, 27(1): 55–75.
Gerth, K. (2011). Consumer nationalism. In D. Southerton (ed.), *Encyclopedia of Consumer Culture*. London: Sage.
Gerth, K. (2012). *As China Goes, So Goes the World: How Chinese Consumers are Transforming Everything*. New York: Hill and Wang.
Giannarakis, G. and Theotokas, I. (2011). The effects of financial crisis in corporate social responsibility performance. *International Journal of Marketing Studies*, 3(1): 2–10.

Lekakis, E. J. (2013). *Coffee Activism and the Politics of Fair Trade and Ethical Consumption in the Global North: Political Consumerism and Cultural Citizenship.* Basingstoke: Palgrave.

Lekakis, E. J. (2014). Ethnocentric consumption, political consumerism and austerity cultures in the Eurozone: 'Buy Greek to save the economy? Paper presented at the *Midwest Political Science Association Annual Meeting,* Chicago, IL, 3–6 April.

McGoey, L. (2012). Philanthrocapitalism and its critics. *Poetics,* 40(2): 185–199.

Metaxas, T. & Tsavdaridou, M. (2012). Corporate Social Responsibility in Greece during the crisis period. *MPRA Paper,* No. 41518. Available: http://mpra.ub.uni-muenchen.de/41518/ [26 February 2014].

Nasioulas, I. (2012). *Greek Social Economy Revisited: Voluntary, Civic and Cooperative Challenges in the 21st Century.* Oxford: Peter Lang.

Panorama of Greek Supermarkets (2005) Athens: Boussias Communications.

Rakopoulos, T. (2014). The crisis seen from below, within, and against: From solidarity economy to food distribution cooperatives in Greece. *Dialectical Anthropology,* 38(2): 189–207.

Robinson, P. K. (2010). Responsible retailing: The practice of CSR in banana plantations in Costa Rica. *Journal of Business Ethics,* 91: 279–289.

Rogers, C. & Vasilopoulou, S. (2012). Making sense of Greek austerity. *The Political Quarterly,* 83(4): 777–785.

Scholz, T. (2012). *Digital Labor: The Internet as Playground and Factory.* London: Routledge.

Seeger, M. (1997). *Ethics and Organizational Communication.* Cresskill, NJ: Hampton Press.

Sellnow, T. L. & Seeger, M. W. (2013). *Theorizing Crisis Communication.* Chichester, West Sussex: John Wiley & Sons Inc.

Stolle, D., Hooghe, M. & Micheletti, M. (2005). Politics in the supermarket: Political consumerism as a form of political participation. *International Political Science Review,* 26(3): 245–269.

Wernick, A. (1991). *Promotional Culture: Advertising, Ideology and Symbolic Expression.* London: Sage.

Part II
Informal Modes of Civic Engagement, Enacting Alternatives and Sustaining Involvement

4
Technologies of Self-Mediation: Affordances and Constraints of Social Media for Protest Movements

Bart Cammaerts

Introduction

Despite the many critiques (Cammaerts, 2008), it also has to be acknowledged that, in line with some of the more optimistic accounts, social media and so-called Web 2.0 applications have played both an instrumental and a constitutive role for activists worldwide in their efforts to disseminate social movement discourses, to mobilize for direct actions online as well as offline, to coordinate direct action, and to self-mediate acts of resistance potentially leading to movement spill-overs. In this chapter I seek to provide a conceptual framework to make sense of the roles that social media play for protest movements and the interplay between affordances and constraints inherent to social media. The affordances, I will argue, map onto what I call a set of self-mediation logics, which in turn correspond to Foucault's Stoic technologies of the self: disclosure, examination, and remembrance.

Furthermore, by adopting the notion of self-mediation, this chapter aligns itself with the mediation tradition as outlined by Martín-Barbero (1993) and Silverstone (2002). Mediation in this tradition is understood to be a dialectical, communicative process that encompasses but also complicates a variety of dichotomies; the production of media and symbols versus their reception or use, alternative media versus mainstream media, traditional media versus new media, and the symbolic versus the material. The latter refers to the double articulation of mediation, as referring both to symbolic power and to the process of technological innovation. From this perspective the notion of mediation is deemed to be productive. Besides this, as Martín-Barbero (1993: 188) pointed out, mediations can also be seen as 'the articulations between communication practices and social movements and the articulation of different tempos of development and practice'.

Throughout this chapter, a number of examples will be provided to illustrate conceptual points. First, however, the notion of technologies of the self and its relationship to self-mediation will be theorized.

Technologies of the self and of self-mediation

It is proposed here that Foucault's notion of technologies of the self is a useful way to theorize the interplay between the affordances and constraints of social media for protest movements and activists. Foucault (1997) spoke of technologies of the self in relation to the way in which individuals internalize rules and constraints. Through technologies of the self, we ultimately discipline ourselves, Foucault explained. However, at the same time, technologies of the self are also those devices, methods, or 'tools' that enable the social construction of our personal identities; they

> permit individuals to effect by their own means or with the help of others a certain number of operations on their own bodies and souls, thoughts, conduct, and way of being, so as to transform themselves in order to attain a certain state of happiness, purity, wisdom, perfection, or immortality. (Foucault, 1997: 225)

It is thus through the technologies of the self and the construction of personal identities that self-compliance to the structures of coercion is being instilled, but it is also the space where resistance can be given shape and is exercised. Commenting on Foucault's work, Burkitt (2002: 224) contends that the technologies of the self are:

> a form of practical action accompanied by practical reason, which aims to instil in the body certain habitual actions – either moral virtues (that is, right ways of acting in a situation) or technical skills – and, later, to give people the reflexive powers to reason about their virtues or skills, providing them with the capacity to refine, modify or change them.

Foucault identified three distinct Stoic technologies of the self; (1) disclosure, (2) examination, and (3) remembrance. The first, disclosure, relates to what Foucault (1997: 234) called 'the cultivation of the self', the second, examination, is concerned with the reflexive powers Burkitt talks about; 'taking stock' and making 'adjustments between what he wanted to do and what he had done, and to reactivate the rules of conduct' (Foucault, 1997: 237). The final Stoic technology of the self that Foucault refers to is remembrance, which we can relate to capturing and recording: they are 'memorizations of deeds' (ibid: 247).

Bakardjieva and Gaden (2012) mobilize Foucault's concept of technologies of the self to make sense of Web 2.0's role in terms of self-constitution and in linking up the technologies of the self with other technologies such as the production of signs and ultimately power. By applying technologies of the self not to individual actors, but to collective ones, I take this experiment further. However, at the same time, by doing this, I argue that there is a need for a more complex understanding of what Honneth (2012) recently called 'the I in We', or the way in which we all negotiate and navigate the relationship between our own complex individual identities and a panoply of collective identities.

I will use technologies of self-mediation here as a metaphor, pointing to the way in which, amongst other things, social media platforms and the communicative practices they enable can potentially become constitutive of the construction of collective identities and have become highly relevant in view of disseminating, communicating, recording, and archiving a variety of movement discourses and deeds. Technologies of self-mediation are thus both shaping and constraining action and imagination; they are to some extent determining the horizon of the possible. Technologies of self-mediation are, in other words, the tools through which a social movement becomes self-conscious.

Furthermore, as outlined in the introduction, mediation, as a concept, is chosen carefully. Mediation refers, amongst other things, to the ritualistic characteristics of communication, to an *in-betweenness*, and ultimately to (symbolic) power. Mediation also enables us to analyze the interactions and intersections between dichotomies such as private and public, alternative and mainstream, production and reception, the material and the symbolic, as intricate and dialectical.

All this points to adopting a post-structuralist approach to understand and make sense of the various ways in which social media are relevant to protest movements. The post-structural paradigm in combination with a mediation approach is particularly helpful precisely because it defines power as diffused and operating at a micro as well as macro level; it also considers opportunities and constraints to be dynamic and two sides of the same coin; and, finally, it foregrounds resistance as intrinsic to the exercise of power, also highly relevant for the field of study in this chapter.

The communicative affordance of social media for protest movements

Gibson (1977), working in the field of ecological psychology, coined the notion of affordances to explain how the environment surrounding an animal constitutes a given set of affordances, which are both objective and subjective. Affordances, Gibson (1977: 75) explains, are a 'unique combination of qualities that specifies what the object affords us', and they represent opportunities or potentialities for a set of actions, which we perceive or not. Also, as we use these objects, they become an extension of ourselves, overcoming the subject-object dichotomy. As Gibson (1979/1986: 41) points out:

> the capacity to attach something to the body suggests that the boundary between the animal and the environment is not fixed at the surface of the skin but can shift. More generally it suggests that the absolute duality of 'objective' and 'subjective' is false.

The notion of affordances became popular in technology and innovation studies to make sense of our relationship with and our shaping of technologies. ICTs such as the Internet, mobile technologies, and the social media platforms that run on them thus hold a set of affordances that are inherent to them but need to be recognized as such by activists. The affordances we can attribute to social media in relation to activists' use of them are intrinsically related to the affordances of other tools of self-mediation such as print media, broadcasting media, or classic telecommunication.

From this perspective, usage of networked technologies by activists and protest movements situates itself at the 'intersection between social context, political purpose and technological possibility' (Gillan et al., 2008: 151).

Communicative affordances of social media for self-mediation

On the one hand, reminiscent of broadcasting and telecommunication, social media enable instant – real-time – forms of communication, which tends to be fleeting (unless recorded or harvested). However, just like print, a delayed asynchronous form of communication is also possible, which is potentially more permanent and easier to archive.

On the other hand, social media afford both public/open forms of communication – akin to broadcasting and private/protected forms of communication – more salient to traditional postal services and

Table 4.1 Communicative affordances

	Real-Time	Asynchronous
Public/Outward	Streaming, Twittering	Blogs, Comments, iLike, Photo Repositories
Private/Inward	Chatting, VoIP	Email, SMS, Mailing lists, Forums

telecommunication. Social media combine one-to-many, one-to-one, and many-to-many forms of communication. This produces a matrix of affordances that can be attributed to various types of social media leading to a variety of possible actions for protest movements and activists (Table 4.1).

It has to be said, though, that when it comes to private communication the distinction between real-time and asynchronous communication is increasingly blurring; for example, email is presented as a chat dialogue on mobile devices.

Self-mediation logics

These communicative affordances of various social media platforms can be mapped onto a set of activist self-mediation logics – or the rationale activists ascribe to the use of a certain type of media for a certain purpose. In my view, we can identify six inter-connected but analytically distinct *self-mediation logics* for activists and protest movements.

The first logic refers to the need for protest movements to disseminate as widely as possible their various movement discourses through a variety of channels. The second logic has relevance for the crucial task of movements to mobilize and recruit for (direct) actions, online as well as offline. The third logic has to do with the need of movements to organize themselves internally, which is increasingly mediated through communication technologies. The fourth logic of self-mediation refers to instant, on-the-spot coordination of direct actions, which also increasingly takes place on or through social media platforms. The fifth logic of self-mediation relates to the act of (self-)recording protest events increasingly facilitated amongst others through mobile technologies. The final self-mediation logic is the need to archive protest artefacts which then subsequently enable connections between movements and the articulation of alternative imaginaries.

The first and second logics align with the first Stoic technology of the self, namely disclosure. The third and forth logics are in tune with examination and self-reflexivity, the second Stoic technology of the self. The final two logics, recording and archiving, enable remembrance, the third Stoic technology of the self.

1. To Disseminate and To Mobilize (Disclosure)
2. To Organize and Coordinate (Examination)
3. To Record and Archive (Remembrance)

Networked technologies play a variety of roles in terms of facilitating or enabling practices of disclosure, examination, and remembrance.

Combining affordances with logics of self-mediation

When we combine the affordances of social media identified above with the sets of logics of self-mediation it becomes apparent that social media play a variety of roles for protest movements at different levels of analysis.

The asynchronous affordances of public forms of communication fuel strategies of *disclosure*. Here movements use technologies of self-mediation to construct and sustain collective identities, to articulate a set of demands and ideas and in effect to become self-conscious as a movement. At the same time, their asynchronous nature also enables the capturing and recording of movement discourses, protest events, slogans, and the subsequent memorization of them, the combination of which in turn enables *remembrance*; here technologies of self-mediation play a crucial role in archiving the past, and through that transmitting practices, tactics and ideas across space and time. Subsequently, these disclosures and remembrances are amplified through as many channels and platforms as there are at a given moment, with a view to garnering support, recruiting new sympathizers and mobilizing for action. Remembrance and disclosure processes are also neither bounded by national boundaries anymore; they can gain global attention and bypass national censorship strategies. All this can potentially lead to what in the social movement literature is called 'movement spill-overs' (Meyer & Whittier, 1994) These spill-overs occur across time and space, and potentially contribute to the sustaining of collective identities and of commitment to the cause. From this latter perspective, the dynamic between disclosure and remembrance also ties in with the 'beyond protest' theme of this book.

A pertinent recent example of this asynchronous self-mediation process, facilitated and to some extent even propelled and sustained by social media as a technology of self-mediation, is the way in

Figure 4.1 The appropriation of the V for Vendetta mask in various parts of the world

Note: Photo at the top taken at Anti-Scientology Protest, New York, 10 February 2008; Photo at the bottom taken at Gezi Park Protests, Istanbul, 8 June 2013.

Source: Wikimedia Commons. All content on this page is freely licenced. Furthermore, permission to use the two pictures in Figure 4.1 has been obtained from the photographers.

which movement discourses, protest tactics, slogans, and symbols oscillated between Anonymous, WikiLeaks, the Arab Spring protests, the Indignados in Spain, Occupy Wall Street/LSX, the Pirate Parties, MoVimento 5 Stelle in Italy, and the V for Vinagre protests in Turkey and Brazil. We could refer here to the appropriation of the V for Vendetta mask by protesters across the world (cf. Figure 4.1). I am not hereby claiming that these movements align totally – on the contrary, but they do pick and choose from a similar and above all mediated set of symbols, tactics, ideas, and critiques.

The asynchronicity which social media affords is also relevant to private forms of communication. This mainly refers to the establishment of internal communication channels between the core and periphery of a movement and within the core of a movement. As such, this very much relates to a permanent process of *examination* and adaptation to new circumstances and self-reflection on the precise articulation of movement discourses and at times also mediated decision-making. This asynchronicity in private communication also enables (some) participants of protest movements to better balance their political engagements with everyday life and family, social, and professional commitments. A few years ago a radical environmental activist explained it as follows:

> Most of the activists and sympathisers have a full-time job. Being called up during working hours for urgent co-ordination or actions would be considered too intrusive ... Sympathisers that are being informed and mobilised through email can decide themselves when to dedicate time and attention to 'the action'. As such, they can easily adapt their action-rhythm to the highs and lows in their own personal and professional timeframes. (Quoted in Cammaerts, 2007: 276)

Besides asynchronous communication, social media also affords real-time public communication. When it concerns public or outward forms of communication, this enables activists and protest movements to in effect broadcast in real time, reaching those who want to tune into their stream or twitter feed. This can obviously be linked to the logic of *disclosure*. A recent example of this was the way in which Greenpeace streamed their direct action in July 2013 against drilling for oil in the Artic by sending six women to climb the Shard, a landmark building in London resembling ice.

Another more intricate example was the way in which mobile phones and social networking platforms became, in effect, broadcasting tools in the hands of protesters in the Middle East during the Arab Spring. Mainstream media broadcasters across the world began using the protesters' feeds to make sense of what was happening on the ground (Hermida et al., 2012). Protesters' strategies of *disclosure* became part of mainstream media archives, feeding *remembrance* and documenting atrocities committed by state actors through synoptic tactics of sousveillance or the 'many watching the few' (Mathiesen, 1997). Furthermore, through the use of social media platforms, 'individualized, localized, and community-specific dissent [turned] into structured movements with a collective consciousness about both shared grievances and opportunities for action' (Howard & Hussain, 2011: 41).

Real-time social media is also increasingly used as a tool for 'on-the-spot' *examination* when we approach it from the perspective of the coordination of offline direct actions. In 2010, students in the UK were actively using Google maps to update the positions of the police throughout central London thereby providing all protesters who had access to smartphones with real-time information to avoid being kettled or contained by police (Cammaerts, 2012). Along the same lines, activists using flash-mob tactics for political purposes also rely on the real-time affordances social media offers to mobilize and direct their sympathizers towards possible targets; in the UK context we could refer to UK Uncut, an organization targeting high street retailers, banks and multinationals for not paying any (or very little) corporate tax in the UK by (briefly and thus symbolically) occupying their branches and using social media to coordinate their direct actions.

The last category – private real-time communication – is most suited to fit examination practices or the organization and coordination of protest movements, at times replacing face-to-face encounters between figureheads of movements and enabling point-to-point communication between two or more members of the movement to discuss strategy and tactics or to examine movement discourses and action, and to make adjustments if need be. Decisions on these important matters tend to be easier in real time rather than through an asynchronous communication process. It also has to be said that despite the affordance of real-time multi-point group communication through, for example, a 'conference call' on Skype, many activists and movements tend to prefer face-to-face meetings and decision-making processes over and above mediated ones. This is certainly the case for more radical and anti-systemic movements who are often the object of state repression and surveillance (cf. Diani, 2001).

This last point brings us to the constraints which are inherent in the use of social media by collective actors and which I argue also need to be carefully assessed in order to get a fuller picture of the role social media play for activists and protest movements.

Constraints of social media for protest movements

If, as Burkitt (2002: 235) posits, 'technologies of the self are forms of pro-duction as well as means of domination', then it follows that technologies of self-mediation also encapsulate a set of constraints, which is in line with a post-structuralist account of power. Besides the productive charac-teristics of technologies of self-mediation there are thus also disciplinary ones. While for analytical purposes I treat the constraints separately from the opportunities, they operate in conjunction with each other.

Technologies of self-mediation thus not only afford, but at the same time also constrain and limit. In line with a Foucauldian perspective on power, these constraints should not be defined exclusively in negative terms, but as 'the conditions and relationships amongst attributes which provide structure and guidance for the course of actions' (Kennewell, 2001: 106). As such, constraints are by no means 'the opposite of affor-dances; they are complementary, and equally necessary for activity to take place' (ibid.). This concurs with a view of the relationship between structure and agency as being productive or generative, and whereby power inevitably invokes strategies of resistance (Foucault, 1978). Such strategies of resistance are employed by activists (as outlined in the previous section) as well as by those actors that resist activists' efforts towards change, which is more the focus of this section.

As such, the relationship and links between technologies of the self and technologies of domination are invoked here – i.e. 'the points where the techniques of the self are integrated into structures of coer-cion and domination' (Foucault, 1993: 203). Foucault denoted this point of contact between technologies of the self and technologies of domination as governmentality, shaping not only the possibilities of action for subjects but also instilling a sense of self-control and limita-tions of the possible:

> Governing people, in the broad meaning of the word, governing people is not a way to force people to do what the governor wants; it is always a versatile equilibrium, with complementarity and conflicts between techniques which assure coercion and processes through which the self is constructed or modified by himself. (ibid.: 204)

Before dealing with the particular constraint of state repression and surveillance, some other constraints in relation to social media and protest movements will be addressed. In this regard, structural issues relating to access and reach will be addressed, but also tensions between the individualistic nature of social media and the collective identities protest movements aim to build. Furthermore, besides state control and surveillance we also need to acknowledge that social media and the Internet in more general terms is first and foremost a corporate and hyper-commodified space.

Access and narrowcasting

Despite some voices heralding the ubiquity of networked technology and of screens in our everyday lives, we should not forget that digital as well as skills divides in the West and beyond remain a reality when it comes to access and types of usage of the Internet and of social media platforms. True, penetration rates have been rising consistently, but it would be an illusion to think that access to social media is universal. Furthermore, those who do have access and the skills do not necessarily use the Internet and social media for political purposes. All this can potentially hinder processes of disclosure and especially limit the reach that social movements have.

Across the EU, 24% of households do not have access to the Internet at home (Eurostat, 2012). In the UK about 17% of the population above 15 years old has never used the Internet. The penetration rate of Facebook amongst over-15-year-olds is deemed to be 57%, while if we consider Twitter the penetration rate reduces to 19% of 15 years and older. For Italy, 33% of the population that is 15 years or older does not use the Internet, Facebook has a penetration rate of about 43% amongst over-15-year-olds and Twitter about 6%. In Egypt, however, Internet penetration amongst over-15-year-olds is at 54%, while Facebook attracts a mere 25% of the population older than 15 years and Twitter just about 1%. (cf. Figure 4.2)

In this regard, we should also take into account that the use of social media requires a set of skills and prior knowledge, which some argue requires new forms of literacies and leads to new forms of illiteracies. These skills situate themselves at the level of production and dissemination of movement discourses through social media as well as the reception of these discourses (Hall, 2011; Livingstone, 2008).

Besides this, even if we consider access to be less of an issue and the skills divide to be closing, then there is still the problem that only a minority of Internet users are interested in politics when they go online. While almost 60% of Internet users in the EU purchased goods online in 2011, only about 20% read or posted opinions on civic

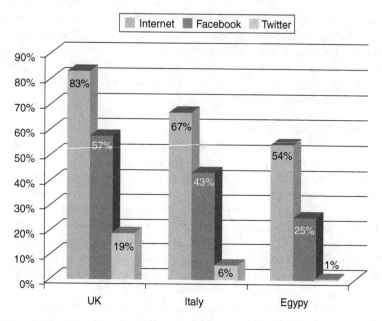

Figure 4.2 Penetration of Internet, Facebook, and Twitter amongst those older than 15 years
Source: Wikimedia Commons. All content on this page is freely licenced.

or political issues online and a mere 7% took part in online consultations or voting (Seybert, 2011).

In addition to this, social media typically require citizens to opt in through liking or through following a particular feed. As such, the use of social media, especially in terms of disclosure, could be approached as a form of narrowcasting. This implies that there is a high probability that activists and protest movements that exclusively use social media only reach those who are already more or less aligned with the aims and goals of the movement; through social media, movements mainly preach to the converted. All this explains why many scholars point to the continuing importance of mainstream media in communicating beyond the likeminded when it comes to the logic of disclosure (see Rucht, 2013).

Social media promote individualism first and foremost

While social media is presented as inherently 'social' and geared towards sharing with others, building networks, it is at the same time all rather 'Me'-centric. In many countries the word 'Selfie' was voted new word of the year in 2013. The navel-gazing act of taking your own picture and uploading it on social media is symptomatic of the primacy of individualism in our current technology-obsessed societies. Social media and the ubiquity of screens in everyday life arguably feed fragmentation and individualism, which makes the articulation of firm connections between the individual and society more difficult. This in turn is potentially detrimental to building the strong collective identities deemed to be of crucial importance to protest movements (della Porta & Diani, 2006).

In addition to this, there is increasing evidence that the ubiquity of screens in our everyday lives is leading to an extreme fragmentation of attention spans and has drastically reduced the ability to focus, concentrate, and memorize. This can be related to the arguments being developed by Carr (2011); the way the Internet is wired changes the way we think and, crucially for this chapter, the way we remember.

There is an intrinsic tension and conflict here between the individualistic nature of social media platforms – it is 'I'-Like, not 'we'-Like – and the need for movements to build and sustain collective identities and to organize collective actions. The fragmentation of attention spans is arguably mirrored by a radical fragmentation of demands and causes online. The 'global web movement' Avaaz.org was launched in January 2007 and has in the meantime started almost 146 million different actions. There is also the common critique that the cost of participation in these kinds of online actions is minimal and therefore easier to disregard by the powers that be. This explains why some observers speak of slacktivism as being inconsequential (Morozov, 2009). In this regard, we could also refer to Bennett and Segerberg's (2012: 744) arguments relating to changes at the level of collective action, group affiliation, and organizational participation, all influenced by multifaceted processes of individualization.

The radical fragmentation of demands and causes as witnessed online is in my view a symptom of a much broader problem, namely that of the de-ideologization of social, economic, and political struggles. Bauman's (2001: 9) account of what individualism amounts to in our times is highly appropriate here; he contends that

> The distinctive feature of the stories told in our times is that they articulate individual lives in a way that excludes or suppresses (prevents from articulation) the possibility of tracking down the links connecting individual fate to the ways and means by which a society as a whole operates.

A good illustration of this is Change.org, a 'social good company' that offers individuals and organizations the opportunity to set-up and sign online petitions, some of which are sponsored. The company claims to have a 'business model that provides value to both our users and our advertisers'.[1] Change.org is a certified 'B Corp', which is a new label that is given to social enterprises that use 'the power of business to solve social and environmental problems' and that thereby 'redefine success in business'[2]. One of Change.org's most recent success stories was a campaign to 'Keep a woman on the English banknotes'.[3]

Phenomena like this thrive through the viral characteristics of social media platforms, but at the same time they reflect the emptying of signifiers such as (social) change and reform of their radical meanings; they decouple emancipatory struggles from the structural inequalities and the unequal distribution of resources that form the basis of most injustices. To put it bluntly, capitalism is seen here as the solution rather than the problem.

Social media are commercial/corporate spaces

This de-ideologization of social struggles and lack of examination in relation to the use of social media for activist purposes is not entirely unsurprising given that the Internet and social media in particular are first and foremost corporate spaces promoting capitalist values. They are geared towards creating added value rather than advocating for radical social change or protecting collective interests. The fact that social media are profit-driven spaces is reflected in the way in which corporate actors unashamedly commodify the digital footprint we leave behind online (Fuchs et al., 2012). As such, everything we do in these corporate spaces is monitored and controlled by these companies.

While social media platforms are often heralded as liberal spaces – advocating freedom of speech, facilitating democratic struggles against authoritarian regimes, fueling revolutions, etc., when it comes to radical protest in Western democracies the Internet and social media platforms in particular often become illiberal and repressive spaces. Usually, the justification provided by Internet companies for such repressive actions relates to breaches of their terms and conditions of use.

In the wake of the WikiLeaks disclosures of the US diplomatic cables, Amazon Web Services (AWS), the company hosting its content, blocked access to the WikiLeaks site. They denied this was due to government pressure, but stated instead that AWS 'does have terms of service that must be followed. WikiLeaks was not following them. There were several parts they were violating'.[4]

In addition to this, Twitter closed an account of the hacktivist collective Anonymous (#Anon_Operation),[5] who had mounted a campaign to support WikiLeaks and Assange. Furthermore, PayPal, Moneybookers, Visa, MasterCard, BankAmerica, and the Swiss bank PostFinance also closed, froze, or restricted the accounts of WikiLeaks. Again, the main justification used by these corporations was that WikiLeaks had breached their terms and conditions. PayPal, for example, sent out a press release on 3 December 2010, stating that the account of WikiLeaks was

> permanently restricted ... due to a violation of the PayPal Acceptable Use Policy, which states that our payment service cannot be used for any activities that encourage, promote, facilitate or instruct others to engage in illegal activity.[6]

Another example of corporate clampdowns and purges was the sudden and unannounced removal by Facebook of a large number of political groups that rallied against the UK government's austerity measures and were mobilizing against the royal wedding of William and Kate (Table 4.2).

Facebook justified the removal of these political groups by stating that Facebook profiles can only represent individuals, not (anonymous) organizations:

> As you may know, Facebook profiles are intended to represent individual people only. It is a violation of Facebook's Statement of Rights and Responsibilities to use a profile to represent a brand, business, group, or organization. As such, your account was disabled for violating these guidelines.[7]

All this shows the vulnerability of radical activists when relying too much on the corporate structures that own the Internet, the popular social media platforms, and the companies that facilitate financial transactions online. At any time these companies can decide to close down spaces of contention and the use of these platform by activists. This also potentially impedes remembrance as activist content online can disappear without prior warning.

However, processes of examination and self-reflexivity mean that this also leads to an increased awareness by activists of the dangers, as a student activist from University College London (UCL) attests:

> Ultimately, the anti-cuts movement in the UK will need to start organising through self-hosted, open source platforms to avoid reliance upon the very corporate power structures we are aiming to challenge.[8]

Table 4.2 List of deactivated political Facebook Groups (28–29 May 2011)

Anarchista Rebellionist	Free Ricardo Palmera group	Ourland FreeLand
Anti-Cuts Across Wigan	Freedom Isa StateofMind	PROUD TO BE A MEMBER OF THAT
ArtsAgainst Cuts	Frfi Students	LEFT-WING FRINGE GROUP CALLED WOMEN*
Beat'n Streets	Goldsmiths Fights Back	Rochdale Law Centre*
BigSociety Leeds	IVA Womensrevolution	Rock War
Bootle Labour	Jason Derrick	Roscoe 'Manchester' Occupation*
Bristol Anarchist Bookfair*	Leeds City College Against Fees and Cuts	Save NHS
Bristol Ukuncut	London Student Assembly	Sheffield Anti-libdemconference
Camberwell AntiCuts	NETWORK X	Sheffield Occupation*
Canadians Against Proroguing Parliament	Newcastle Occupation*	Slade Occupation*
Canadians don't care about the Royal Wedding*	No Cuts	Socialist Unity
Canadians Rallying to Unseat Harper	No Quarter Cutthewar	Southwark Sos
Central London SWP*	NO STEPHEN HARPER WE WON'T SHUT THE F*ck UP	SWP Cork
Chesterfield Stopthecuts	North East Walkout	Teampalestina Shaf
Claimants Fightback	North London Solidarity	Tower Hamlet Greens*
Cockneyreject	Not Stephen Harper 2011*	UWE Occupation*
Comrade George Orwell	Notts-Uncut Part-of UKUncut	Westiminster Trades Council
Don't Break Britain United	Occupied Oxford	Whospeaks Forus*
Ecosocialists Unite*	Occupy Monaco	WOMEN WHO R CREEPED OUT BY STEPHEN HARPER*
Firstof Mayband	Open Birkbeck	York Anarchists

Note: * These groups were up again by May 2011
Source: Open Rights Group.

Figure 4.3   Still from removed You Tube clip called 'William and Kate'
Source: Permission has been obtained from the author.

It is not only radical activists but also ordinary citizens who suffer from this type of corporate censorship. Around the time of the 2011 royal wedding in the UK, Lucy Willow from Cornwall uploaded a video of her pigs on YouTube (cf. Figure 4.3). The title of the video was William and Kate, the names of the two pigs. In March 2012, the video was removed by YouTube, who argued that the music which accompanied the images contravened the copyright of Warner Media Group. Why then was this taken down, while the over 6.5 million video-clips on You Tube using the world-hit 'Gangnam Style' are not?

Social media is highly susceptible to state control and surveillance

One of the affordances described above relates to inverse surveillance or sousveillance. However, this does not mean that the Foucauldian Panopticon has disappeared. On the contrary, the Internet and social media in particular are highly susceptible to state, as well as corporate, surveillance (Fuchs et al., 2012; Leistert, 2013). Our digital footprint is recorded and commodified by corporate actors, but it is also the object of omni-optic surveillance practices by state actors. Some countries have developed dragnet surveillance strategies whereby all the data that is produced by their citizens, but also by citizens in other countries, is being collected and recorded, enabling security services to access all types of data produced by those they seek to follow, monitor, or track down.

These types of omni-optic or ubiquitous surveillance practices are not only prevalent in authoritarian countries, but as much – if not more so – in mature democracies. Given the disclosures relating to the US programme PRISM, set-up by the NSA,[9] but also of TEMPORA, directed by the UK's GCHQ[10], and of a similar programme run by the secret services of France (DGSE)[11], it is becoming increasingly obvious that we are close to realizing the dystopian vision of a truly Orwellian surveillance society; about 30 years later than 1984. We have been '[s]leepwalking into the surveillance society' (Hayles, 2009).

The main rationale provided by democratic leaders for this frightening degree of state surveillance is national security and the war on (Islamist) terrorism. However, in recent years ample evidence has emerged of these anti-terrorism laws and discourses being used against unions, anti-capitalist groups, as well as radical environmental groups (Monaghan & Walby, 2012; Salter, 2011). It goes without saying that anti-systemic or radical protest movements and those that are active in organizations aligned with such movements are also prime targets of these forms of very intrusive state surveillance.

Furthermore, it is becoming ever more apparent that the US and the UK have backdoor keys to the encryption software provided by Microsoft, Google, Yahoo, other email-providers, social network platforms, banks, e-commerce services, cloud services, etc. (Ball et al., 2013). Even the open-source alternatives, which were considered to be very secure up until recently, are now deemed to be highly vulnerable.

Software relying on the Tor-network to remain anonymous is used by many activists, NGOs, journalists. Tor was originally built by the US Navy to secure government communication and it 'helps to reduce the risks of both simple and sophisticated traffic analysis by distributing your transactions over several places on the Internet, so no single point can link you to your destination'. [12] Following the recent disclosures by Edward Snowden, however, cryptographers are convinced that earlier versions of Tor, which 90% of users are still using, are now insecure, hacked and readable by the NSA (Graham, 2013).

Another worrisome tactic democratic countries are increasingly contemplating and in effect also implementing is the strategic and temporal shutdown of networked services. Unlike Hosni Mubarak's decision to close down the Egyptian Internet for three days during the Arab Spring

(January 2010), Western governments do not envisage closing down the whole of their Internet infrastructure, but seek to intervene, rather, at a localized level in places where dissent is taking place. In the wake of the UK riots in 2011 there were strong calls by MPs and government to have the ability to close down all social media platforms in times of social unrest. David Lammy, the Labour MP for Tottenham, where the riots started, blamed Blackberry Messenger as 'one of the reasons why unsophisticated criminals are outfoxing an otherwise sophisticated police force' (quoted in Prodhan & Sharp, 2011: n.p.). Furthermore, during an emergency debate in the UK Parliament a few days later, Prime Minister David Cameron stated the following:

> Everyone watching these horrific actions [the riots] will be struck by how they were organised via social media. Free flow of information can be used for good. But it can also be used for ill, and when people are using social media for violence we need to stop them. So we are working with the police, the intelligence services and industry to look at whether it would be right to stop people communicating via these websites and services when we know they are plotting violence, disorder and criminality.[13]

A few days after the UK riots, in the US, the Bay Area Rapid Transit (BART) police services actually shut down cell services at four San Francisco stations in an attempt to disrupt protests taking place against the killing of Charles Blair Hill by police at the Civic Center station. This in return prompted a reaction by Anonymous starting an #OpBART-campaign targeting the San Francisco subway system (Goodman, 2011; Spencer, 2012).

As all these examples demonstrate, surveillance by the state is first and foremost geared towards monitoring disclosure as well as hindering coordination and examination efforts by social movements and activists.

Conclusions

Social media certainly hold a set of affordances that are highly beneficial to protest movements and activists. These affordances enable activists to develop a range of self-mediation strategies through asynchronous and real-time communication, inward and outward oriented, and less constrained by time and space. These affordances map onto a set of logics of self-mediation which in turn can be related to the Stoic technologies of the self as identified by Foucault – (1) disclosure,

(2) examination and (3) remembrance. Mediation is a crucial component of how these technologies of the self operate in terms of facilitating the dissemination of movement discourses, the organization of social movements, and the coordination of protest events, the recording of movement discourses and protest artefacts, and the long-term archiving of them. This last role also has relevance for the 'beyond the protest' theme of this book.

While these affordances and opportunities inherent to them are real and used profusely by protesters across the whole world, they are also vulnerable and at times problematic. At the level of disclosure, questions regarding the actual reach of social media remain pertinent. The Arab Spring was arguably fuelled more by the amplification of protesters' strategies of disclosure through mainstream media than by social media as such. We also need to actively opt in, which can potentially lead to the emergence of ideological echo chambers (Boutyline & Willer, 2013) – mediating discussion amongst the likeminded and impeding amplification beyond them.

Movement discourses also tend to be geared towards the building of collective identities, and they would generally advocate for collective solutions and call for collective actions. This is at odds with the individualistic and capitalist values inherent to the rationale and raison d'être of social media platforms. Facebook only accepts and recognizes individuals on its platform, not collectivities. This also aligns with their advertisers, who are interested in the details of the online behaviour of individuals, not of collective actors. The use of social media platforms may also lead to a decoupling of social and political struggles with ideology, and feed a lack of examination and self-reflection.

The corporate nature of social media spaces also means that these spaces are permanently watched and potentially closed down, either because the companies exploiting those spaces are easily swayed by government pressure or because they use the small print of their terms and conditions to close down whatever they do not like; for an online political group or a blog, all its contacts and content can suddenly be removed from the public space, hindering remembrance.

This also exposes a tension between on the one hand a liberal discourse of freedom of speech and democratization when it comes to authoritarian regimes – think of claims such as the Twitter Revolution, and on the other hand the repressive behaviour of these same corporate actors towards anti-systemic dissent in Western democracies. All this has detrimental effects on the ability of activists to disclose, amplify, and archive movement discourses and protest artefacts through social media.

Finally, state surveillance and repression is a genuine constraint when it comes to disclosure and examination mediated through social media. Activists are increasingly aware that everything they do online can potentially be under the extreme scrutiny of the security forces. In a sense the very notion of private communication for activists might not exist anymore, certainly not online. However, examination will subsequently lead to new communicative practices which take these constraints into account.

Surveillance also brings the Foucauldian concept of the Panopticon back into the fray, as well as the broader philosophical question as to what social media as technologies of the self do. Foucault argued that through technologies of the self we regulate our bodies, constrain our thinking, and become aware of the stipulated expectations of how to behave in a society. Is a similar mechanism at play for social/political actors, for technologies of self-mediation such as social media? Are social media constraining collective actors more than they are enabling them? Do corporate as well as state actors regulate what is acceptable and what is not? Do they limit the amplification of radical discourses, reward good behaviour, and discipline bad behaviour?

In many respects, the answer to these questions is a resounding yes. Foucault (1978: 94) does also leave us with a way out, though, allowing us to overcome the pessimism of the intellect. While power (and surveillance) is omnipresent, so is resistance. In a sense, throughout history we can witness a permanent dialectic between the appropriation of and experimentation with various forms of media and mediations by resisting subordinate actors, and the subsequent attempts of dominant forces in society to close down these emancipatory fissures, after which new ways to circumvent and pervert the limits and controls are sought. Long may it continue!

Acknowledgements

The author would like to thank the editors, Fausto Colombo, Giovanni Boccia Artieri, and those present at the research seminar organized by the University of East Anglia for their valuable comments on earlier versions of this chapter.

Notes

1. http://www.change.org/en-GB/about/business-model.
2. http://www.bcorporation.net/what-are-b-corps/the-non-profit-behind-b-corps.

3. http://www.change.org/en-GB/petitions/bank-of-england-keep-a-woman-on-english-banknotes.
4. http://aws.amazon.com/message/65348/ (retrieved 1 June 2011).
5. See: http://twitter.com/#!/Anon_Operation (suspended 8 December 2010).
6. See: https://www.thepaypalblog.com/2010/12/paypal-statement-regarding-wikileaks/ (last consulted 28 May 2013).
7. http://digitaljournal.com/article/306162.
8. Ibid.
9. http://www.theguardian.com/world/edward-snowden.
10. http://www.theguardian.com/uk/2013/jun/21/gchq-cables-secret-world-communications-nsa.
11. http://www.lemonde.fr/societe/article/2013/07/04/revelations-sur-le-big-brother-francais_3441973_3224.html.
12. https://www.torproject.org/about/overview.html.en.
13. http://www.theguardian.com/media/2011/aug/11/david-cameron-rioters-social-media

References

Bakardjieva, M. & Gaden, G. (2012). Web 2.0 Technologies of the self. *Philosophy & Technology*, 25(3): 399–413.

Ball, J., Borger, J. & Greenwald, G. (2013). How US and UK spy agencies defeat Internet privacy and security. *The Guardian*, 6 September: http://www.theguardian.com/world/2013/sep/05/nsa-gchq-encryption-codes-security.

Bauman, Z. (2001). *The Individualized Society*. Cambridge: Polity Press.

BBC (2013). Egypt Profile. 6 August: http://www.bbc.co.uk/news/world-africa-13313373.

Bennett, L. W. & Segerberg, A. (2012). The logic of connective action, *Information, Communication & Society*, 15(5): 739–768.

Boutyline, A. & Willer, R. (2013). The social structure of political echo chambers: Ideology and political homophily in online communication networks. Working Paper, 24 May: http://www.ocf.berkeley.edu/~andrei/EchoChambers.pdf.

Burkitt, I. (2002). Technologies of the self: Habitus and capacities. *Journal for the Theory of Social Behaviour*, 32(2): 219–237.

Cammaerts, B. (2007). Media and communication strategies of glocalized activists: Beyond media-centric thinking. In Bart Cammaerts and Nico Carpentier (eds), *Reclaiming the Media: Communication Rights and Expanding Democratic Media Roles* (pp. 265–288). Bristol: Intellect/Chicago: Chicago University Press.

Cammaerts, B. (2008). Critiques on the participatory potentials of Web 2.0. *Communication, Culture & Critique*, 1(3): 358–376.

Cammaerts, B. (2012). Protest logics and the mediation opportunity structure. *European Journal of Communication*, 27(2): 117–134.

Carr, N. (2011). *The Shallows: How the Internet is Changing the Way We Think, Read and Remember*. London: Atlantic Books.

della Porta, D. & Diani, M. (2006). *Social Movements: An Introduction*. Oxford: Blackwell Publishing.

Diani, M. (2001). Social movement networks: Virtual and real. In Frank Webster (ed.), *Culture and Politics in the Information Age: A New Politics?* (pp. 117–128). London: Routledge.

eMarketer (2013). Facebook sees growth in UK monthly users, but nears saturation point, 15 August: http://www.emarketer.com/Article/Facebook-Sees-Growth-UK-Monthly-Users-Nears-Saturation-Point/1010136.

Eurostat (2012) Internet access and use in 2012. 18 December. URL: http://europa.eu/rapid/press-release_STAT-12-185_en.htm

Foucault, M. (1978). *History of Sexuality, Part 1: An Introduction*. New York: Pantheon.

Foucault, M. (1993). About the beginning of the hermeneutics of the Self. *Political Theory*, 21(2): 198–227.

Foucault, M. (1997). Technologies of the Self. In Paul Rabinow (ed.), *Michel Foucault, Essential Works, Volume 1: Ethics, Subjectivity, and Truth* (pp. 223–251). New York: New Press.

Fuchs, C., Boersma, K., Albrechtslund, A. & Sandoval, M. (eds) (2012). *Internet and Surveillance: The Challenges of Web 2.0 and Social Media*. London: Routledge.

Gibson, J. J. (1977). The theory of affordances. In Robert Shaw and John Bransford (eds), *Perceiving, Acting, and Knowing: Toward an Ecological Psychology* (pp. 67–82). Hillsdale, NJ: Lawrence Erlbaum Associates.

Gibson, J. J. (1979/1986). *The Ecological Approach to Perception*. Hillsdale, NJ: Lawrence Erlbaum Associates.

Gillan, K., Pickerill, J. & Webster, F. (2008). *Anti-War Activism: New Media and Protest in the Information Age*. Basingstoke: Palgrave Macmillan.

Goodman, A. (2011). Hacktivism's global reach, from targeting Scientology to backing WikiLeaks and the Arab Spring. *Democracy Now*, 16 August: http://www.democracynow.org/2011/8/16/hacktivisms_global_reach_from_targeting_scientology.

Graham, R. (2013). Tor is Still DHE 1024 (NSA Crackable), *Errata Security*: http://blog.erratasec.com/2013/09/tor-is-still-dhe-1024-nsa-crackable.html.

Hall, W. (2011). The ever evolving web: The power of networks. *International Journal of Communication*, 5: 651–664.

Hayles, K. (2009). Sleepwalking into the surveillance society. *Surveillance and Society*, 6(3): 2–9.

Hermida, A., Lewis, S. C. & Zamith, R. (2012). Sourcing the Arab Spring: A case study of Andy Carvin's sources during the Tunisian and Egyptian revolutions. Paper presented at the International Symposium on Online Journalism in Austin, TX, April: https://online.journalism.utexas.edu/2012/papers/Hermida.pdf.

Honneth, A. (2012). *The I in We: Studies in the Theory of Recognition*. Cambridge: Polity Press.

Howard, P. N. & Hussain, M. M. (2011). The role of digital media. *Journal of Democracy*, 22(3): 35–48.

Index Mundi (2013). Country facts: http://www.indexmundi.com/.

Kennewell, S. (2001). Using affordances and constraints to evaluate the use of information and communications technology in teaching and learning, *Journal of Information Technology for Teacher Education*, 10(1&2): 101–116.

Leistert, O. (2013). *From Protest to Surveillance – The Political Rationality of Mobile Media Modalities of Neoliberalism*. New York: Peter Lang.

Livingstone, S. (2008). Internet literacy: Young people's negotiation of new online opportunities. In T. McPherson (ed.), *Unexpected Outcomes and Innovative Uses of Digital Media by Youth* (pp. 101–121). Cambridge, MA: The MIT Press.

Martín-Barbero, J. (1993). *Communication, Culture and Hegemony: From the Media to Mediation*. London: Sage.

Mathiesen, T. (1997). The viewer society: Michel Foucault's 'Panopticon' revisited. *Theoretical Criminology*, 1(2): 215–134.

McLuhan, M. & McLuhan, E. (1988). *Laws of Media: The New Science*. Toronto: Toronto University Press.

Meyer, D. S. & Whittier, N. (1994). Social movement spillover. *Social Problems*, 41: 277–298.

Monaghan, J. & Walby, K. (2012). Making up 'Terror Identities': Security intelligence, Canada's Integrated Threat Assessment Centre and social movement suppression. *Policing and Society: An International Journal of Research and Policy*, 22(2): 133–151.

Morozov, E. (2009). The brave new world of slacktivism. *Foreign Policy*, 19/05. See: http://neteffect.foreignpolicy.com/posts/2009/05/19/the_brave_new_world_of_slacktivism.

Mourtada, R. & Salem, F. (2013). Arab social media report. Dubai: Dubai School of Government.

ONS (2013). *Internet Access Quarterly Update*, Q1 2013: http://www.ons.gov.uk/ons/dcp171778_310435.pdf [last accessed 20 September 2013].

Prodhan, G. & Sharp, A. (2011). MP calls for BlackBerry Messenger suspension to calm UK riots. Reuters, 9 August: http://www.reuters.com/article/2011/08/09/us-britain-riots-blackberry-idUSTRE7784EE20110809.

Rucht, D. (2013). Protest movements and their media usages. In B. Cammaerts, A. Matoni & P. McCurdy (eds), *Mediation and Protest Movements* (pp 249–268). Bristol: Intellect.

Salter, C. (2011). Activism as terrorism: The green scare, radical environmentalism and governmentality. *Anarchist Developments in Cultural Studies*, 1: 211–238. – http://www.anarchist-developments.org/index.php/adcs/article/view/45

Seybert, H. (2011). Internet use in households and by individuals in 2011. *Eurostat Statistics in Focus*, 66: 1–8.

Silverstone, R. (2002). Complicity and collusion in the mediation of everyday life, *New Literary History*, 33(4): 761–780.

Spencer, J. (2012). No service: Free speech, the Communications Act, and BART's cell phone network shutdown. *Berkeley Technology Law Journal*, 27: 767.

Telecom Paper (2013). Facebook use grows in Italy as Twitter use declines. 31 May: http://www.telecompaper.com/news/facebook-use-grows-in-italy-as-twitter-use-declines-946888.

5

When Narratives Travel: The Occupy Movement in Latvia and Sweden

Anne Kaun

Introduction

In autumn 2011, the Occupy movement emerged as a global phenomenon with camps all over the world. Since then it has changed considerably. The encampments have disappeared, but a number of working groups – such as Occupy Sandy, a group mainly active in New York City and New Jersey supporting communities that suffered as a result of Hurricane Sandy in October 2012 – have developed specific causes loosely related to the initial Occupy movement (Kellner, 2012). These changes are to be expected over time; however, the movement also changed as a result of travelling to different localities around the world. In that sense, it provides an example of transnational activism linking different places across the globe characterized by various political contexts (Cohen & Rai, 2000). In this context, Occupy as a movement has often been considered a global protest network consisting of nodes linked by the communicative infrastructure of blogs, digests, and social networking platforms (Castells, 2012; Cohen & Rai, 2000; Sassen, 2011). This approach to analyzing Occupy highlights the importance of specific media practices for the movement's internal identification, organization, and mobilization.

While the network metaphor has been helpful in developing an understanding of communicative connectivity worldwide and identifying central nodes within the network, the approach also has been criticized for technological determinism and a focus on central nodes while dismissing the peripheries and, in that sense, establishing new hierarchies. Hence, the first main concern of this chapter is to argue for radical contextualization of media practices (Radway, 1984), especially in times of Big Data (Mayer-Schonberger & Cukier, 2013) and datafication of the public realm (van Dijck & Poell, 2013). Secondly, the chapter suggests combining diachronic historization with synchronic analysis of protest movements' social media practices. Thirdly, it argues for narrative analysis as a useful approach to studying media participation in protest movements. Relying on in-depth interviews with activists, media content produced by Occupy Stockholm and Occupy Latvia/ Riga, and a discourse analysis of mainstream media reporting, these points are illustrated through an analysis of Occupy Latvia and Occupy Stockholm.

The Occupy movement and its recontextualization in Latvia and Sweden

In July 2011, Adbusters,[1] the notorious facilitator of anti-consumerism campaigns, launched a call to occupy Wall Street by introducing the hashtag #occupywallstreet on Twitter. The organization was, however, later reluctant to claim to have founded the movement. On 17 September 2011, after online mobilization, a few dozen people followed the call. Since Wall Street was strongly secured by police force, the Occupiers turned to nearby Zuccotti Park. This small, privately owned square became the place for camping, campaigning, and deliberating for the weeks until the first eviction in November 2011 (Graeber, 2013). Initially, there were only a handful of activists. The numbers grew quickly, however, and the encampment became a diverse group of Occupiers based on what has been characterized as leaderlessness and non-violence (Bolton et al., 2013). At the same time, there was a 'division over conventional politics, over reform and revolution' (Gitlin, 2012: p.xv). This varied group of people with different political visions and ideas about how to organize the movement appropriated elaborate means of consultation, including the People's Microphone, which amplified an individual speaker's voice through a repeating choir, a system of hand signals to organize discussions in large groups, and a system of working groups and breakout sessions that all gathered at the general assembly to reach consensus (Graeber, 2013).

Mainstream media initially reported little about the movement – although what it did report was rather sympathetic (Gitlin, 2012). At the same time, word of Occupy Wall Street (OWS) spread around the world, not least to the main capitals of Europe, leading to the adoption of tactics and different versions of OWS, spearheaded by the London St. Paul's Cathedral occupation (Conztanza-Chock, 2012). It was not only in the financial centres of Europe, such as London and Frankfurt, that people had begun to occupy public spaces promoting the slogan 'we are the 99%'; in cities and areas usually seen as peripheral to global capitalism, too, the ideas and ideals of Occupy were adapted to the specific context – as, for example, by Occupy Stockholm and Occupy Latvia, which are the focus here.

Despite earlier occupations of various public spaces and protests related to the economic crisis in 2008/2009, Latvia has never seen an actual occupation connected with the global Occupy movement. Linked to the general growth of Occupy worldwide, however, loose online groups associated with the movement appeared, discussing economic greed and politics in the Latvian context.

In Stockholm, by contrast, occupations had been taking place for almost a year.[2] During the first weeks, Occupy Stockholm quickly diversified into several subgroups and committees working with specific questions. The media group was one of the biggest of these, consisting of several divisions working on the homepage[3] (discontinued), Facebook, Twitter, and YouTube, printed news outlets and posters, as well as graphics. Other subgroups were dedicated to demonstrations and to a study group that met weekly between January and May 2012. Their discussions about democracy, participation, economics, and neoliberal ideology were streamed live online. As two interviewees who were involved with Occupy Stockholm suggested, many first-time activists joined the group when it began. During late summer 2012, however, more and more activists vanished from the encampment and the last campsite was cleared voluntarily. A core group of five people remained and held a general assembly on a regular basis until October 2012, when they decided to pause Occupy Stockholm indefinitely.

Network society

As the Occupy movement spread globally, research efforts also grew. Special journal issues emerged (for example *Social Movement Studies* (vol. 11, no 3–4) and *Cultural Anthropology* ('Hot Spots' on Occupy), articles and books were published, conferences were held, research collectives (e.g. the Occupy Research Collective) were set up, and a scholarly journal appeared (*Journal for Occupied Studies*). Among these research endeavours, several scholars also engaged in the specific analysis of Occupy as a global phenomenon (Conztanza-Chock, 2012; Juris, 2012; Postill, 2013; Uitermark & Nicholls, 2012). In particular, social networking sites such as Facebook, Twitter, Reddit, and Tumblr have been identified and emphasized as crucial components of the global Occupy movement (Castells, 2012; Gleason, 2013; Milner, 2013; Penney & Dadas, 2014; Wang et al., 2013).

In contrast to this earlier research, this chapter focuses on the question of activists' media practices and the role of mainstream news media in the process of recontextualizing a globally shared frame of activism. In this way, it connects to previous studies of the repertoire of collective action (Tilly, 1986, 1993), which suggest that an increasingly important part of the collective action repertoire is constituted by questions of media representation and media practices (Couldry, 2012) or, more specifically, forms of media participation in and through the media (Carpentier, 2011). Participation *in* the media refers to contributions of lay people to the decision-making processes and governance of (mainstream) media, while participation *through* the media refers to own productions, but also to the visibility of different voices in media content (Carpentier, 2011). Generally it is argued that all of these forms of media participation become increasingly important in societies characterized by mediatization (Couldry & Hepp, 2013; Hepp, 2011). One of the most prominent approaches to analyzing the role of media participation in social movements, suggested by Manuel Castells, is the notion of the network society that is largely based on communicative power (Castells, 2009, 2011, 2012).

Castells argues that 'the social dynamics constructed around networks appear to dissolve society as a stable social form of organization' (Castells, 2009: 19) and explains further that 'a network society is a society whose social structure is made around networks activated by microelectronics-based, digitally processed information and communication technologies' (Castells, 2009: 24). This notion of the network society has been identified as being of value for the analysis of protest and social movements as it describes a common culture that is based not on shared values, but on the shared understanding of the importance of communication. Network societies are based on communication protocols that interlink different cultures. The interlinking of different cultures without diminishing their inherent differences makes the approach especially appealing for the analysis of global protest movements that struggle for communicative power.

Communicative power is central to the network society, as power is exercised through the control over minds 'by means of coercion ... and/or by the construction of meaning on the basis of the discourses through which social actors guide their action' (Castells, 2009: 10). Social movements then join the 'battle of images and frames' (Castells, 2009: 302) that is taking place in multimedia communication networks:

> By using both horizontal communication networks and mainstream media to convey their images and messages, they increase

their chances of enacting social and political change – even if they start from a subordinate position in institutional power, financial resources, or symbolic legitimacy. (Castells, 2009: 302)

However, several problems with Castells' notion of the network society have been raised. Firstly, it has been argued that the notion of the network society overemphasizes technological aspects and downplays the question of access to resources and agency (Hands, 2011; van Dijck, 1999). Secondly, it has been suggested that Castells overemphasizes social formation over social action by proposing that society is a network. Furthermore, networks – and, hence, the network society – are based on ties or relationships between nodes. These relationships determine the centrality of certain nodes and the peripherality of others (Mansell, 2010). The relational logic establishes a different kind of hierarchy – namely, that between central and peripheral nodes, which are visible and invisible respectively, while downplaying the character and activities constituting a node as such (Halvorsen, 2012). Furthermore, one could argue that emphasizing the role of communication technologies, especially commercial social networking platforms, maintains communicative capitalism as conceptualized by Jodi Dean (2008, 2012) as the network metaphor. Dean argues that within the current landscape of social networking sites, exchange value is of more importance than the use value of messages. It is hence not the shared content that is of major interest and bears the potential for change, but the mere exchange of messages that is endorsed as it contributes to the generation of surplus value for the platforms being used. Arguing that protest movements are inherently characterized by the network logic among others embodied by social networking sites strengthens the power of these commercial players and the logic of communicative capitalism rather than critically deconstructing it.

There have also been general discussions about which aspects of the global Occupy movement could be analyzed in terms of network logics. Taking Occupy as an example, Halvorsen (2012) argues that the movement did not establish global convergence spaces where central nodes for a transnational network emerged, as was the case for the alter-globalization movement that was largely organized around events such as the World Social Forum and G8 or G20 meetings. No such attempts have been made within Occupy, except for the Alternative Day of Action on Human Rights Day (10 December 2011). In that sense, the movement was very locally anchored, combining network logic with the logic of aggregation (Juris, 2012; Uitermark & Nicholls, 2012).

The network notion has certainly contributed to developing an understanding of Occupy on a global scale, but less to an understanding of the relevance and transformation of Occupy as a shared frame that is concretely enacted in different contexts. Hence, I would like to suggest considering Occupy as a meta-narrative that has been very specifically reshaped and reinterpreted in different contexts, while taking the limits of narratives as heuristic into account (Polletta, 2006). The aim is not to completely dismiss the notion of the network, but to point out its limitations and consider relevant extensions.

Empirical entry points

I would like to illustrate the points made above, especially the argument for radical contextualization and historization, with an analysis of Occupy Latvia and Occupy Stockholm. Neither Sweden nor Latvia took a central position within the global Occupy network. However, they can be considered as exemplifying the recontextualization of the movement.

The analysis is twofold and could be described as multi-sited narrative analysis considering a variety of materials such as interviews with activists, media productions by Occupy Stockholm and Occupy Latvia, and articles published in major Swedish and Latvian news outlets.

Firstly, the analysis focuses on the recontextualization by activists' media practices and secondly on the recontextualization by mainstream news media in both countries. The first part is based on in-depth interviews, participant observations and an analysis of documents produced by activists in Latvia and Sweden in autumn 2012. Besides materials documenting activists' media practices, the movement's recontextualization is traced through a discourse analysis of major mainstream newspapers in both countries. The discourse analysis focuses on the first two months after the first encampment of OWS on 17 September 2011, which is the time when Occupy groups and encampments mushroomed all over Europe.

The discourse analysis sample consists of *Dagens Nyheter*, *Svenska Dagbladet*, *Aftonbladet* and *Expressen* for the Swedish part and *Diena*, *Neatkarīgā Rīta Avīze*, *Latvijas Avīze* (all in Latvian), *Chas* and *Vesti* (both in Russian) for the Latvian part. The choice of newspapers represents a broad spectrum of political positions (from liberal to conservative) as well as quality and tabloid newspapers. For the Latvian case, the sample includes the most important Russian daily newspapers, which are mainly read by the Russian-speaking minority (comprising approximately 27% of the Latvian population).

The Swedish sample consists of 63 articles in total, whereas the Latvian newspapers published only 17 articles during the same period (from September to November 2011; the period was chosen based on the main activities of the OWS). The first report in Sweden appeared on 29 September 2011 in *Svenska Dagbladet* and was a comparably long article in the economy section. In Latvia, the first article concerning the Occupy movement was published on 3 October 2011.

Narrative analysis of protest movements

Instead of focusing on central nodes of a global protest network, this chapter suggests considering the reshapings of a shared meta-narrative in different contexts. Narrative analysis originating from literature, history, anthropology, sociology, and linguistics encompasses a variety of research practices and analytical strategies, such as biographical studies, autobiographical approaches, and life- and oral histories (Creswell, 2007). Despite, or because of, the intensive engagement with narrative analysis within qualitative research, the field is characterized by ambiguities and controversies. Hence, it is difficult to point to a coherent tradition of narrative analysis (Rogan & de Kock, 2005). The focus of narrative semiotics is on how stories are told through the media, e.g. movies, by focusing on different levels of analysis, such as technical aspects, plot development, and character. In general, the notion of narrative may refer to an actual text or more abstract discourse. Narrative analysis enables, therefore, the inclusion of individual voices and more abstract discourse. The inclusion of individual voices is of particular importance in the context of the Occupy movement, which is and was characterized by a broad diversity of political views and actors.

Stories and narratives are also considered as expressions of emplotment. On the micro level of stories, as well as the more abstract discourse level, they provide coherence in a world of disorder (Ricoeur, 1984). Hence, focusing on narratives allows us to follow the emplotment of experiences here in the sense of recontextualization (Bennett, 2013; van Leeuwen, 2007; van Leeuwen & Wodak, 1999). Recontextualization refers to the idea – in line with van Leeuwen's framework – that all social practice is reformulated as talk and texts in discourse. Through discursive articulation, practices become meaningful from a specific point of view. This view establishes discourse as being clearly grounded in a material world transcending pure exercise of ideology (van Leeuwen, 2008; van Leeuwen & Wodak, 1999). Van Leeuwen constructs, furthermore, a chain of recontextualization, moving from social practices to discursive, signifying practices to discourse. He further identifies participants, actions, performance modes, presentation, time and location, as well as resources, as key elements within this chain of recontextualization.

Occupy narrative/s

It seems difficult, however, to establish a coherent narrative of Occupy in the first instance, in order to trace the recontextualization of its meta-narrative. At the beginning of the movement, the leaderlessness, multi-voiced character, and openness in terms of demands were the fundamental features of OWS, making it obsolete to tell one story of the movement. The difficulty of defining the movement was part of the initial organizing and mobilizing period of OWS, when different (political) groups aimed to establish narrative power (Graeber, 2013). Graeber nicely describes this struggle – which manifested itself, for example, in one of the first meetings (the general assembly on 2 August 2011), where members of the Workers World Party (WWP) seemed to have been dominating the discussion initially (pp. 24–26), but anarchist activists successfully questioned their position. This had consequences for the character of the movement that consequently emerged organically, in terms of organizational structures without hierarchies and the deep commitment to multi-voicedness, which means that carving out one major narrative appears counter-intuitive (Bolton et al., 2013).

However, in order to develop an understanding of the narrative structure of Occupy, a distinction between story and narrative is crucial, as the individual stories of occupiers feed into a grander web of the Occupy narrative. In this context, Occupy Together[4] establishes an international platform that gathers shared narratives of the movement with an emphasis on diversity, multiplicity of voices, and the individual. The openness of the defining Occupy narrative allows for different political subject positions and contributes to the 'opening up of the radical imagination that Occupy allowed' (Graeber, 2013: xxvii). This radical imagination that enables the construction of chains of equivalence concerning concrete local concerns allowed for a global appropriation and spread of the movement to numerous places in the world. By April 2014, Occupy.net listed, for example, 1,518 occupations worldwide.

Activists' stories: Negotiating the global and the local

In terms of recontextualization, Occupy Latvia activists were faced with a generally negative attitude towards the term 'occupy'. Two of my Latvian interviewees suggested that the name Occupy appealed little to the Latvian population and potential activists given Latvia's German and Russian occupation in the first half of the twentieth century. For this reason, one of the aims of the Occupy movement – to overturn and reclaim the notion of occupation (Pickerill & Krinsky, 2012) – failed in the Latvian context. Adam, one of my interview partners, remembered:

> There wasn't Occupy as such in Latvia. The problem started with the word Occupy. It reminds very much of the occupation in Soviet times and the German occupation. That's not really inviting. But the movement has been discussed – for example, in our blog. Mainly, what was discussed was how it looks in the US and Spain, but not in Latvia, where people are not used to protests and demonstrations. One exception was 2009, when – during the winter – there were demonstrations and a small encampment in front of the parliament for a couple of weeks, but these were considered as hippy-like activities, in a way. (Interview with Adam[5] – Latvian activist)

For Adam, one of the main reasons that Occupy never took off in Latvia was the problematic naming of the movement, although the country had already seen crisis-related protest mobilizations, including occupations in 2008/2009. Adam recounts that on 13 January 2009, a protest against the government's handling of the crisis turned into a violent riot. Protesters – mainly students – were pressing for the resignation of the government. During the time of mobilization, a number of protesters tried to hinder MPs' entry into parliament and camped in front of the building. However, after the resignation of the government on 20 February 2009, the protest quickly faded; it seemed that the activists had achieved their goal. Additionally, in autumn 2009, a group of approximately 20 activists was camping in front of the Cabinet of Ministers, the main Latvian government building. They remained in this self-organized camp until summer 2010, promoting a broad range of demands of the Latvian government. Some of the main issues were unemployment and the recently introduced austerity measures. This illustrates the importance of considering the historical situatedness of global movements such as Occupy and the need for including diachronic analyses.

Although there were no Occupy camps in Latvia, Occupy narratives were circulating in blogs, e.g. http://politika.lv/ and on social networking platforms such as Facebook, e.g. the Occupy Latvia Facebook page, which describes itself and its aims as follows:

> We will publish here information about events that are connected with the movement against the financial terrorism of banks and corporations.

Dear citizen! We are not some kind of organized group that will try to convince you what you should do. There will be no Lenin or Ulmanis[6] who will give orders to others from above. That would be against the nature of the action for which we were inspired by the occupation of Wall Street and its followers in the whole world. We have painful credits from banks too, we have also tightened belts because of reduced budgets, and we also have relatives and friends who have been forced to leave the fatherland in order to earn money in exile. Meanwhile the 1% – owners and managers of banks, oligarchs, as well as the 'cream' of government and state administration – earn money on that. But the sovereign power in the Republic of Latvia belongs to the people – thus, to those 99%, and not to the elite that is only 1% of the population. It is time to use this power. It is time to occupy Latvia so that it really belongs to us and not to a handful of greedy men of wealth.

We do not intend to keep silent!

Only together can we achieve something!

Yours, 99% of the citizens of Latvia (Occupy Latvia Facebook group[7])

This section of the Facebook page opens with a general statement about the group's aim to inform people about the Occupy movement. Readers are firstly addressed as 'citizens' and then invited to join the group, which is open to everyone and welcomes all kinds of ideas. This call follows a reference to the OWS encampment as a source of inspiration. A clear distinction is drawn between the debt-ridden, exploited 99% of Latvian society and the 1% of elite politicians and bankers. The description closes with a mission statement, a call for participation and the signature of the 99%. The description of the group is an attempt to include both first-time activists and interested citizens. It establishes the group members as distinct from others (greedy bankers, politicians, and those not yet involved), while at the same time offering points of identification by describing a life of debt and insecurity for the majority of Latvian society. Hence, the section provides possibilities for group internal identifications, which are based on marking the difference from others – here, the elite.

In the case of Occupy Stockholm, the activists emphasized very strongly the general features of the OWS narrative: an open space for discussion and the aim to restructure the economy and democratic organization fundamentally, as the following press release for the one-month anniversary of the Occupy Stockholm camp illustrates:

Occupy Stockholm is going to celebrate its one-month anniversary of occupation at Brunkebergstorg tomorrow – Saturday, November

12. As far as we know, this occupation has been the longest open-air occupation in the history of modern Sweden and you are warmly welcomed to celebrate! Occupy Stockholm is in solidarity with all other occupations and protests that take place around the world. Now that our planet faces global economic and environmental crises, we have reclaimed our voices against the propaganda of corporations. The change we are aiming for includes all levels of society: culture, healthcare, education, agriculture, energy, financial politics, and so on. If we want to build a better life, all these areas need to be developed. These responsibilities live with us as society. Only if we are united beyond our individual goals will there be a responsible future for coming generations. In order to make this happen, we need to support each other. The solution needs much more than a camp at Brunkebergstorg, but we are going to be in the park to remind you of what is going on in the world, what needs to be done, and what we can do together to realize it. You are always welcome to join us. We are going to be there ... (Occupy Stockholm website)[8]

The general demands for change at all levels of society, which resonate with those of OWS, are anchored in the local presence of the activists, making the aim for change visible on a daily basis (Hayduk, 2013). The more context-specific recontextualization of the local encampments was especially visible in the demonstrations and particular events that Occupy Stockholm either organized or supported. The causes for mobilization on the local level stretched from protests against the further privatization of housing in Stockholm, to homelessness, Swedish weapon deals with Saudi Arabia, and the data retention directive (FRA).[9] Furthermore, Occupy Stockholm mobilized people to take part in Europe-wide protests against public debt and the ESM funds, and advocated for a European directive for the increased regulation of banks at the European level. Globally, it supported World Environment Day, protests against US war politics, and May Day marches. Combining global Occupy features with local causes, the encampment became a site of negotiation between the global and the local – which also affects the individual. Thomas, for example, describes his previous (remote) involvement with OWS, which paved the way for his mobilization and support of Occupy Stockholm. The physical mobilization meant for him:

the biggest challenge personally, because almost all my interests and a large share of my normal social context are technology-based. I grew up in the context of the BBS-scene – that's what the Internet was called before – and was one of the first users of a private Internet provider in Sweden. This form of social engagement is expressed today in the fact that I spend almost all the time I am awake consuming media – commenting on and forwarding current developments in social media (Twitter and the like). So to go – within an afternoon – from intensive activity around, for example, OWS (New York and other branches) and the North-African/Middle East revolutions with little sleep to not knowing anything about the world beyond the 100–200 metres or so around you (except for the little things that you pick up from passers-by) ... is a big change. (Interview with Thomas[10] – Occupy Stockholm)

Thomas also describes in the interview how he was involved with setting up the online infrastructure of OWS in New York City and how activism came to mean being a relay or hub for information on a global scale. Being one of the longest and most involved occupiers meant, for him, not having access to global news, since the technological infrastructure and hardware in the Stockholm encampment did not allow for it. In more general terms, Thomas's shift from being a broker in a network to an occupier reflects the double articulation combining networking logic and logic of aggregation that Jeffrey Juris (2012) describes. Both logics are of importance in terms of sustaining a global protest movement, although the focus might be shifting over time. Juris argues, for example, that networking logic – 'that is shaped by our interactions with networking technologies and ... gives rise to specific kinds of social and political networking practices' (Juris, 2012: 266) – was of utmost importance during the initial mobilizations for Occupy and after the disappearance of the camps.

Ultimately, the narratives of Occupy Stockholm and Occupy Latvia activists reflect the negotiation of a global frame with the local conditioning that has been discussed in scholarly literature, especially in the context of new social movements (Cohen & Rai, 2000). Occupy emerges as a multi-level movement reflecting a nation station that is being continuously challenged by globalization of finance capitalism (della Porta & Piazza, 2008). Part of the multi-level character of the movement is the integration of the logic of the network and of aggregation that is expressed in multiple forms of action that link local protest to global movements (della Porta & Piazza 2008). Following only Castells' network society argument would preclude the aggregation aspect. However, both logics are of importance for the global movement, although for different reasons, and their impact shifts over time (Nayak, 2013). In the Latvian context, the movement remained within the logic of networking, never leading to physical aggregation in a public space, while in the Swedish context, both logics were fully played out.

News media stories: Global trumps local

This section analyzes the recontextualization of the Occupy movement in Sweden and Latvia by mainstream news media. By way of a discourse analysis, four major strategies of emploting the narrative in a different context were identified: nomination, predication, perspectivation, and mitigation (van Leeuwen, 2008).

Nomination refers to the discursive construction of social actors, objects, events, and actions and ultimately asks who gets to talk about which kinds of event. In general, the reports about OWS, and Occupy in the Swedish and Latvian context, are rather few and dominated by elite actors such as politicians, artists, and intellectuals. Rarely are activists themselves given voice in the articles. In the Swedish case, activists appear in the articles more frequently after the first encampments in Stockholm. In the Latvian case, no local activists or politicians are mentioned in the articles.

In terms of the motivations for and causes of the emergence of the Occupy movement, the newspapers in both Latvia and Sweden focus on the greed of individual bankers and corporations, and make some mention of the growing inequality. However, as the following example from the Swedish *Expressen* illustrates, this is only justified and evidenced for the American and not the Swedish or Latvian context, and remains rather non-specific in terms of Occupy's suggested criticisms:

The average income in the US has marginally increased the last 30 years. At the same time, the income of the richest part has exploded. The large productivity growth has not reached the middle class, however, the richest are paying ever less and the middle class ever more. (*Expressen*, 22 October 2011)[11]

Predication, the second discursive practice prevalent in the articles, refers to the qualification of actors, objects, events, and action, in comparison to other actors, objects, events, and actions, and hence to which kinds of category they potentially belong. In both contexts, Occupy is associated with other protest movements, such as the Global Justice Movement, the Arab Spring, and the Indignados, but also with WikiLeaks and Anonymous, as well as the Tea Party movement, as shown in *Diena*:

The activists of Occupy Wall Street like to stress that they are a repercussion of the so-called Arab Spring protests. The internet edition of *International Business Times*, however, rather links the American movement with the 15M movement, which started in May in Madrid, followers of which stay in the parks of the biggest cities for weeks and months, in order to demand that the government carries out social and political reforms. 15M can be proud of real achievements, because the socialist Prime Minister José Luis Zapatero announced extraordinary parliamentary elections in the summer. (*Diena* 14 October 2011)[12]

There are, however, no links to traditional political organizations such as trade unions, although they have been supporting specific mobilizations of, for example, Occupy Stockholm. Through this kind of predication, the movement is ideologically depoliticized, especially as the comparison to all kinds of protest and social movements from the radical left to the right contextualizes the movement as ideologically and structurally arbitrary.

In terms of perspectivation, it is clear that both Latvian and Swedish newspapers create only weak links between Occupy and the local/national context. The movement is largely considered in foreign news sections and as having little relevance for the local political and economic context:

Started as a rather marginal movement against the bankers of Wall Street, the protest campaign Occupy Wall Street concerns almost everybody in American society. (*Latvijas Avīze* 14 October 2011)[13]

This also links with the discursive strategy of mitigation: the down-toning to minimize the act of protesting and occupying public space itself. *Expressen* downplays the movement in the following way:

It is not true. 99 percent of the Swedes do not have to choose at all between paying for food *or* the rent. Of course the differences have increased during the last couple of years, but most parts of the Swedish population do not suffer economically. (*Expressen* 22 October 2011)[14]

In the Latvian context, mitigation of the movement in general is executed by completely delinking it from the Latvian crisis experience while, in Sweden, commentators question the severity of the crisis and consequently the motivation of the local activists.

In general, the movement is depoliticized by disconnecting it from its initial cause of questioning and criticizing the global financial capitalism that led to the economic crisis. Furthermore, the movement is disconnected from other forms of critiquing or countering capitalist practices – for example, through institutionalized forms of political organization such as unions. Additionally, the causes of the movement are mitigated by delinking it from the crisis experience in the local context of both Sweden and Latvia. Hence, Occupy is largely constructed as foreign and less relevant in the north-European context. In terms of negotiating the global movement and the local context, mainstream news media in both Latvia and Sweden attribute more importance to the global level of the movement than to its local relevance, leading to a crude discrediting of the root causes for the emergence of the movement.

Conclusion

The main aim of this chapter was to show that the protest network metaphor that has been invoked by, for example, Castells (2009 and 2012) might be helpful for certain kinds of analysis. In order to grasp the relationship between the global movement and its local expressions, I would argue, however, that it overemphasizes the technological aspects and downplays the contextual considerations of how global narratives and practices are appropriated and recontextualized. Besides the problems that have been pointed out, the network metaphor emphasizes the newness of how protests are organized and places communication technologies at the centre without investigating changes or the legitimacy of newness claims. In order to develop an in-depth understanding of the media practices of current protest movements, they have to be put, however, in the historical context of previous movements and their (social) media practices. Consequently, I have suggested focusing on the discursive practices of activists and mainstream news media that constitute a global movement in local contexts. In line with this, radical (re)contextualization is stressed as an approach that allows for an analysis of the local contexts in which Occupy emerged. Furthermore, the chapter argues for comparative research to develop a deeper understanding of local particularities and shared characteristics of global social movements. The comparative analysis conducted here aimed to articulate structural differences and commonalities in order to show the linkages while preserving the particularities of the movement in specific localities. Furthermore, analyzing narratives provided by the activists in contrast with mainstream news media narratives shows how the global and the local are negotiated differently, and the consequences of these diverse appropriations. While activists' stories emphasize the local specifics of their activism in relation to a global cause, mainstream news reports that have been analyzed here merely consider the global scope. In so doing, they mitigate the importance of the movement in the local context and question its origins as inappropriate in terms of the political and economic realities in Sweden and Latvia.

In addition to the investigation of how the global and the local are negotiated in different contexts, the multi-sited narrative analysis exercised here allows an understanding of the double articulation of networking logic in combination with the logic of aggregation. Network analysis as a dominant perspective on global social movements only partially makes sense of this double articulation.

As earlier studies have pointed out, global social movements today emerge in the nexus of the global and local. The Occupy encampments around the world are vivid expressions of contentious politics against global (finance) capitalism, expressed on the local level through physical presence in public spaces as well as mobilizing for direct action with specific local foci. While the network metaphor emphasizes global connectedness and contributes to an understanding in terms of visibility versus non-visibility, centre versus periphery, multi-sited narrative analysis contributes to an understanding of the actual negotiation process between the local and the global.

Acknowledgements

The author would like to thank Iveta Jurkane Hobein, PhD student in the Sociology Department at Södertörn University, for her substantial contributions to the discourse analysis.

Notes

1. For a critical analysis of Adbusters as a facilitator of social and political criticism, see Haiven (2007).
2. 15 October 2011–29 February 2012: Brunkebergstorg; 2 March 2012–4 April 2012: Rålambshovsparken; 7 April 2012–17 May 2012: Fittja; 27 June 2012–31 July 2012: Tantolunden.
3. Occupystockholm.com
4. http://www.occupytogether.org/aboutoccupy/ [Accessed 12 April 2014].
5. Name changed by the author.
6. Kārlis Ulmanis was the Latvian president from 1936 to 1940.
7. Dārgais pilsoni! Mēs neesam nekāda organizēta grupa, kura tev mēģinās iestāstīt, kas tev ir jādara. Te nav un nebūs neviena Ļeņina vai Ulmaņa, kas komandēs citus no varas pjedestāla. Tas būtu pretrunā ar pasākuma būtību, kuram iedvesmu esam smēlušies no Volstrītas okupācijas un tās sekotājiem visā pasaulē. Arī mums ir grūti atdodami kredīti bankās, arī mēs

esam savilkuši jostas valsts budžeta samazināšanas dēļ, arī mums ir radi un draugi, kuri ir bijuši spiesti pamest dzimteni, lai pelnītu naudu svešatnē. Mēs esam 99% Latvijas iedzīvotāju, kuri iznes visu krīzes smagumu uz saviem pleciem. Tikmēr 1% – banku īpašnieki un vadība, oligarhi, kā arī valdības un valsts pārvaldes 'krējums' – uz to visu pelna naudu. Taču suverēnā vara Latvijas Republikā pieder tautai. Tātad tiem 99%, nevis elitei, kas ir tikai 1% no iedzīvotājiem. Ir pienācis laiks izmantot šo varu. Ir pienācis laiks okupēt Latviju, lai tā tiešām piederētu mums, nevis saujiņai mantrausīgu bagātnieku. Mēs vairs nedomājam klusēt! Tikai kopā mēs varam kaut ko panākt! Ar cieņu,99% Latvijas pilsoņu. Available from: https://www.facebook. com/OccupyLatvia [Accessed 14 April 2014].

8. Occupy Stockholm kommer att fira sitt ettmånadersjubileum av ockupationen på Brunkebergstorg imorgon lördag, den 12 november. Så vitt vi vet har detta varit den längsta utomhusockupationen i modern historia i Sverige, och du är varmt välkomna att delta i firandet! Occupy Stockholm rörelsen är i solidaritet med alla de andra ockupationer och protester som äger rum runt om i världen. Då vår planet står inför globala ekonomiska och miljömässiga kriser har vi åtagit oss att ha våra röster hörda i ansiktet av företagens propaganda. Den förändring vi söker omfattar alla sektorer i samhället; kultur, hälsovård, utbildning, jordbruk, energi, ekonomisk politik, etc. Om vi skall kunna bygga ett bättre liv, måste alla dessa sektorer utvecklas. Detta ansvar lever med oss som mänsklighet. Om vi förenas genom omvandling av våra individuella åtgärder kommer vi först då att manifestera en framtid som är hänsynsfull för kommande generationer. För att göra detta behöver vi stödja varandra. Lösningen beror på så mycket mer än ett läger på Brunkebergstorg, men vi kommer att vara i parken att påminna dig om vad som händer i världen och vad som behöver göras och tillsammans arbeta för att detta blir verklighet. Du är alltid välkommen till oss. Vi kommer att vara här. Available from: http://web.archive.org/ web/20120201000000*/http://occupystockholm.org/ [Accessed 14 April 2014].

9. The FRA law enables Swedish authorities to wiretap telephone and internet communication that passes a Swedish border without a warrant.

10. Name changed by the author.

11. Medelinkomsten i USA har nämligen knappt ökat alls på 30 år, samtidigt som den rikaste procentens inkomster exploderat. Den stora produktivitetsökning som skett har knappt alls kommit medelklassen till del, ändå har skattesystemet gjorts om så att de rikaste betalar allt mindre och medelklassen mer.

12. Kustības Occupy Wall Street aktīvistiem patīk uzsvērt, ka viņi ir tā sauktā Arābu pavasara protestu atskaņa. Interneta izdevums International Business Times amerikāņu kustību gan vairāk saista ar maijā Spānijas galvaspilsētā Madridē aisākušos kustību 15M, kuras sekotāji nedēļā un mēnešiem ilgi uzturas lielāko pilsētu centrālajos laukumos, lai pieprasītu valdībai politiskās un sociālās reformas. 15M var lepoties ar reāliem panākumiem, jo sociālistu premjerministrs Hosē Luiss Sapatero vasarā izsludināja ārkārtas parlamenta vēlēšanas.

13. Sākusies kā samērā margināla kustība pret Volstrītas baņķieriem, protesta akcija 'Okupē Voltstrītu' vienaldzīgu neatstāj nevienu amerikāni.

14. Ändå skaver det i ögonen. Det är ju inte sant. 99 procent av svenskarna måste inte alls välja mellan att betala mat och hyra. Visst har klyftorna ökat på senare år, men de flesta svenskar har det ekonomiskt rätt bra.

References

Bennett, J. (2013). Moralising class: A discourse analysis of the mainstream political response to Occupy and the August 2011 British riots. *Discourse and Society*, 24(1): 27–45.

Bolton, M., Welty, E., Nayak, M. & Malone, C. (2013). We had a front row seat to a downtown revolution. In E. Welty, M. Bolton, M. Nayak. & C. Malone (eds), *Occupying Political Science. The Occupy Wall Street Movement from New York to the World* (pp. 1–24). New York: Palgrave Macmillan.

Carpentier, N. (2011). *Media and Participation. A Site of Ideological-Democratic Struggle*. Bristol: Intellect.

Castells, M. (2009). *Communication Power*. Oxford University Press.

Castells, M. (2011). A network theory of power. *International Journal for Communication*, 5: 773–787.

Castells, M. (2012). *Networks of Outrage and Hope. Social Movements in the Internet Age*. Cambridge: Polity Press.

Cohen, R. & Rai, S. M. (2000). Global social movements. Towards a cosmopolitan politics. In R. Cohen. & S. M. Rai (eds), *Global Social Movements* (pp. 1–17). London: Athlone Press..

Conztanza-Chock, S. (2012). Mic Check! Media cultures and the Occupy movement. *Social Movement Studies: Journal of Social, Cultural and Political Protest*, 11(3–4): 375–385.

Couldry, N. (2012). *Media, Society, World. Social Theory and Digital Media Practice*. Cambridge: Polity Press.

Couldry, N. & Hepp, A. (2013). Conceptualizing Mediatization: Contexts, Traditions, Arguments. *Communication Theory*, 23(3): 191–202.

Creswell, J. (2007). *Qualitative Research and Research Design. Choosing Among Five Approaches*. Thousand Oaks, CA: Sage Publications.

Dean, J. (2008). Communicative Capitalism: Circulation and the Foreclosure of Politics. In M. Boler (ed.), *Digital Media and Democracy* (pp. 101–121). Cambridge: MIT Press.

Dean, J. (2012). *The Communist Horizon*. London: Verso.

della Porta, D. & Piazza, G. (2008). *Voices of the Valley. Voices of the Straits. How Protest Creates Communities*. New York: Berghahn Books.

Gitlin, T. (2012). *Occupy Nation*. New York: Harper Collins.

Gleason, B. (2013). #Occupy Wall Street: Exploring informal learning about a social movement on Twitter. *American Behavioral Scientist*, 57(7): 966–982.

Graeber, D. (2013). *The Democracy Project. A History, a Crisis, a Movement*. New York: Spiegel and Grau.

Haiven, M. (2007). Privatized resistance: AdBusters and the culture of neoliberalism. *Review of Education, Pedagogy, and Cultural Studies*, 29(1): 85–110.

Halvorsen, S. (2012). Beyond the network? Occupy London and the global movement. *Social Movement Studies: Journal of Social, Cultural and Political Protest*, 11(3–4): 427–433.

Hands, J. (2011). *@ is for activism. Dissent, Resistance and Rebellion in a Digital Culture*. London: Pluto Press.

Hayduk, R. (2013). The anti-globalization movement and OWS. In E. Welty, M. Bolton, M. Nayak & C. Malone (eds), *Occupying Political Science. The Occupy*

Wall Street Movement from New York to the World (pp. 225–245). New York: Palgrave Macmillan.

Hepp, A. (2011). *Medienkultur. Die Kultur mediatisierter Welten.* Wiesbaden, VS: Verlag für Sozialwissenschaften.

Juris, J. (2012). Reflections on #Occupy Everywhere: Social Media, public space, and emerging logics of aggregation. *American Ethnologist*, 39(2): 259–279.

Kellner, D. (2012). *Media Spectacle and Insurrection, 2011. From the Arab Uprisings to Occupy Everywhere.* London: Bloomsbury.

Mansell, R. (2010). The life and times of the information society. *Prometheus*, 28(2): 165–186.

Mayer-Schönberger, V. & Cukier, K. (2013). *Big Data: a Revolution that will Transform how we Live, Work, and Think.* Boston, MA: Houghton Mifflin Harcourt.

Milner, R. (2013). Pop polyvocality: Internet memes, public participation, and the Occupy Wall Street movement. *International Journal of Communication*, 7: 2357–2390.

Mörtenböck, P. & Mooshammer, H. (2012). *Occupy. Räume des Protests [Occupy. Spaces of Protest].* Bielefeld: Transcript.

Nayak, M. (2013). The politics of the 'global'. In E. Welty, M. Bolton, M. Nayak & C. Malone (eds), *Occupying Political Science. The Occupy Wall Street Movement from New York to the World* (pp. 247–274). New York: Palgrave Macmillan.

Penney, J. & Dadas, C. (2014). (Re)Tweeting in the service of protest: Digital composition and circulation in the Occupy Wall Street movement. *New Media & Society*, 16(1): 74–90.

Pickerill, J. & Krinsky, J. (2012). Why does Occupy matter? *Social Movement Studies: Journal of Social, Cultural and Political Protest*, 11(3–4): 279–287.

Polletta, F. (2006). *It was Like a Fever. Storytelling in Protest and Politics.* University of Chicago Press.

Postill, J. (2013). Democracy in an age of viral reality: A media epidemiography of Spain's Indignados movement. *Ethnography.*

Radway, J. (1984). *Reading the Romance. Woman, Patriarchy, and Popular Literature.* Chapel Hill, NC: University of North Carolina Press.

Ricoeur, P. (1984). *Time and Narrative, 1.* Chicago: University of Chicago Press.

Rogan, A. & de Kock, D. (2005). Chronicles from the classroom: Making sense of the methodology and methods of narrative analysis. *Qualitative Inquiry*, 11(4): 628–649.

Sassen, S. (2011). *The Global Street Comes to Wall Street.* [Online] Available from: http://etc [Accessed 24 January 2014].

Tilly, C. (1986). European violence and collective action since 1700. *Social Research*, 53(1): 159–184.

Tilly, C. (1993). Contentious repertoires in Great Britain, 1758–1834. *Social Science History*, 17(2): 253–280.

Uitermark, J. & Nicholls, W. (2012). How local networks shape a global movement: Comparing Occupy in Amsterdam and Los Angeles. *Social Movement Studies: Journal of Social, Cultural and Political Protest*, 11(3–4): 295–301.

van Dijck, J. (1999). *The Network Society. Social Aspects of New Media.* London: Sage Publications.

van Dijck, J. & Poell, T. (2013). Understanding social media logic. *Media and Communication*, 1(1): 2–24.

van Leeuwen, T. (2007). Legitimation in discourse and communication. *Discourse and Communication*, 1(1): 91–112.

van Leeuwen, T. (2008). *Discourse and Practice. New Tools for Critical Discourse Analysis.* Oxford University Press.

van Leeuwen, T. & Wodak, R. (1999). Legitimizing immigration control: A discourse-historical analysis. *Discourse Studies*, 1(1): 83–118.

Wang, C-J., Wang, P-P. & Zhu, J. J. H. (2013). Discussing Occupy Wall Street on Twitter: Longitudinal network analysis of equality, emotion, and stability of public discussion. *Cyberpsychology, Behavior, and Social Networking*, 16(9): 679–684.

6
Corporate Management of Visibility: Social Media and Surveillance

Julie Uldam

Introduction

Social media have been welcomed as arenas with the potential to provide civil society with increased possibilities for debating and publicizing business-society relations and holding corporations to account by 'potentially increas[ing] the importance of individual citizens relative to corporations and their (functional/formally organized) stakeholders' (Whelan et al., 2013: 778). However, what tends to be overlooked is the fact that the proliferation of social media also provides corporate actors with new possibilities for monitoring social movements that they consider a potential risk. Government surveillance of activists is well-documented in both scholarly research and the media (Juris, 2005). At the intersection of social movement and media studies, particularly, government monitoring of activists and protest activities in the wake of the Seattle protests against the World Trade Organization in 1999 has been examined (e.g. Eagleton-Pierce, 2001; Juris, 2005; Kahn & Kellner, 2004), as well as the exposure of several undercover officers from London's Metropolitan Police who infiltrated activist groups across Europe, primarily in the climate justice movement.[1] However, corporate monitoring of social movements remains significantly under-researched (Lubbers, 2012; Pickerill, 2003). In surveillance studies, recent research has started to critically address corporate organizations' uses of the predictive capabilities of 'big data' from social media for identifying issues, contexts, events, and groups that could potentially damage their reputations (Andrejevic, 2014; Trottier & Lyon, 2012). In the management and corporate communications literature, corporate monitoring is often studied from the perspective of the corporation, discussing corporate strategies for circumventing the reputational risks of critical voices in social media, for example through PR initiatives and stakeholder engagement (e.g. Fieseler et al., 2010; Jones et al., 2010). In this chapter I examine corporate monitoring in relation to the empowering potential of social media and argue that certain corporate practices of monitoring impede this potential. In doing so, I focus on the multinational oil company BP, information they have gathered on their critics, and responses to criticism in social media.

BP provides a pertinent case of corporate surveillance and monitoring. Climate change, oil exploration in the Arctic, human rights violations, and high-profile disasters have brought BP into the limelight of public scrutiny, with civil society groups drawing attention to these issues, notably through online media (Du & Vieira, 2012). In response, oil companies such as BP have tried to protect and repair their reputation by participating in voluntary initiatives and sponsorships, typically under the headings of sustainability and corporate social responsibility (Fleming & Jones, 2013; Lam et al., 2013). However, such initiatives are often met by civil society actors with accusations of greenwashing. This has propelled a culture of monitoring and surveillance as oil companies try to anticipate and contain criticism that challenges the sincerity and ethico-political implications of their sustainability and CSR initiatives (Fieselier et al., 2010; Hansen, Hans Krause & Uldam, 2015). These emerging regimes of online corporate surveillance raise questions about the wider power relations in which social media are embedded and the role of antagonism in civic engagement and contestation.

The chapter is organized in four sections. First, I outline the theoretical framework which draws on Thompson's (1995, 2005) concept of management of mediated visibility and Mouffe's concept of the post-political. Second, I describe the methods and data that I draw on for this study. Third, I introduce the case of BP and the company's CSR initiatives, focusing on their sponsorship activities, as well as responses to the sponsorships from BP's critics. Fourth, I examine the ways in which BP employees and BP's security division discuss and develop counter-responses to individual critics.

Mediated visibility and the post-political

This section begins by discussing some of the interrelations between social media, corporate reputation, and visibility. It links these to the fantasy of the post-political, arguing that corporations' management of visibility in social media plays a key role in constructing the fossil fuel industry and energy provision as a consensual arena. In doing so, it draws together perspectives from management and organization studies with perspectives from media and communication studies.

Visibility and corporate reputation

In the management literature focused on CSR, social media are often examined in terms of reputational threats that corporations need to reduce (e.g. Schultz et al., 2013). Less corporate-centric accounts provide optimistic views of the empowering potential that social media afford civil society actors vis-à-vis corporations. For example, Whelan et al. (2013) suggest that

> within social media-augmented 'public arenas of citizenship', individual citizens are empowered, relative to corporations and their (functional/formally organized) stakeholders, when it comes to creating, debating, and publicizing, CSR relevant issues. (777)

While this optimism is tempered with the acknowledgement that such civic empowerment is 'partly contingent upon the corporations (and governments) who control social media (and who continue to possess significant capacities more generally) doing so in a responsible way' (Whelan et al., 2013: 786), the role of non-ICT companies in influencing the empowering potential of social media remains unexplored.

In media and communication studies, corporate surveillance has been given attention in relation to ICT companies' and private security companies' surveillance of activists, often in collaboration with government agencies (Fuchs, 2011; McChesney, 2013), as well as the ways in which the internet and its regulation often facilitate government and corporate surveillance of dissenting views (Cammaerts, this volume; Dahlgren, 2013). However, specific cases of online corporate monitoring and censoring remain few (see e.g. Pickerill, 2006 for an exception). Thompson's (2005) notion of mediated visibility can help capture and further explore the ambiguous properties of online media.

In pointing to the role of the media as key to the relation between visibility and power, Thompson (2005) departs from Foucault's notion of the Panopticon and the idea that the visibility of the many works as a means of control. Instead he argues that in our media-saturated society political actors are increasingly visible to wider publics, and that this entails both reputational opportunities and challenges. On the one hand, the media grant visibility to (media-savvy) political actors independent of spatio-temporal locales. On the other hand, the conduct of politicians is made visible in uncontrollable ways by the media. This development is augmented and made more complex by the proliferation of Internet technologies as they simultaneously provide new possibilities for staging self-representations and render political leaders increasingly vulnerable to the scrutiny of civil society actors (Thompson, 2005). These challenges are no less relevant to corporations. Internet technologies enable civil society to expose corporate practices and misconduct to wider publics (Bennett, 2005). In this way, it is those in power, including political and corporate actors, for whom it has become more difficult to hide their activities and control the disclosure of information (Chouliaraki & Morsing, 2010). This increased synoptic visibility has brought about new reputational challenges for companies (Whelan et al., 2013). However, Internet technologies grant visibility not only to political and corporate actors, but also to civil society actors – the visibility on which the exposure of corporate practices and misconduct relies. Activists' uses of social media to plan and mobilize for protest events and to circulate images and footage to wider publics after protest events enable companies to monitor and collect information about their activities.

CSR and the fantasy of the post-political

As social media render companies more visible, investing in Corporate Social Responsibility (CSR) activities gains renewed value (Whelan et al., 2013; Zyglidopoulos & Fleming, 2011). Furthermore, companies' willingness to engage in dialogic debate with their stakeholders is increasingly considered an inherent part of CSR. In this respect, a rational, consensus-based approach to public debate informs both stakeholder theory and the CSR literature more generally (Gilbert & Rasche, 2007; Scherer & Palazzo, 2011). However, this Habermasian–inspired approach has been criticized for not allowing for disagreement, or 'dissensual CSR' (Whelan et al., 2013: 762), and for negating radical negativity and antagonism (Edward & Willmott, 2013). Mouffe (2005) stresses antagonism as inherent to politics and a democratic society. She argues that eliminating conflict and dissent from society risks seeing democratic confrontation 'replaced by a confrontation between non-negotiable moral values or essentialist forms of identifications' (1998: 13–14). Mouffe (2005) sees this situation as post-political because it presupposes that we have reached a stage where conflict and antagonism can be transcended. This post-political vision underpins many contemporary regulatory practices, including CSR practices (Garsten & Jacobsson, 2011; Hansen & Uldam, forthcoming 2015). If we approach the post-political as a fantasy – i.e. a discursively produced (unobtainable) imaginary

(Stavrakakis, 1999) – then contradictions must remain hidden from the public sphere. In the context of CSR and the oil industry, the expression of disagreement from critical stakeholders would disturb the fantasy that there are no inherent contradictions between a market-driven agenda and social and environmental concerns – that economic growth, with its requirement for continual expansion and search for new sources of raw materials, does not entail detrimental consequences in a world of finite natural resources (Böhm et al., 2012). Therefore, when civil society actors point to discrepancies between corporations' practices and self-representations as 'good corporate citizens', consensus assumptions of the post-political are challenged. For example, activists' critique of oil companies' sponsorships as greenwashing constitute a potential disturbance of the fantasy of the post-political. In this light, oil companies' management of visibility vis-à-vis civil society groups can be seen as a response to controversies and conflicts. In this (Lacanian) view, the fantasy of the post-political provides an expectation that CSR activities are not contradictory to the profit-driven raison d'être of the corporation. By holding forth the promise that voluntary CSR and sustainability activities offer a win-win solution to contemporary social and environmental issues in a society organized and governed on the basis of market-driven logics, the fantasy of the post-political obscures unequal power relations and contradictory interests.

The ways in which oil companies manage visibility in relation to civil society groups serve to sustain the fantasy of the post-political. By not engaging with – and in some cases silencing – critique from civil society groups, oil companies treat them as antagonists without a legitimate claim to visibility. Corporate counter-attacks often aim to discredit or obscure activists' opposing views (MacKay & Munro, 2012). Without contestation, the possibility of contesting the wider implications of the extraction and promotion of fossil fuels is blocked. In this light, activists' exposure of discrepancies between companies' CSR discourses and their wider operations and deeds can be seen as struggles over the construction of the corporation as a post-political actor.

The following analysis provides an empirical illustration of this argument. The social and environmental consequences of fossil fuel extraction have seen civil society groups bring problematic practices into the limelight, notably through online media (Du & Viera, 2012; Uldam, 2013). In response, companies have tried to protect and repair their reputations by participating in voluntary initiatives and sponsorships, typically under the heading of sustainability and corporate social responsibility (Livesey, 2001; Palazzo & Scherer, 2006). This article sheds light on the ways in which companies try to anticipate and pre-empt critique that might challenge these initiatives so as to construct an impression of consensus and thus sustain the fantasy of the post-political.

Studying corporate surveillance of activists

The study in this chapter draws on a variety of data related to criticism of oil companies in the UK. The material includes files on specific civil society individuals obtained through Subject Access Requests under the Data Protection Act 1998.[2] The files are based on four Subject Access Requests submitted to BP. Each file is between 14 and 28 pages long and dates from between April and August 2012. They contain email correspondence between BP employees (including photos and links to video footage), emails sent to other critics and activist networks by the individuals who have submitted the Subject Access Requests, and a 'BP AGM 12 April 2012 Major Personality Report' with biographical information about individual critics. The BP files have been redacted. In particular, the names of senders and receivers are crossed out, as are references to individuals other than those who have submitted SARs. Furthermore, some documents have been omitted, because the requested information 'no longer exists' or might 'prejudice commercial interests'.[3] In addition to this, the study draws on interviews with activists from the climate justice movement in the UK conducted in 2013.

I was able to obtain the data for this study through my involvement with the climate justice movement in the UK. In this respect, I consider myself a member of the UK climate justice movement first and a researcher second (Roseneil, 1995; Uldam & McCurdy, 2013). While this position helps shed light on power relations from the perspective of marginalized groups (McCurdy & Uldam, 2014), it inevitably entails taken-for-granted observations, as the researcher has both blind spots and shared sympathies (Plows, 2008). In this case, particularly, this has had ethical implications, as activists often experience repression from those they contest (Hintz & Milan, 2010). Therefore, informed consent has been obtained from all individuals who have contributed data for this study, both in relation to Subject Access files and interviews. Furthermore, all individuals have been anonymized.

In exploring the case of BP, the chapter particularly focuses on the company's practices of visibility management in the UK. BP is listed on the London Stock Exchange, and is a constituent of the FTSE 100. Therefore, much of their effort to manage their visibility vis-à-vis non-institutional actors is focused on the UK, even when it relates to issues in countries where the extraction takes place such as Nigeria (Cherry & Sneirson, 2011; Holzer, 2008).

Controversy, sponsorships, and critique

Since the late 1990s oil companies have tried to counter the (reputational) impact of social and environmental problems brought about by their operations by participating in various forms of voluntary initiatives and sponsorships, typically under the headings of sustainability and corporate social responsibility (Livesey, 2001). The growing engagement of corporations in these issues reflects the way in which the oil industry has become an arena for controversies and conflicts (den Hond et al., 2012; Du & Vieira, 2012).

Controversial issues in the oil industry

One of the most notorious events in the oil industry is the Brent Spar incident. In 1995, Shell's plans to dump the Brent Spar oil storage platform in the North Atlantic were blocked, as Greenpeace initiated a campaign that brought the plans into the limelight (Livesey, 2001). The same year Shell was criticized for not making an effort to intervene when the Nigerian military regime of Sani Abacha executed nine Ogoni activists who had opposed Shell for exploiting their people and land and for the devastating environmental and social consequences of oil exploration and production in the Niger Delta (Livesey, 2001).

In 2010 BP was brought into the limelight when their Deepwater Horizon platform spilled 780,000m³ of oil into the Gulf of Mexico (Du & Viera, 2012). Following BP's attempt to clean up the area, local communities are still experiencing oil surface in areas deemed 'clean' by BP, sickness from toxic exposure, and a collapse in fish stocks and local livelihoods. Not only major environmental and social disasters have caused controversy, but also growing political and public attention to climate change, with civil society actors contesting the political economy and ethics of fossil fuel extraction more broadly. Most recently, both BP's and Shell's plans to drill in the Arctic have generated criticism.

Countering controversy: CSR and sponsorships

BP has responded to mounting criticism by establishing CSR departments, publishing sustainability reports and inviting NGOs to develop partnerships with them. The company withdrew from the Global Climate Coalition, a lobby group against reductions in greenhouse gas emissions, in 1997 (Livesey, 2001). BP was rebranded as 'bp: beyond petroleum' in 2000, intended to conjure up an image of BP as an energy company rather than just an oil company (Beder, 2002). BP also approached NGOs such as Save the Children and Oxfam to propose 'partnership' (Beder, 2002).

These CSR initiatives can be seen as part of oil companies' management of visibility. As such they are complemented by yet another set of activities: sponsorships. The sponsorships that BP provides cover a wide range of activities, including conferences on climate change, educational initiatives, and cultural and sports related activities and events. This chapter focuses on sponsorships of cultural and sports related activities and events. Such sponsorships constitute a popular strategy for companies to appear as conscientious corporate citizens (Lam et al., 2012). Over the course of the last two decades BP has been increasing its sponsorships of art and culture in the UK (Chong, 2013; Liberate Tate, 2012). In 2011, BP renewed its sponsorship of four of the UK's major cultural institutions, the British Museum, the National Portrait Gallery, the Royal Opera House, and Tate Britain. Between them, the four cultural institutions will receive nearly £10 million from 2011 to 2016 (BP, 2011). BP was one of the 'Tier One' sponsors of the 2012 Olympics. In addition to this, the company sponsored the Cultural Olympiad, which included a Shakespeare Festival. The sponsorship involved the appointment of BP as Sustainability Partner of the Games. BP publicizes the sponsorships as 'a meaningful contribution to society [...] enabling people around the country and the world to connect through the experience of outstanding exhibitions and performances, promoting ideas and encouraging creativity' (BP, 2011). Together, sustainability initiatives and sponsorships help portray oil companies such as BP as good corporate citizens that make a positive contribution to our society. However, activists contest these initiatives as greenwashing, designed to divert attention from their business operations and their effect on people and the environment.

Climate justice activism and the empowering potential of social media

A wide variety of activist groups and networks have criticized oil companies' management of visibility practices, including they ways in which they have engaged with the issues of sustainability and sponsorships. The diversity of the actors can be seen as a spectrum ranging from mainstream NGOs at one end to radical groups campaigning for systemic change at the other. The mainstream end of the spectrum includes established NGOs such as Oxfam and WWF who work within existing structures of governance by lobbying, and sometimes forming partnerships with, governments, policy-makers, and corporations. In addition to lobbying, their repertoires for action revolve around petitions, research, and aid (Den Hond & De Bakker, 2007).

Towards the radical end of the spectrum of civil society groups campaigning in this area, oil companies' sustainability initiatives and sponsorships are seen as a false solution that serves to create a defence for the socially and environmentally detrimental consequences of fossil fuels. In the UK, for more than a decade, a variety of activist groups and organizations have provided critique specifically of oil companies' sponsorships, contesting them as measures to protect the companies' reputation and distract attention from the controversial issues mentioned above.

In bringing to the fore and criticizing these practices and their consequences, the groups draw on a range of different tactics. Despite their diverse organizational and resource-related make-up, the groups collaborate on their common causes as a part of the climate justice movement. In protesting against oil sponsorships of the UK's cultural institutions and events, their repertoires for action involve creative interventions.

In 2012 these included the Greenwash Gold campaign which contested the choice of BP, Dow Chemicals, and Rio Tinto as sponsors for the London2012 Games by inviting members of the public to vote online for the worst corporate sponsor of the Olympics. It culminated with a mock award ceremony in Trafalgar Square where three activists who pretended to be corporate representatives from BP, Dow, and Rio Tinto were awarded gold medals for being the worst corporate sponsors of the Olympics, before having green custard poured over their heads. Another 2012 intervention consisted of a series of pop-up performances of Shakespeare-inspired scripts at the BP-sponsored Shakespeare exhibition at the British Museum and before the Royal Shakespeare Company's performances at the World Shakespeare Festival in Stratford.[4]

The online mediation of these interventions plays a key role in reaching wider publics. To achieve this, the groups use a range of online platforms. These include both commercial and alternative online media: their websites, YouTube, Vimeo, Facebook, Twitter, and Indymedia. These online platforms serve two main purposes when drawing attention to the discrepancies between oil companies' operations and their reputation construction through sponsorships: (1) to facilitate the viral circulation of visual and multimodal documentation of actions after the event has taken place, and (2) to access traditional mass media. The former relies on the capacity of social media for reaching beyond the confines of the activist community, but due to the Internet's properties as a 'pull medium' which is argued to merely connect likeminded users (Cammaerts, 2007), traditional mass media still play a central role in reaching new sympathizers and influencing public opinion. The online mediation of offline actions, such as spectacular or exceptional videos or images, can help generate mass media attention (Uldam & Askanius, 2013). This was a key aspect of the campaigns discussed here so as to ensure visibility beyond those present at the events. The best-attended interventions had up to 2,500 spectators (inside the Royal Festival Hall), while some interventions had as little as a few hundred. Therefore, social media played a key role in enabling footage and photos from the interventions go viral, both in terms of numbers and reach. Without online mediation – and its uptake in traditional mass media – the interventions would remain largely unnoticed. For example, the video and tweets from the Reclaim Shakespeare Company's first guerrilla Shakespeare intervention at the Royal Shakespeare Company's performance of 'The Tempest' in April 2012 helped gain coverage in mainstream media outlets, including the *Guardian*[5] and *LA Times*.[6] In this way, social media potentially enable the circulation of visual and multimodal documentation of actions so as to reach users beyond their immediate constituency of activists and access traditional mass media. However, this mediated visibility simultaneously enables oil companies to monitor activists' activities in these online media.

Management of visibility: BP's responses to critique in social media

This section analyses how oil companies, and more specifically BP and Shell, as part of their broader projects of management of visibility, monitor activists' activities in online social media. This is often done through contracting with risk assessment and PR agencies. One example is the risk assessment agency Exclusive Analysis. Exclusive Analysis produces analyses of socio-political environments so as to 'forecast reputation risks' for a variety of sectors, including the oil and gas industry.[7] In May 2012 the Head of Indicators and Warning from Exclusive Analysis contacted a freelance documentary photographer who had covered political protest in the UK for news media, including the *Guardian*. In the email, he described his job as 'produc[ing] objective forecasts of civil unrest in the UK'. He explained that he had been 'analysing the actions of many of the groups that you have encountered over the years', just as he had 'follow[ed] Climate Camp, Rising Tide, UK Tar Sands Network and UK Uncut and others regularly on social media' (email 2 May 2012). This illustrates the importance that companies attach to the role of social media in their assessment of risk, including reputational risks, and that attention is paid to specific groups rather than just social movements more broadly.[8] While there is no specific mention of oil companies, Exclusive Analysis specializes in providing risk assessment to the energy sector. Moreover, several of the groups that the agency monitors are concerned with issues of climate change, and with a history of criticizing oil companies such as BP.

Two strategies of management of visibility can be discerned: (1) a strategy of anticipation and (2) a strategy of containment. Both strategies work to contain criticism and thus eliminate (the visibility of) conflict from the public sphere so as to sustain the fantasy of the extractive industries as a post-political arena. Social media constitute the main arena in which these practices of surveillance take place. In emails obtained under the Data Protection Act, BP[9] report on the activities of their critics based on their online mediation via social media, including Vimeo and Twitter. As a cover letter from BP's Regional Privacy Adviser explains:

> BP plc collects information about you and UK Tar Sands Network from a range of publicly available sources, including Facebook and Twitter. (Letter from BP's Regional Privacy Adviser, 24 October 2012)

The focus in the material obtained through Subject Access Requests is on individual citizens rather than the general sentiment of (a particular group of) activists. The documents include information about and photos of individuals who have submitted Subject Access Requests to BP.

Monitoring activists: anticipating the visibility of individuals

Monitoring of critics in social media as part of BP's regular stakeholder regime entails the singling out of individuals for further monitoring. This is illustrated by the two documents 'Individuals of note' and 'Major Personality Report' (see Figures 6.1 and 6.2).

The Major Personality Report from BP's 2012 AGM is compiled by the company's security division, Group Security. It contains biographical information, protest history briefs and photos of protesters who have been ejected from or 'known to have gained entry' to the BP AGM. For example, the note on Sophie Harvey states that 'The female below is Sophie Harvey and was ejected after staging a demonstration inside

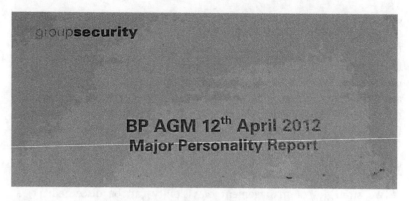

Figure 6.1 The front page of BP's 'Major Personality Report' 2012

Figure 6.2 Snapshot from top of a profile page in BP's 'Individuals of Note' document

the meeting. She also attended 2011 year AGM and was ejected after taking part in a protest'. The 'Individuals of Note' document contains photos of activists from protest contexts as well as portrait photos from activists' online profiles. Much of the biographical data on individual activists seems to be circulated within BP in connection with specific events such as the AGM. The following email from 14 April 2010, the day before BP's 2010 AGM, illustrates this (Figure 6.3).

The attachment to the email includes a photo of Sophie Harvey as well as biographical details, including her name, position, company, educational degree, and previous position and workplace. This points towards a practice of identifying specific individuals for further monitoring

Indeed, the Subject Access Request files also show how BP monitors known 'anti-BP protesters' in relation to protest activities against other companies. This is captured in the following email with the subject line 'Web footage from CON protest: anti-BP protesters present'.[10] The email identifies two members of the Reclaim Shakespeare Company (Figure 6.4).

The CON protests were organized by the Counter Olympics Network to protest against the corporatization of the Olympics. The email thus illustrates how BP's monitoring of activists' participation extends

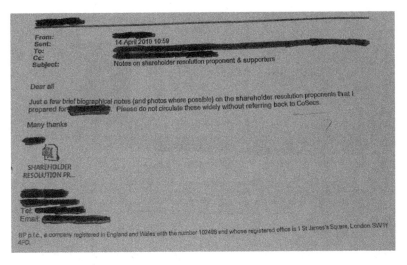

Figure 6.3 BP email – sender and receiver redacted by BP and activist names anonymized by author

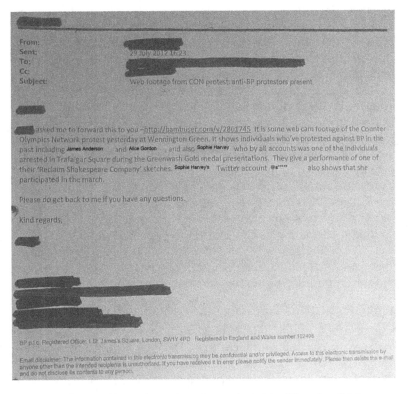

Figure 6.4 BP email – sender and receiver redacted by BP and activist names anonymized by author

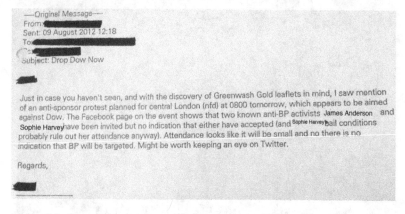

Figure 6.5 BP email – sender and receiver redacted by BP and activist names anonymized by author

beyond critique levelled specifically against BP to protest activities against sponsorships more generally. Furthermore, BP monitors protest events against other companies on Facebook to anticipate potential criticism levelled against the company. This is further exemplified by the following email in which BP is alerted that 'two known anti-BP activists' are on the list of 105 invited participants for a protest event organized by the campaign group Drop Dow Now and targeted against the company Dow Chemicals:[11] [12] (Figure 6.5).

The main concern in the email is whether BP will be targeted specifically and if the protest will have a large attendance and thus increased visibility. While both these perceived risks are taken to be unlikely, the sender nonetheless suggests monitoring Twitter. While anticipating civil society criticism may serve the purpose of improving standards or engaging in debate (whether by providing counter-arguments or trying to find common ground) (Den Hond & De Bakker, 2007; Whelan et al., 2013), the concern with individuals and with protests against other companies in this email exchange suggests that it also serves the purpose of preparing for the containment of the visibility of critics.

Monitoring activists: containing the visibility of individuals

In some cases the monitoring of individuals leads to further action so as to ensure the containment of criticism. The ways in which BP's mechanisms of containment are brought into play are illustrated by the company's response to the 'f***ing the future' campaign, which attempted to subvertize billboards with BP's 'fuelling the future' advertisements in connection with BP's sponsorship of the 2012 Olympics and the Cultural Olympiad, and particularly their role as 'Sustainability Partner'. BP took action to have first the websites f-ingthefuture.org and later f-ingthefuture.org.uk removed. The f-ingthefuture.org website was taken down following accusations from BP of 'brand infringement' (Claire Smith, November 2012, personal communication). The accusation of brand infringement highlights BP's concern with protecting a veneer of sustainability and legitimacy (Zyglidopoulos & Fleming, 2011). Maintaining this image requires sustaining the fantasy that there are no inherent contradictions between a profit-driven agenda and social and environmental concerns. It was possible for BP to have the f-ingthefuture.org website removed, because the people behind the f***ing the future campaign had breached the terms of service[13] of the hosting platform (Wordpress.com) by not providing a real name and address for the site and domain name registration. Therefore, Wordpress. com administrators did not hesitate to remove the blog when BP's representatives contacted them with allegations of 'brand infringement' in relation to the website's domain name, f-ingthefuture.org (Claire Smith, November 2012, personal communication). The people behind the f***ing the future campaign had not provided their real name and address, because Wordpress.com has a history of handing over the identities of their bloggers.[14] This was seen as an important precaution, as authorities were clamping down on most protest activity in London in the run-up to and during the Olympic Games (Tom Parry, November 2012, personal communication). Concerns about anonymity are of central importance for activists using online media, not only in the context of the contestation of CSR and greenwashing, but also more generally in a diverse range of other groups and movements such as media activists and protesters in the Arab Spring (Hintz & Milan, 2010). The case of BP instructing Wordpress to take down the f-ingthefuture.org website illustrates what Youmans and York (2012: 317) call a 'mismatch between the commercial logic of platforms [...] and the needs of activists'. Profit-driven online platforms such as Wordpress.com, Facebook and Youtube rely on boosting revenue generation and access to new markets, which requires avoiding negative publicity and appealing to advertisers and other commercial actors (Youmans & York, 2012). In contrast, independent platforms that rely on open source technologies and volunteer support can better disregard take-down notices from companies and allow critical content to remain online. In this way, the content from the f-ingthefuture.org website was moved to the independent hosting platform Network23 with the new domain name f-ingthefuture.org.

uk. BP also contacted Network23, requesting to have the website taken down (Claire Smith, November 2012, personal communication). But the platform's independent status enabled its administrators to circumvent such requests, e.g. by not keeping users' details and by continuing to host the website at https://network23.org/f-ingthefuture/. However, independent platforms such as Network23 have very limited resources and do not have the capacity to cater for more than a fraction of content publishers. In this way, the current governance and architecture of social media privilege corporate and elite interests over counter-hegemonic voices (Curran et al., 2012; Dahlgren, 2013). In the case of the f***ing the future campaign this enabled BP to impede the circulation of the campaign's criticism and thus eliminate the appearance of disagreement from the public sphere.

Conclusion

In this chapter, I have argued that relying on a dialogue of consensus risks negating inherent contradictions between a market-driven agenda and social and environmental concerns. From the perspective of the fantasy of the post-political, oil companies' monitoring of activists with the intention to anticipate *and contain* their criticism reflects a concern with protecting the construction of a brand related to sustainability and CSR. The circulation of criticism to wider publics would disturb the fantasy that oil companies' CSR initiatives provide a win-win situation by rendering visible antagonism and conflicting interests over the ethico-political values of CSR.

Exploring BP's monitoring of and responses to critics of their sponsorships in social media this chapter contributes to the growing literature that stresses the importance of recognizing that the potential of social media for empowering citizens to hold corporations accountable is deeply enmeshed in wider power relations, often privileging commercial over civil society interests (e.g. Bennett & Segerberg, 2013; Carpentier, 2011; Couldry, 2012; Curran et al., 2012; Dahlgren, 2013; Mansell, 2012). One of the key affordances of social media that can potentially help empower citizens in business-society relations is their capacity for granting increased visibility to citizens. However, this mediated visibility can be doubly construed as granting both power and vulnerability to citizens: as social media grant visibility to citizens, they simultaneously enable companies to monitor and contain their activities in social media. It is in this respect that wider power imbalances come into play. Companies have greater resources that they can commit to monitoring critics in social media, which enables them to react swiftly with counter-mobilizing strategies that serve the purpose of defusing any criticism that might generate public or media attention (Kraemer et al., 2012). As the analysis above has illustrated, BP monitors its critics closely in social media, including their potential involvement in protest activities against other companies. This requires significant material resources, e.g. for staff, which are readily available to large corporations such as BP. Moreover, when companies deem that action is required to contain criticism, the market-based logics of social media – including social networking site Facebook, microblog Twitter, and blog hosting platform Wordpress.com – enable them to impede the visibility of their critics. Whelan and colleagues (2013) argue that social media enable individual citizens to voice their concerns about the conduct of specific companies. They contrast this possibility with traditional mass media, arguing that corporate control of advertorial and advertising budgets provide corporations with 'a strong position from which to directly and indirectly influence the reporting of CSR issues within old media-enabled public arenas of citizenship (e.g., newspapers)' (782). However, we need to remember that social media (and most Internet technologies) also operate along market-driven logics.

This is not to suggest that social media (or Internet technologies more generally) are entirely devoid of any potential for empowering civil society vis-à-vis corporate actors or that all corporate management of visibility serves the purpose of eliminating dissent, foreclosing possibilities for questioning the wider implications corporate power and (in)accountability. Indeed, small activist groups such as the Reclaim Shakespeare Company and the f***ing the future campaign may be poor in terms of material resources, but they do have flexibility and abundant creative talent for both actions and media publicity, which are key ingredients in social movement visibility (Bennett & Segerberg, 2013), and alternative platforms such as Network23 continue to evolve (Milan, 2013). Rather, I want to reiterate Brighenti's (2007) point that '[p]erhaps never before has the distinction between empowerment and vulnerability, between recognition and control, been thinner' (33) and suggest that we need to pay attention to both the political economy of the Internet and media practices at organizational and individual levels, including those that are not readily visible. With the cases examined in this chapter I aim to contribute to our understanding of the role of corporations in influencing the empowering potential of social media. Specifically, I want to suggest that corporate surveillance can significantly impede the visibility of fundamental disagreement over the ethico-political aspects of CSR in the public sphere, and thus possibilities for activists' online criticism to go beyond protest and sustain involvement or enact alternative imaginaries. Here, Foucault's notion of disciplinary power through the visibility of the many still bears relevance to the dynamics of visibility vis-à-vis online media. More research is needed to better understand the self-disciplining effects on activists as they are monitored by the companies they critique on the basis of 'big data' and as individuals – in the north and in the global south.

Notes

1. Some of the most notorious cases are Mark Kennedy who was undercover between 2003 and 2009 and Bob Lambert who was undercover between 1984 and 1988 (Lubbers, 2012). These cases have been particularly notorious because both police officers had long-term sexual relationships with some of the women they were spying on, and were complicit in actions for which activists were later prosecuted (Lubbers, 2012).
2. The Data Protection Act allows individuals to request copies of personal information that UK based organizations hold on them http://www.legislation.gov.uk/ukpga/1998/29/contents.
3. http://www.ico.gov.uk.
4. http://vimeo.com/46239547, http://bp-or-not-bp.org/news/british-museums-shakespeare-late-sees-surprise-anti-bp-performances/.
5. http://www.theguardian.com/stage/video/2012/apr/25/rsc-bp-protesters-video.
6. http://www.latimes.com/entertainment/arts/culture/la-et-cm-bp-shakespeare-festival-20120424,0,5074811.story#axzz2n0fS7TOf.
7. http://www.exclusive-analysis.com/public%20affairs.html.
8. Corporate monitoring of civil society groups extends beyond online media. See Lubbers (2012) for examples of corporations employing risk analysis agencies to infiltrate and spy on specific civil society groups.
9. The emails obtained under the DPA are from 'relevant departments and individuals' within BP and Shell (processed by BP's and Shell's respective legal departments), but in most cases the senders and recipients of the emails have been redacted.
10. CON stands for Counter Olympics Network.
11. The Facebook event referred to can be found here: https://www.facebook.com/events/447315678636083/447420018625649/?notif_t=plan_mall_activity.
12. Alice Gordon was charged with criminal damage after spilling green custard in Trafalgar Square at the Greenwash Gold ceremony in July 2012, see e.g. http://www.theguardian.com/sport/2012/jul/20/police-arrested-actors-olympic-custard.
13. http://en.wordpress.com/tos/, as in accordance with the governance of the Internet's domain name system which requires the domain name registrar (in this case Wild West Domains) to register the contact information of the registrant (the people behind the f***ing the future campaign), see https://www.icann.org and http://who.wildwestdomains.com.

14. See http://en.flossmanuals.net/tech-tools-for-activism/anonymous-blogs-and-websites/, see Dutton et al. (2010) for a general discussion.

References

Andrejevic, M. (2014). Surveillance in the Big Data era. *Emerging Pervasive Information and Communication Technologies (PICT)*, 11: 55–69.

Beder, S. (2002). bp: Beyond petroleum? In E. Lubbers (ed.), *Battling Big Business: Countering Greenwash, Infiltration and Other Forms of Corporate Bullying*. Devon: Green Books. pp. 26–32.

Bennett, W. L. (2005). Social movements beyond borders: Organization, communication, and political capacity in two eras of transnational activism. In D. della Porta & S. Tarrow (eds), *Transnational Protest and Global Activism* (pp. 203–226). Oxford: Rowman and Littlefield.

Bennett, W. L. (2003). Communicating global activism. *Information, Communication & Society*, 6(2): 143–168.

Bennett, W. L., & Segerberg, A. (2013). *The logic of connective action: Digital media and the personalization of contentious politics*. New York: Cambridge University Press.

Bourdieu, P. & Haacke, H. (1995). *Free Exchange*. Cambridge: Polity Press.

Brighenti, A. (2007). Visibility: a category for the social sciences. *Current Sociology*, 55(3): 323–342.

Böhm, S., Misoczky, M. C. & Moog, S. (2012). Greening capitalism? A Marxist critique of carbon markets. *Organization Studies*, 33(11): 1617–1638.

BP (2011). BP and Leading UK Cultural Institutions Extend Partnerships with £10 Million Sponsorship. 18 December 2011. Retrieved from http://www.bp.com/en/global/corporate/press/press-releases/bp-and-leading-uk-cultural-institutions-extend-partnerships-with-10-million-sponsorship.html

Cammaerts, B. (2013). Networked resistance: The case of WikiLeaks. *Journal of Computer-Mediated Communication*, 18(4): 420–436.

Cammaerts, Bart. (2007). Activism and media. In B. Cammaerts & N. Carpentier (eds), *Reclaiming the Media: Communication Rights and Democratic Media Roles* (pp. 217–224). Bristol: Intellect.

Carpentier, N. (2011). Policy's hubris: Power, Fantasy, and the limits of (global) media policy interventions. In R. Mansell & M. Raboy (eds), *The Handbook of Global Media and Communication Policy* (pp. 113–128). Malden, MA: Wiley-Blackwell.

Carpentier, N. (2012). *Media and Participation. A Site of Ideological-Democratic Struggle*. Bristol: Intellect.

Cherry, M. A., & Sneirson, J. F. (2011). Beyond profit: Rethinking corporate social responsibility and greenwashing after the BP oil disaster. *Tulane Law Review*, 85(4), 983.

Chong, D. (2013). Institutions trust institutions critiques by artists of the BP/Tate partnership. *Journal of Macromarketing*, 33(2), 104–116.

Chouliaraki, L. & Morsing, M. (2010). *Media, Organizations and Identity*. Basingstoke: Palgrave Macmillan.

Costanza-Chock, S. (2004). The whole world is watching: Online surveillance of social movement organizations. In P. N. Thomas & Z. Nain (eds). *Who Owns the Media* (pp. 271–292). London: Zed Books.

Couldry, N. (2012). *Media, society, world: Social theory and digital media practice.* Cambridge: Polity.

Couldry, N., & Turow, J. (2014). Advertising, big data and the clearance of the public realm: Marketers' new approaches to the content subsidy. *International Journal of Communication, 8,* 1710–1726.

Curran, J., Fenton, N. & Freedman, D. (2012). *(Mis)understanding the Internet.* New York, NY: Routledge.

Dahlgren, P. (2013). *The Political Web: Media, Participation and Alternative Democracy.* Basingstoke: Palgrave Macmillan.

Den Hond, F. & De Bakker, F. G. (2007). Ideologically motivated activism: How activist groups influence corporate social change activities. *Academy of Management Review.* 32(3): 901–924.

Den Hond, F., De Bakker, F. G., & Doh, J. (2012). What prompts companies to collaboration with NGOs? Recent evidence from the Netherlands. *Business & Society,* 0007650312439549.

Du, S. & Vieira Jr., E. T. (2012). Striving for legitimacy through corporate social responsibility: Insights from oil companies. *Journal of Business Ethics, 110*(4), 413–427.

Eagleton-Pierce, M. (2001). The Internet and the Seattle WTO protests. *Peace Review,* 13(3): 331–337.

Edward, P. & Willmott, H. (2013). Discourse and normative business ethics. In C. Luetge (ed.), *Handbook of the Philosophical Foundations of Business Ethics* (pp. 549–580). Springer.

Fieseler, C., Fleck, M. & Meckel, M. (2010). Corporate social responsibility in the blogosphere. *Journal of Business Ethics,* 91(4): 599–614.

Fleming, P. and Jones, M.T. (2013). *The end of corporate social responsibility: Crisis and critique.* London: Sage.

Fleming, P. & Spicer, A. (2003). Working at a cynical distance: Implications for power, subjectivity and resistance. *Organization,* 10(1): 157–179.

Flyverbom, M. (2012). Big data meets politics: Advocacy, mobilization and governance at a distance. Presented at Workshop on Media, Discursive Struggles and Political Agency. Free University of Brussels, November 2012.

Foucault, M. (1977). *Discipline and Punish. The Birth of the Prison.* London: Penguin Books.

Fuchs, C. (2011). Web 2.0, prosumption, and surveillance. *Surveillance & Society,* 8(3): 288–309.

Gilbert, D. U. & Rasche, A. (2007). Discourse ethics and social accountability: The ethics of SA 8000. *Business Ethics Quarterly, 17*(2), 187–216.

Garsten, C., & Jacobsson, K. (2011). Transparency and legibility in international institutions: the UN Global Compact and post-political global ethics. *Social Anthropology, 19*(4), 378–393.

Hansen, Hans Krause and Uldam, Julie. (2015). The Intersections of Corporate Social Responsibility and Corporate Surveillance: On the Policing Practices of Extractive Multinationals to Corporate Resistance. In Barak, G. (ed.) *Routledge Handbook on Corporate Crimes.* Chapter 12. London: Routledge.

Hestres, L. E. (2013). Preaching to the choir: Internet-mediated advocacy, issue public mobilization, and climate change. *New Media & Society,* 1–17.

Hintz, A. & Milan, S. (2010). Social Science is police science: Researching grassroots activism. *International Journal of Communication,* 4: 837–844.

Holzer, B. (2008). Turning Stakeseekers into stakeholders: A political coalition perspective on the politics of stakeholder influence. *Business Society,* 47(1): 50–67.

Juris, J. (2005). The new digital media and activist networking within anti–corporate globalization movements. *The Annals of the American Academy of Political and Social Science,* 597: 189–208.

Kahn, R. & Kellner, D. (2004). New media and internet activism: From the 'Battle of Seattle' to blogging. *New Media & Society,* 6: 87–95.

Kraemer, R., Whiteman, G., & Banerjee, B. (2013). Conflict and astroturfing in Niyamgiri: The importance of national advocacy networks in anti-corporate social movements. *Organization Studies, 34*(5-6), 823–852.

Lam, S., Ngcobo, G., Persekian, J., Thompson, N., Witzke, A. S., & Tate, L. (2013). Art, ecology and institutions: A conversation with artists and curators. *Third Text, 27*(1), 141–150.

Leander, A. (2005). The power to construct international security: On the significance of private military companies. *Millennium – Journal of International Studies,* 33: 803–826.

Lee, R. M. (1993). *Doing Research on Sensitive Topics.* London: Sage Publications

Liberate Tate (2012). Disobedience as performance, *Performance Research: A Journal of the Performing Arts,* 4(17): 135–140.

Livesey, S. M. (2001). Eco-identity as discursive struggle: Royal Dutch/Shell, Brent Spar, and Nigeria. *Journal of Business Communication,* 38: 58–91.

Lubbers, E. (2012). *Secret Manoeuvres in the Dark. Corporate and Police Spying on Activists.* London: Pluto Press.

Lyon, D. (2007). *Surveillance Studies: An Overview.* Cambridge: Policy Press.

MacKay, B., & Munro, I. (2012). Information warfare and new organizational landscapes: An inquiry into the exxonmobil–greenpeace dispute over climate change. *Organization Studies, 33*(11), 1507–1536.

Mansell, R. (2011). New visions, old practices: policy and regulation in the internet era. *Continuum: Journal of Media & Cultural Studies,* 25(1): 19–32.

Mansell, R. (2012). *Imagining the Internet: Communication, Innovation, and Governance.* Oxford: Oxford University Press.

McChesney, R. W. (2013). *Digital Disconnect: How Capitalism Is Turning the Internet against Democracy.* New York: The New Press.

Milan, S. (2013). *Social movements and their technologies: Wiring social change.* Basingstoke: Palgrave Macmillan.

Mouffe, C. (2005). *On the Political.* London: Taylor & Francis.

Nahon, K., Hemsley, J., Walker, S., and Hussain, M. (2011). Fifteen minutes of fame: The power of blogs in the lifecycle of viral political information. *Policy & Internet,* 3(1): 1–28.

Palazzo, G. & Scherer, A. G. (2006). Corporate legitimacy as deliberation: A communicative framework. *Journal of Business Ethics,* 66: 71–88.

Papacharissi, Z. & J. Fernback (2005). Online privacy and consumer protection: An analysis of portal privacy statements. *Broadcasting & Electronic Media,* 49(3): 259–281.

Pickerill, J. (2003). *Cyberprotest: Environmental Activism Online.* Manchester: Manchester University Press.

Plows, A. (2008). Social movements and ethnographic methodologies: An analysis using case study examples. *Sociology Compass,* 2(5): 1523–1538.

Roseneil, S. (1995). *Disarming Patriarchy: Feminism and Political Action at Greenham*. Buckingham: Open University Press.

Sandoval, M. (2012). A critical empirical case study of consumer surveillance on Web 2.0. In C. Fuchs, K. Boersma, A. Albrechtslund & M. Sandoval (eds), *Internet and Surveillence. The Challenges of Web 2.0 and Social Media*. New York: Routledge.

Scherer, A. G., & Palazzo, G. (2011). The new political role of business in a globalized world: A review of a new perspective on CSR and its implications for the firm, governance, and democracy. *Journal of management studies, 48*(4), 899–931.

Schultz, F., Castelló, I., & Morsing, M. (2013). The construction of corporate social responsibility in network societies: A communication view. *Journal of business ethics, 115*(4), 681–692.

Stavrakakis, Y. (1999). *Lacan and the Political*. London: Routledge.

Thompson, J. B. (1995). *The Media and Modernity. A Social Theory of the Media*. Cambridge: Polity.

Thompson, J. B (2005). The new visibility. *Theory, Culture and Society, 22*(6): 31–51

Trottier, D. & Lyon, D. (2012). Key features of social media surveillance. In C. Fuchs, K. Boersma, A. Albrechtslund. & M. Sandoval (eds), *Internet and Surveillance. The Challenges of web 2.0 and Social Media*. London: Routledge. pp. 89–105.

Uldam, J. (2013). Activism and the online mediation opportunity structure: Attempts to impact global climate change policies?. *Policy & Internet, 5*(1), 56–75.

Uldam , J. & Askanius , T. (2013). Calling for Confrontational Action in Online Social Media: video activism as auto-communication. In B. Cammaerts, P. McCurdy and A. Mattoni (eds) *Mediation and Protest Movement*, Bristol: Intellect Books.

Uldam, J., & McCurdy, P. (2013). Studying social movements: challenges and opportunities for participant observation. *Sociology Compass, 7*(11), 941–951.

Unerman, J. & Bennett, M. (2004). Increased stakeholder dialogue and the Internet: Towards greater corporate accountability or reinforcing capitalist hegemony? *Accounting, Organizations and Society, 29*: 685–707.

Vestergaard, A. (forthcoming). Mediatized humanitarianism. Trust and legitimacy in the age of suspicion. *Journal of Business Ethics*.

Whelan, G., Moon, J. & Grant, B. (2013). Corporations and citizenship arenas in the age of social media. *Journal of Business Ethics, 118*(4): 777–790.

Yossarian (2008). Indymedia and the enclosure of the Internet. Indymedia London, 9 November 2008, http://london.indymedia.org/articles/203 (Accessed 4 October 2013).

Youmans, W. L., & York, J. C. (2012). Social media and the activist toolkit: User agreements, corporate interests, and the information infrastructure of modern social movements. *Journal of Communication, 62*(2), 315–329.

Zyglidopoulos, S. & Fleming, P. (2011). Corporate accountability and the politics of visibility in 'late modernity'. *Organization, 18*(5): 691–705.

7
From Creation to Amplification: Occupy Wall Street's Transition into an Online Populist Movement

Emil Husted

Introduction

Within recent years, an array of public protests has swept across the globe with remarkable force, from the Arab Spring and the Spanish Indignados to Occupy Wall Street and the recent uprisings in Ukraine and Thailand. Besides constituting convenient platforms for citizens to express frustration and discontent with the established system, these movements seem to signal a shift in the way we conceive of public participation in politics. Instead of participating through conventional means, these protest movements allow citizens to bypass traditional institutions of liberal democracy, and influence political processes through extra-institutional activities (West, 2013). As a consequence, several scholars have suggested that we broaden our conception of democracy to encompass this novel type of political participation (e.g. Angus, 2001; della Porta, 2013; Maeckelbergh, 2009; Zukin et al., 2006).

Particularly since the advent of social media technologies, praise of protest movements' democratic potential has reached new heights (Loader & Mercea, 2011). This mainly has to do with activists' ability to mobilize and engage thousands of citizens through online technologies, such as Facebook and Twitter, in almost no time (Warren et al., 2014). Today, citizens from all corners of the world are not only able to follow protest movements at a distance; they are also allowed to participate and collaborate in the mutual 'mass-construction' (Leadbeater, 2009) of the movements. Through the so-called 'architecture of participation', which is a defining feature of Web 2.0 technologies (O'Reilly, 2005), citizens today have a 'chance to claim a greater share of participation – they have a renewed chance to become active participants in the pro-dusage of democracy' (Bruns, 2008: 10). Through social media, the boundaries between producers and consumers are allegedly blurred to such an extent that new avenues for political participation emerge; and via these avenues, democracy is supposedly broadened. At least, this is how the argument often goes.

What these scholars suggest is that social media and protest movements converge well, because both are based on non-hierarchical and leaderless structures that afford practices of participation and collaboration (della Porta, 2013; Diamond, 2010; Juris, 2005; Milan, 2013). As Michael Hardt and Antonio Negri proclaim, social media technologies are excellent tools for protest movements, because 'they correspond in some sense to the horizontal network structure and democratic experiments of the movements themselves' (Hardt & Negri, 2011: 2). And as Manuel Castells (2012: 229) proposes in his recent account of contemporary global uprisings, social media technology 'creates conditions for a form of shared practices that allows leaderless movements to survive, deliberate, coordinate and expand'. According to this argument, when protest movements utilize social media technologies, they not only expand the reach of their political project across time and space, they likewise enhance their participatory and collaborative potential.

In this chapter, however, I will strive to explore and challenge the merits of this claim. By employing Occupy Wall Street (OWS) on Facebook as a case, I will advance the argument that social media technologies do not always provide citizens with ample opportunities to participate in democracy. On the contrary, the technological affordances of Facebook often seem to constrain the participatory and collaborative structure embodied by these movements. This, I will argue, is due to the fact that content on Facebook is distributed much more hierarchically, and that users are much more passive than is usually claimed by proponents of the optimistic view on social media's democratic potential. On Facebook, protest movements are neither leaderless nor horizontal. In fact, they tend to be quite the opposite.

I base my argument on a qualitative content analysis of nearly 1,400 Facebook posts, collected during OWS's first year (2011–2012). Through this analysis, I show how OWS underwent a transition from being a predominantly *offline* movement, based on active participation and collaboration, to becoming a predominantly *online* movement, based on passive participation and amplification of content that is distributed top-down. The focal point of this chapter is thus the displacement of protest movements from the offline to the online world. My overall claim is that protest movements, such as OWS, are important platforms for ordinary citizens to participate in democracy. However, when these movements replace their offline activities with purely online activities, their participatory and collaborative structure is seriously compromised.

In order for me to advance this argument, I draw on the concept of 'populism', as proposed by Ernesto Laclau (2005a, 2005b, 2007). I do so to provide a theoretical basis for describing the social consequences of OWS's transition into what I call an 'online populist movement'. Despite the negative connotations commonly associated with the word populism, this chapter employs a more progressive understanding of the concept than what is usually proposed. Instead of perceiving populism as a vaguely defined type of *ideology*, frequently attributed to especially right-wing movements, following Laclau, I perceive it as a particular *organizing principle*, inherent to certain enactments of public protests (Laclau, 2005a: 14).

Laclau's conception of populism is also important to my argument because it allows me to frame a critique of online populist movements that centres on a particular social dynamic referred to as 'inverse representation'. For now, it suffices to say that inverse representation signifies those moments where political ideas travel not only from represented to representative but also vice versa (Laclau, 2005a: 158). According to Laclau, inverse representation is not necessarily a bad thing. However, in the case of OWS's transition into a purely online movement, I will argue that, today, political ideas hardly ever travel upwards. In OWS on Facebook, political ideas are articulated by the administrators of the page and amplified by ordinary members. And this, I argue, constitutes a problem for the movement's ideals of participation and co-creation.

I have divided the analysis into two parts. The first part centres on the explicit articulation of popular demands by the OWS Facebook administrators. By categorizing and aggregating the frequency with which certain popular demands are published on the movement's Facebook page, I strive to show how OWS can be considered populist in the Laclaudian sense – and how this condition has changed concurrently with OWS's transformation into an online movement. The second part centres on ordinary OWS participants' reactions to these articulations. By comparing the frequency of 'likes', 'shares', and 'comments', I show how the move from online to offline has transformed the very structure of the movement, from being horizontal and co-creational to being vertical and based on passive amplification.

Laclau's theory of populism

Above, I claimed that Laclau's conception of populism is much more productive than previous attempts to define the phenomenon. This is the case because Laclau was the first to add a positive element to the definition of populism. While other accounts have treated populism as the mere absence of traditional political practices or a particular type of ideology (e.g. Canovan, 1981; Ionescu & Gellner, 1969; Lukacs, 2006), Laclau perceives it as nothing but a specific organizing principle, inherent to certain instances of social reality. Due to the many negative connotations often associated with populism, I will use this section to explain why the concept should not be perceived as a negative feature per se.

Instead of outlining Laclau's entire theoretical framework, for the purpose of this chapter, I will limit myself to describing a few concepts related to the notion of populism. These concepts are 'social demands', 'empty signifiers', and 'chains of equivalence'. To grasp the meaning of these three concepts, however, it will be necessary to dwell briefly on the concepts of 'discourse', 'dislocation', and 'articulation', as these concepts are paramount to comprehending Laclau's perception of populism. I begin with the perhaps most fundamental concept of all, namely discourse.

Even though the idea of discourse is often associated with actual writing or speech, Laclau's conception of the term is much broader. In fact, discourse should be understood as 'any complex of elements, in which relations play a constitutive role' (Laclau, 2005a: 67). Accordingly, not only words and expressions, but also more composite aspects of social reality, such as culture and technology, can be considered parts of prevailing discourses. As long as these elements' relations are constitutive, they are discursive (Laclau & Mouffe, 1985: 105). This is an important observation for the following analysis, since I will analyze not only written articulations, but also technologically constituted/constitutive elements. What I will be looking for in the analysis are different types of articulations, published on Facebook by the participants of OWS. First, I will look for articulations made by the OWS administrators (posts), and then I will look for ordinary participants' articulated reaction to the messages proposed by the administrators ('likes', 'shares', and 'comments').

These objectives immediately lead to an explanation of the concepts of 'articulation' and 'dislocation'. In the etymological sense, the word dislocation signifies something which is out of place. In Laclau's discourse theory, the term is used to describe moments where the linguistic structure permits re-articulations of certain elements (Laclau, 1990). To put it in another way, dislocations happen when linguistic elements are opened up for redefinition. In the analysis, we shall see how discursive elements, such as 'occupy' and 'the people', are opened up for re-articulations by OWS. Accordingly, this must entail the social objectivity, which previously fixed the notion of e.g. 'the people', being dislocated, which is why we today see a vigorous struggle to re-fix the term through various types of articulations. This brings me to the concept of populism, since the persistent re-articulation of 'the people' is fundamental to all populist movements (Laclau, 2005b: 40).

Populism and emptiness

In relation to the question of populism, Laclau operates with a smallest unit of analysis called 'social demands' (Laclau, 2005a: 73). According to Laclau, two types of social demands can be identified: *Democratic* demands and *popular* demands. While the former are defined as social demands that remain isolated from other demands, the latter are defined as social demands that are bundled together with other demands. The former types of demand are labelled 'democratic', not because of their internal relation to other demands, but because of their external relation to the system. When social demands remain isolated they can potentially be addressed and satisfied by the system in a democratic manner. When social demands, on the other hand, become unified and popularized, they become increasingly hard for the system to deal with, as they are extremely difficult to exhaust or satisfy. In the case of populism, these are the demands we will focus on, as popular demands are fundamental elements of populist movements (Laclau, 2005a: 74).

In the following analysis, we shall see how OWS bundles together multiple popular demands, by connecting one demand (say, anti-capitalism) with a second demand (say, anti-climate change), which is then connected to a third demand (say, anti-war) and so on. The reason this makes sense for OWS is because the movement is constituted by so-called 'chains of equivalence', which means that the only common denominator, shared by the many demands, is their universal opposition to the hegemonic order (Laclau, 2007: 36). What makes these chains of demands equivalent is thus the universal correlation, which exists despite crucial differences in particular content. This is what Griggs and Howarth (2008) have called the 'paradox of political engagement': A universal connection between seemingly disconnected social demands. In this sense, 'equivalence' therefore means to surrender some particularity in the quest for universality (Laclau, 2005a: 78); and this is exactly what we will see happening in OWS on Facebook.

Such chains of demands require political representation. Not just by human representatives, but also through symbolic signification.

This leads us to the concept of 'empty signifiers'. Empty signifiers are discursive elements/demands, deprived of particular meaning and elevated to a universal level (Laclau, 2007: 36). By emptying these elements of meaning, they can be made to represent – or signify – entire chains of popular demands. A classic empty signifier in relation to populism is that of 'the people'. In the following analysis, we will get to know this signifier as the well-known OWS construct, 'the 99%'. In this sense, the empty signifier of 'the 99%' is made to signify the chain of equivalent demand, which constitutes the OWS movement. This, however, is only possible because no particular meaning is attributed to the signifier itself.

The above implies that, instead of being a vaguely defined type of ideology, for Laclau, populism is a specific circumstance inherent to certain instances of social reality (Laclau, 2005a: 14). In the first part of the analysis, we will thus see why it makes sense to speak of OWS on Facebook as an online populist movement. However, before getting to that, we need to dwell briefly on the previously mentioned dynamic of inverse representation, as this concept is crucial to my critique of online populist movements.

Inverse representation

As we have seen thus far, a chain of equivalent demands, unified at a universal level, generally constitutes populist movements. There is, however, another characteristic, which defines these movements – or, rather, a consequence that stems from populism. This consequence is the social dynamic of inverse representation. According to Laclau, political ideas do not only travel from represented to representative, as often argued by proponents of elitist models of democracy, but also vice versa. In order to apply political ideas and demands to a context of realpolitik, the representatives will inevitably have to transform the ideas of the represented. In the words of Laclau (2005a: 158):

> It is in the nature of representation that the representative is not merely a passive agent but has to add something to the interest he represents. This addition, in turn, is reflected in the identity of the represented, which changes as a result of the very process of representation. Thus, representation is a two-way process: A movement from represented to representative, and a correlative one from representative to represented.

The represented, Laclau argues, is thus dependent on the representative for the construction of their identity. It seems straightforward to conclude that democratic representation exists only when the first movement (from represented to representative) prevails over the other. As Lisa Disch (2012) has argued, this must be the 'bedrock norm' of all democratic representation. According to Laclau, however, this is not the case. What he calls the 'impunity' of representation, or inverse representation, is not necessarily a symptom of democratic deficit, since the 'bedrock norm' argument fails to take into account the represented's desire to be represented. This, then, makes the whole issue of representation a question of identity: Does the constitution of identity precede or coincide with the moment of representation? Proponents of elitist democracy often assume the former, while Laclau and other radical democrats emphasize the latter (Laclau, 2005a: 160).

Due to a lack of space, I will leave the issue of democratic representation here. What is worth noting is that representation, for Laclau, is a process through which the represented's identity is constituted. Hence, inverse representation is not, in itself, undemocratic. As I will show in this chapter, the level of inverse representation taking place in online populist movements, exemplified by OWS, does not necessarily render these movements undemocratic. However, it certainly does constrain the participatory and collaborative structure upon which these movements are usually founded.

After this brief outline of Laclau's most essential concepts in relation to the notion of populism, we are now ready to move on to the methodological dispositions guiding the forthcoming analysis. In this section, I will further provide a brief case description which clarifies the circumstances surrounding OWS's transition into an online movement.

Case description and method

On 17 September 2011, a demonstration was scheduled to take place in New York's financial district. A Canadian activist group called Adbusters proposed the demonstration as a protest against what they called 'corporatocracy': a political system controlled by corporate interest. The purpose of the demonstration was thus to show the world what 'real' democracy looks like (Adbusters, 2011). Utilizing the mobilizing potential of Web 2.0, the group encouraged everyone with a feeling of injustice to join the occupation of the (in)famous Wall Street. And people listened. Thousands of people poured into Zuccotti Park in Lower Manhattan. This occupation, which in a matter of weeks turned into a global movement, quickly became known as Occupy Wall Street (Graeber, 2013). Uniting around the signifier of 'the 99%', the ordinary people of OWS joined forces in what, today, is probably one of the most well-known examples of a populist movement.

For almost two months, determined activists occupied Zuccotti Park in an effort to perform a miniature model of 'real' democracy. Discussion groups, general assemblies, libraries, media groups, and plenty of similar initiatives were established, in order to facilitate a more direct democratic environment. Every initiative was thoroughly discussed by OWS participants, and no decisions were taken until full consensus had been reached (Graeber, 2013: 52). Moreover, various practices, such as frequent voting procedures, advanced systems of hand signals, and the so-called People's Microphone, were continuously utilized to ensure that all participants could make their voices heard.

This miniature democracy endured until 15 November, when New York City's then Mayor, Michael Bloomberg, forced the protesters out of Zuccotti Park. The movement continued to stage occupations of different public spaces all over the city, but around spring 2012, the movement seemed to lose momentum. Instead of dissolving completely, however, OWS found another space, in which they could continue the experiment with 'real' democracy, namely, the online world. As we shall see in the following analysis, OWS slowly began to use their Facebook page as a platform for their democratic project. Today, 609,938 users inhabit OWS's Facebook page, and every day new people are joining.

The following analysis centres on these people's interactions. By employing a summative content analysis, I will strive to show how the displacement of OWS from the streets to Facebook has altered the representational structure within the movement.

Summative content analysis

The summative approach to content analysis, which I employ here, is not so much about exploring the *meaning* of discursive elements, but rather exploring their *usage* (Hsieh & Shannon, 2005: 1283). The fundamental idea of summative content analysis is to aggregate chosen elements of the data and to compare their frequency. Accordingly, throughout the analysis, I will first examine the frequency by which various popular demands are presented on Facebook by the OWS administrators. And secondly, I will focus on the frequency of 'likes', 'shares', and 'comments' on the page. This I will do to get two perspectives on the displacement of the movement: one that centres on the practices of the administrators, and another that centres on the practices of ordinary participants.

In order to demarcate the empirical field, I chose time to be the limiting factor. Scattered over the first year of OWS's lifetime, I defined three periods of time, in an effort to cover as much as possible of the movement's first year. I thus mapped and aggregated the activity on OWS's Facebook page from 20 September to 20 November 2011, and again from 20 March to 20 May 2012, and finally from 20 September to 20 November 2012. These three timeslots constitute the empirical domain of the analysis.

In terms of the first focus of the analysis, I coded and counted all the posts published on the page within the three timeslots. This I did to examine how numerous popular demands are connected within OWS. I constructed the coding system by reading through the post to extract the individual demands from the discourse on the page. As we shall see, these demands range from 'anti-capitalism' and 'anti-global warming' to 'anti-racism' and 'anti-war'. I then categorized these articulations according to the demand they were promoting, and aggregated the number of times the various demands had been articulated by the OWS Facebook administrators. I categorized a post as being representative of a certain demand if the post displayed pictures or statements that were directly related to that demand.

In terms of the second focus of the analysis, I counted the number of 'likes', 'shares', and 'comments' on the 20 most active posts in each timeslot. This I did to examine the reactions of ordinary participants to the administrators' articulation of popular demands. Which of the three was the most common practice? And how did the frequency of these practices change over time? This investigation allowed me to explore the level of inverse representation, which, as argued earlier, is a key concept in connection to the overall argument. In relation to this examination, I defined 'high activity' as the level of response to a given post. The 20 most active posts are thus the posts that received the highest number of 'likes', 'shares', and 'comments' combined.

Analysis

As mentioned above, the first objective of this analysis is to determine to what extent OWS on Facebook could be considered an online populist movement, and how this changed during the movement's first year. To briefly recapitulate, following Laclau's theory of populism, I conceive of online populist movements as online articulations of social demands, organized and unified in chains of equivalence. The most obvious way to explore whether OWS on Facebook constitutes a chain of equivalence is to investigate how the participants of the movement articulate social demands (Griggs & Howarth, 2008). More precisely, the first job of this analysis is to determine whether these demands are articulated in a particularistic and isolated manner (which would make them democratic demands), or whether they are articulated in a universal and fused manner (which would make them popular demands). Hence, the analytic gaze of the analysis' first objective is directed at the location of discursive differences: Are a number of differences instituted internally between each particular element in the chain of demands, or is a single difference rather established at a universal level between the chain of demands, as a whole, and something external to itself?

The populism of OWS

Before we engage with the actual content analysis, I will first dwell on perhaps the most visible way of answering the question of populism in OWS, which is to read through the so-called 'Declaration of the Occupation of New York City'. Drafted by a large group of ordinary members in Zuccotti Park on 17 September 2011, and accepted at a general assembly 12 days later, the declaration was the first written statement by the group as a unified movement (Graeber, 2013). The beginning lines of the declaration tell the story of 'one people united', who have assembled in lower Manhattan to tell the world that the 'future of the human race requires the cooperation of its members'. An important thing to note here is the discursive use of 'the people'. Even though the construction of 'the people' as a universal empty signifier is a prerequisite for all populist movements (Laclau, 2005a: 74), the populism of OWS is intensified later in the declaration, where a series of multiple demands is listed. Below is an extract of the listing (Occupy Wall Street, 2011: 1):

They have taken bailouts from taxpayers with impunity, and continue to give Executives exorbitant bonuses. They have perpetuated inequality and discrimination in the workplace based on age, the color of one's skin, sex, gender identity and sexual orientation [...] They have profited off of the torture, confinement, and cruel treatment of countless animals, and actively hide these practices [...] They have purposely covered up oil spills, accidents, faulty bookkeeping, and inactive ingredients in pursuit of profit [...] They have perpetuated colonialism at home and abroad. They have participated in the torture and murder of innocent civilians overseas.

At least two points are crucial in relation to this quote. The first point is the very explicit unification of multiple demands under the same banner. One of the demands listed above is about the federal bailouts of banks and large corporations, which took place during the first years of the financial crisis. Another demand involves the cruel treatment of animals, while yet a third demand focuses on colonialism. In total, 21 grievances are highlighted throughout the declaration, which ends with the words: 'These grievances are not all-inclusive'.

But why are these seemingly differential demands articulated as one coherent statement in OWS's declaration? The answer most likely resides with the location of discursive differences. While the case of corporate bailouts may have no *particular* connection to animal rights, the two demands share a very *universal* connection, namely, the common opposition to the established system. Hence, the 21 demands are not articulated in chains of difference, but rather in chains of equivalence, which serves to transform the movement's demands from democratic demands into popular demands. As the unification of such demands constitute a defining feature of populist movements, the declaration serves as an excellent example of the populism embodied by OWS. When examining the findings of the content analysis, this conclusion will be further emphasized. For now, it suffices to say that in terms of Laclau's first prerequisite for populism, OWS certainly fits the bill.

This leads me to the second prerequisite, which involves the opposition between 'the people' and the establishment. All the demands presented in the declaration start with the articulation of an unspecified antagonist called 'they'. Despite not clarifying what 'they' represent, it is clear that 'they' is the universal signifier of the established system; the hegemonic order of the capitalist system, that is. In this way, a fundamental frontier is erected between the two universal subjects of 'they' and 'the people'. In OWS, this frontier is often articulated as the opposition between the '1%' and the '99%'. Following the first point about the unification of popular demands, the important thing to note in relation to this opposition is the universality. It is not so significant what particular meaning is attributed to either side of the frontier. The important thing is the opposition in itself. This then serves to confirm the second of Laclau's prerequisites for populism, namely, the persistent articulation of a universal frontier between the system and 'the people'.

These two prerequisites, made visible by the quote from the declaration, underpin the populism of OWS in Laclaudian terms. As mentioned, this claim is verified by directing our analytic gaze at the location of discursive differences. By reading through the declaration but also, as we shall see, by exploring the day-to-day articulations on the movement's Facebook page, it becomes clear how a single discursive difference is instituted between the movement, as a whole, and the system, as a whole. Rather than separating particular social demands and treating them independently, OWS constitutes itself through articulations which serve to unify the movement as one equivalent chain. However, it is important here not to lose sight of our overall objective: OWS being populist does not, in itself, render the movement either unproductive or undemocratic. As already mentioned, the adjective 'populism' merely signifies an *organizing principle*, and not a type of ideology. The degree of populism is thus not the overall objective of this analysis. Instead, the objective is to explore how the organizing principle of populism has influenced the flow of (inverse) representation within the movement – and how the movement's transition from an offline to an online movement has affected this condition.

Populism and the offline/online transition

As we have seen, two characteristics, both clearly visible in the movement's own declaration, define OWS as a populist movement, and have done so from the very beginning. However, as we shall see in a moment, these two characteristics significantly intensified within the movement's first year. Once OWS, in the middle of 2012, ceased to stage offline activities, the level of populism within the movement rose considerably. What emerged during the content analysis was, amongst other things, that OWS not only represented a wide span of popular demands, but also that this span widened concurrently with the movement's transition from an offline to an online movement. Below is a figure that illustrates the development in the articulation of popular demands (Figure 7.1).

As can be seen in Figure 7.1, the content analysis immediately confirms the argument about OWS as a chain of equivalent demands. Both in 2011 (when the movement primarily organized offline activities), and much more so in the autumn of 2012 (when the movement solely organized online activities), OWS represented a chain of multiple popular demands. Exemplified by the rapid increase in posts concerning issues such as workers' rights, climate change, war, and the corruption of politics, the important thing to note is that many more demands were articulated much more frequently in the autumn of 2012 than in 2011. During the movement's first months, the vast majority of posts concerned two issues: anti-capitalism and anti-police. These demands took up no less than 93% of all posts. A year later, this picture had changed considerably. While

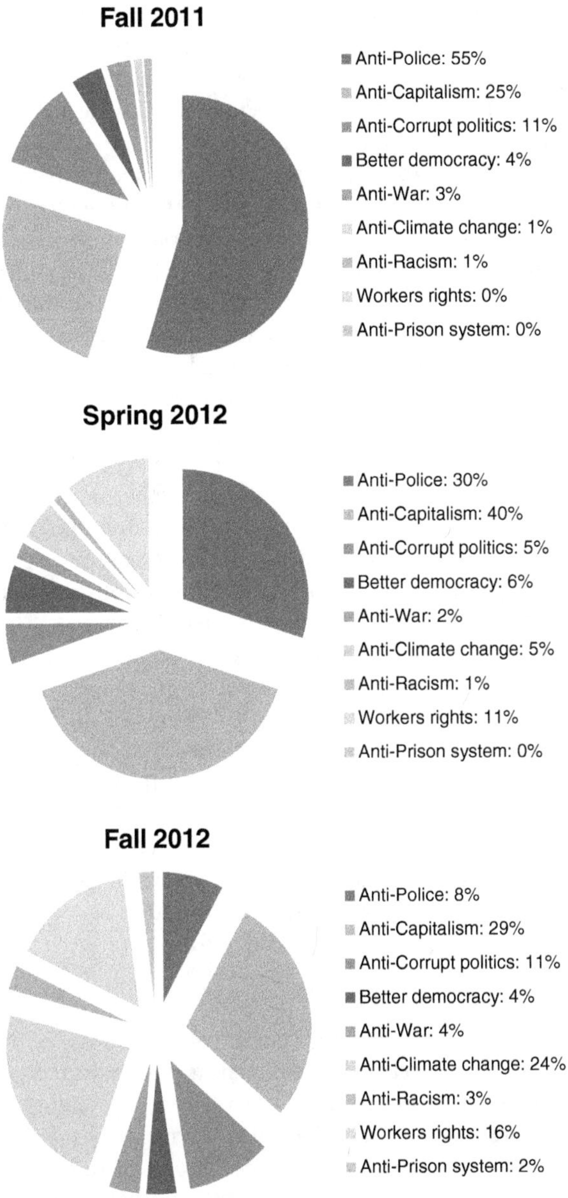

Fall 2011

- Anti-Police: 55%
- Anti-Capitalism: 25%
- Anti-Corrupt politics: 11%
- Better democracy: 4%
- Anti-War: 3%
- Anti-Climate change: 1%
- Anti-Racism: 1%
- Workers rights: 0%
- Anti-Prison system: 0%

Spring 2012

- Anti-Police: 30%
- Anti-Capitalism: 40%
- Anti-Corrupt politics: 5%
- Better democracy: 6%
- Anti-War: 2%
- Anti-Climate change: 5%
- Anti-Racism: 1%
- Workers rights: 11%
- Anti-Prison system: 0%

Fall 2012

- Anti-Police: 8%
- Anti-Capitalism: 29%
- Anti-Corrupt politics: 11%
- Better democracy: 4%
- Anti-War: 4%
- Anti-Climate change: 24%
- Anti-Racism: 3%
- Workers rights: 16%
- Anti-Prison system: 2%

Figure 7.1 The categorization of Facebook posts as 'popular demands' in three timeslots

anti-capitalism still represented a significant share of all posts, demands concerning workers' rights, climate change, and corrupt politicians suddenly enjoyed almost equal attention. Correspondingly, posts concerning anti-war, anti-racism, and better democracy likewise seemed to appear more frequently in 2012 than in 2011.

There are, of course, some apparent explanations for these shifts in the articulation of demands. For one, since the movement ceased to organize offline activities during 2012, the amount of posts concerning the police naturally diminished. There were no longer any mass-arrests or evictions to report, and OWS therefore seemed to turn its gaze towards other issues. Another occurrence which serves to explain the shift was the devastating destruction caused by Hurricane Sandy in late October 2012. In response to this natural catastrophe, OWS morphed into a kind of relief agency called 'Occupy Sandy'. In doing so, OWS used their Facebook page as a medium for drawing attention to the horrible downsides of climate change and, furthermore, as a way of mobilizing relief to those in need. The curious thing about this chain of events is not only that OWS suddenly transformed into a spontaneous relief agency, while for a moment abandoning all other demands, but also the way these efforts were framed discursively.

The transformation of OWS into a relief agency is interesting for this analysis exactly because it emphasizes the non-particularity of the movement. Had OWS been constituted by chains of difference, where particular demands are treated independently, then it probably would not have made sense for a predominantly anti-capitalist movement to provide emergency relief to hurricane victims. However, since the movement, as we have seen, is constituted by chains of equivalence, where popular demands are unified at a universal level, it makes good sense for OWS to respond to the anti-climate change agenda, since both projects seek to challenge the hegemonic order.

Inverse representation in OWS

If the first focus of the analysis centres on articulations posted on Facebook by the OWS Facebook administrators, the second focus is about ordinary members' reaction to these articulations. By 'liking', 'sharing', and 'commenting', ordinary members of OWS are able to respond to the articulations made by the administrators. As part of this second focus, I have counted the number of 'likes', 'shares', and 'comments' on the 20 most active posts during the three timeslots. I have done this in an effort to compare the three practices, and to say something about the populist dynamics that might become visible through such a comparison.

However, before proceeding with the actual numbers, a further methodological note is required. Comparing 'likes', 'shares', and 'comments' is to some extent like comparing apples and oranges. Each practice embodies certain features that might be more or less appealing to Facebook users. While 'liking' is an easy way of signaling sympathies, 'sharing' involves another level of commitment, which is why this practice often plays a significant part in online identity constructions (Zhao et al., 2008). 'Commenting', on the other hand, is a far more time-consuming practice, and furthermore it requires more articulatory skills than the two other practices. In this sense, it is perhaps not so odd that most posts received far more 'likes' and 'shares' than 'comments'. Despite these differences, however, it still makes sense to make the comparison. This is because the whole inequality of these practices embodies an analytical point in itself. This point, however, I will return to at the end of this section.

Below, I have inserted a diagram showing the development in the frequency of practices throughout the three timeslots. Since comparing these practices is the aim of this section, I have displayed the frequency of practices by percentage. The objective is not to compare the total number of, for example, 'likes', but to compare the frequency of 'likes' in relation to the two other practices (Figure 7.2).

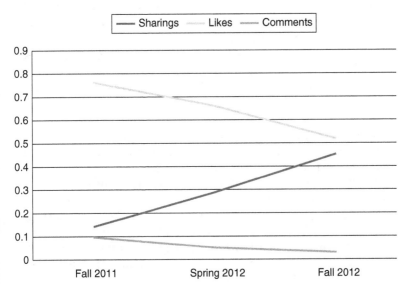

Figure 7.2 Reactions to highly active posts by ordinary members of OWS's Facebook page

As can be seen in this visualization, a clear tendency is detectable: The percentage of 'likes' and 'comments' has steadily *decreased* throughout the timespan, while the percentage of 'shares' has *increased* drastically. In fact, the changes happen in an almost linear fashion. From a level of 76% in 2011, the percentage of 'likes' has decreased to merely 52% in the autumn of 2012. Opposing this trend is the increase in 'shares', which have gone from constituting no more than 14% of the entire user activity in autumn 2011 to 29% in spring 2012 and 45% in autumn 2012.

The conclusion seems to be that as of late 2012, ordinary members of OWS's Facebook page almost equally practice 'liking' and 'sharing'. 'Comments', on the other hand, remain a less frequent practice. As mentioned, this might have a lot to do with the time-consuming nature of writing a comment. However, we still see a relatively sharp decline in comments throughout OWS's first year: from 10% in the first timeslot to 3% in the third. In real numbers, this decline seems even more drastic: From an average of 535 comments per post in autumn 2011 to no more than 216 comments per post in autumn 2012. In many ways, this very decline in 'comments' is quite telling of the populist patterns that emerge from these figures, because, as we shall see, commenting seems to be the only way of opposing the messages distributed by OWS's Facebook administrators.

As we saw previously, the populism of OWS increased within the movement's first year, in the sense that the plurality of popular demands increased. More diverse demands were articulated more frequently in 2012 than in 2011. Following this development was the sharp *decline* in 'comments', and the drastic *rise* in 'shares'. In fact, if one compares these developments, the connection between the increase in the plurality of demands, the increase in 'shares' and the decrease in 'comments' correlates strikingly well. But how is this correlation to be interpreted? One conclusion, which these figures suggest, is that the increased populism of OWS entailed an increase in inverse representation. In other words, the less particular the movements became, the more affirmative its participants became. This tendency is especially made visible by the explosion of 'shares' from 2011 to 2012. This practice is arguably the most committing and affirmative practice on Facebook. By 'sharing' a post from OWS, ordinary member do not only affirm the message (which could also be the act of 'liking'), they furthermore share it with their own network, and thus make it part of their own online identity construction (Zhao et al., 2008). It is striking how almost 50% of the user activity at OWS's page goes into 'shares', and this tendency suggests that representation in OWS flows not only from represented (ordinary members) to representative (the administrators), but surely also the other way around.

In fact, if we keep the idea of inverse representation in mind and employ a sceptical stance on OWS's transition from an offline to an online movement, it is tempting to argue that on Facebook, political ideas hardly ever travel from represented to representative. As the data guiding this analysis shows, the bulk of user activity goes into affirming and sharing the messages proposed by the OWS administrators. This shift from the co-creational environment of the offline protest camps to the affirmative environment of the Facebook page is, in my opinion, best described as a shift from *creation* to *amplification*. In the last section of this analysis, I will strive to explain how this shift should be understood.

From creation to amplification

As has been shown on various occasions, participation is a rather ambiguous term, when speaking of the production of content in online spheres (Bird, 2011). In seemingly participatory environments, such as social media, there are indeed different levels of participation. Van Dijck (2009: 45–46) refers to three levels of online participants: 'creators', 'spectators', and 'inactives', with more than 80% of all users belonging to the two passive categories. Through this categorization, Van Dijck strives to illuminate how the prevailing idea that online users by default participate in the 'mass-construction' of content is far from valid. Most users merely view online content without ever taking on the role of 'creators' by, for example, writing posts or commenting.

In the case of online populist movements, I will go one step further than Van Dijck by arguing that we need to add a fourth level, which could be called 'amplifiers'. At this level, users are by no means passive agents, but in fact very active participants. Certainly, the majority of users on OWS's Facebook page are (just like me) either 'spectators' or 'inactives'. However, as this analysis has shown, online populist movements are also inhabited by a fairly large group of users who labour intensely to amplify the voice of the movement's administrators by liking and sharing their messages. An analogy, which may serve to enhance our understanding of this shift, is the case of the People's Microphone.

The People's Microphone was a mechanism which was used to facilitate the democratic environment that emerged at the OWS protest camps in Lower Manhattan. In fact, the People's Microphone was a mechanism born out of the absence of traditional technology. When the New York City authorities prohibited OWS from using loudspeakers or other tools for 'amplifying sound', the movement made up its own people-powered technology (Wanenchack, 2011: 1). During an assembly, when someone wanted to speak, they simply shouted: 'Mic check'. When the rest of the assembly heard this, they replied: 'Mic check'. Then, the speaker knew that the Microphone was 'on'. Hereafter, the speaker could proceed with their message. They would stop after every sentence to let the assembly amplify their words, and in this way, the technology of the People's Microphone ensured that ordinary participants also got their voices heard.

If we take the analogy of the People's Microphone and apply it to OWS's Facebook page, we see that the People's Microphone, ironically, can be used to describe the exact opposite dynamic. Instead of amplifying the voice of ordinary participants, which the offline Microphone did, the members of OWS's Facebook page now labour intensely to amplify only the voice of the administrators. If we recall Figure 7.2, we see that the practice of 'sharing' increased by no less than 34% during the first year of OWS. Since 'sharing' involves distributing a post to one's own personal network, this practice could very well be interpreted as an act of amplification: a way to allow more people to see/hear the message. The participatory problem, which this example constitutes, is that no one shares the articulations of ordinary people. It is in fact not even possible to share ordinary members' comments on Facebook. Hence, the presentation of a technology that from the outset was designed to allow everyone a voice, should now be re-interpreted, since Facebook's technological affordances allow only the voices of the administrators to be amplified.

In this way, the shift from creation to amplification appears to happen simultaneously with OWS's transition from an offline to an online movement. Not necessarily because the movement consciously chose to alter the participatory structure of the movement (from horizontal to vertical), but most likely because the technological affordances of Facebook has imposed this kind of structure on the movement. As a Facebook engineer proclaimed at a Reddit AMA (Ask Me Anything) in 2013, Facebook is a medium that facilitates *'positive* social interactions' (Guarini, 2013: 1, my emphasis). Hence, by replacing horizontally structured protest camps with a vertically structured online medium that is built to promote only *positive* social interactions, I would argue that Facebook has compromised the participatory and collaborative structure that once made OWS a celebrated example of 'real' democracy.

The once so vigorous and critical deliberation that took place at offline assemblies or discussion groups has today given way to a logic of amplification, where the sole purpose of the movement's participants is no longer to deliberate about politics, but instead to contribute their acclamation, to paraphrase Habermas (1989). The conclusion of this chapter is thus that if we are serious about broadening our conception of democracy to include extra-institutional activities, such as populist movements, we cannot allow social media technologies to compromise these movements' horizontal structure. The case of OWS's transition into an online populist movement, I will argue, thus serves to highlight the dangers of abandoning traditional, offline activism in the face of social media's seemingly democratic affordances.

Conclusion

The purpose of this chapter has been to show how the displacement of protest movements from an offline setting to the online world might alter the organizational structure of such movements. Empirically, the chapter explored Occupy Wall Street's transition into a so-called 'online populist movement', defined as the online enactment of certain public protests, where popular demands are unified in chains of equivalence. By methodologically employing a summative content analysis, the chapter's strove to explain how the affordances of Facebook, as a social media technology, have imposed a hierarchical structure upon OWS. This was done by dividing the analysis into two separate parts.

By categorizing and aggregating almost 1,400 posts on OWS's Facebook page, the first part showed how the movement is constituted by an incredibly wide chain of popular demands, ranging from anti-capitalism and workers' rights to anti-climate change and anti-war. The unification of these demands at a very universal level is what makes the movement populist in a Laclaudian sense. Furthermore, the first part of the analysis showed how this populist condition changed throughout the movement's first year. While OWS could have been characterized as a slightly populist movement with an anti-capitalist agenda in the autumn of 2011, a year later, OWS had morphed into a truly populist movement with a much broader anti-system agenda. The thing to note in relation to this conclusion is that the increase in populism coincided perfectly with OWS's transition into a purely online movement.

The second part of the analysis centred on ordinary members' reaction to Facebook posts, published by the movement's administrators. By comparing the frequency of 'likes', 'shares', and 'comments', this part of the analysis showed how the members of OWS became increasingly affirmative towards content distributed top-down by the movement's administrators. A stark increase in 'shares' combined with a drastic decrease in 'comments' illustrated this shift from active participation to passive affirmation. Combining the insights from the two parts of the analysis, it is notable how (1) the increase in populism and (2) the increase in affirmative practices both coincided with OWS's transition from an offline to an online movement.

In the closing section of the analysis, I proposed the argument that OWS's transition into an online populist movement changed the role of the movement's ordinary members from 'creators' to 'amplifiers'. Instead of actively participating in the mutual co-creation of content, as was the case during the offline protest camps, the sole purpose of ordinary members today is merely to amplify the voice of the OWS Facebook administrators. Returning to the popular claim that democracy should be broadened to include extra-institutional activities, such as social and populist movements, it is crucial that such movements resist the hierarchical structures that certain social media technologies might impose. If not, the horizontal and collaborative structure of protest movements – and, hence, their democratic potential – may be seriously compromised, if not altogether lost.

References

Adbusters. (2011). *#Occupywallstreet: A Shift in Revolutionary Tactics*. Adbusters.org.

Angus, I. (2001). *Emergent Publics: An Essay on Social Movements and Democracy*. Winnipeg: Arbeiter Publishing.

Bird, S. E. (2011). Are we all produsers now?. *Cultural Studies*, 25(4–5): 502–516.

Bruns, A. (2008). The future is user-led: The path towards widespread produsage. *Fibreculture Journal*, 11(1), 1–10.

Canovan, M. (1981). *Populism*. London: Junction Books.

Castells, M. (2012). *Networks of Outrage and Hope – Social Movements in the Internet Age*. Cambridge: Polity Press.

della Porta, D. (2011). Communication in movement. *Information, Communication & Society*, 14(6): 800–819.

della Porta, D. (2013). *Can Democracy be Saved?: Participation, Deliberation and Social Movements*. Cambridge: Polity Press.

Diamond, L. (2010). Liberation technology. *Journal of Democracy*, 21(3): 69–83.

Disch, L. (2012). The impurity of representation and the vitality of democracy. *Cultural Studies*, 26(2–3): 207–222.

Graeber, D. (2013). *The Democracy Project: A History, a Crisis, a Movement*. London: Allen Lane.

Griggs, S. & Howarth, D. (2008). Populism, localism and environmental politics: The logic and rhetoric of the Stop Stansted Expansion campaign. *Planning Theory*, 7(2): 123–144.

Guarini, D. (2013, December). facebook releases 'dislike' button that will satisfy no one. *The Huffington Post*.

Habermas, J. (1989). *The Structural Transformation of the Public Sphere: An Inquiry into a Category Bourgeois Society*. Cambridge: MIT Press.

Hardt, M. & Negri, A. (2011). *The Fight for 'Real Democracy' is at the Heart of Occupy Wall Street*. New York: Council on Foreign Relations.

Hsieh, H. & Shannon, S. E. (2005). Three approaches to qualitative content analysis. *Qualitative Health Research*, 15(9): 1277–1288.

Ionescu, G. & Gellner, E. (eds) (1969). *Populism: Its Meaning and National Characteristics*. New York: Macmillan.

Juris, J. (2005). The new digital media and activist networking within anti-corporate globalization movements. *Annals of the American Academy of Political and Social Science*, 567: 185–208.

Laclau, E. (1990). *New Reflections on the Revolution of Our Time*. New York: Verso.

Laclau, E. (2005a). *On Populist Reason*. London: Verso Books.

Laclau, E. (2005b). Populism: What's in a name? In F. Panizza (ed.), *Populism and the Mirror of Democracy* (pp. 32–50). London: Verso Books.

Laclau, E. (2007). *Emancipation(s)*. London: Verso Books.

Laclau, E. & Mouffe, C. (1985). *Hegemony and Socialist Strategy: Towards a Radical Democratic Politics*. London: Verso Books.

Leadbeater, C. (2009). *We-Think: Mass Innovation, not Mass Production*. London: Profile Books.

Loader, B. D. & Mercea, D. (2011). Networking democracy? *Information, Communication & Society*, 14(6): 757–769.

Lukacs, J. (2006). *Democracy and Populism: Fear and Hatred*. New Haven: Yale University Press.

Maeckelbergh, M. (2009). *The Will of the Many: How the Alterglobalization Movement is Changing the Face of Democracy*. London: Pluto Press.

Milan, S. (2013). *Social Movements and Their Technologies: Wiring Social Change*. Basingstoke: Palgrave Macmillan.

Occupy Wall Street. (2011). *Declaration of the Occupation of New York City*. Zucotti Park, New York.

O'Reilly, T. (2005). *What is Web 2.0?* O'Reilly Media.

van Dijck, J. (2009). Users like you? Theorizing agency in user-generated content. *Media, Culture & Society*, 31(1): 41–58.

Wanenchack, S. (2011). Mic Check! #Occupy, technology and the amplified voice. *The Society Pages, Cyborgology*.

Warren, A. M., Sulaiman, A. & Jaafar, N. I. (2014). Facebook: The enabler of online civic engagement for activists. *Computers in Human Behavior*, 32: 284–289.

West, D. (2013). *Social Movements in Global Politics*. Cambridge: Polity Press.

Zhao, S., Grasmuck, S. & Martin, J. (2008). Identity construction on Facebook: Digital empowerment in anchored relationships. *Computers in Human Behavior*, 24(1): 1816–1838.

Zukin, C., Keeter, S., Andolina, M., Jenkins, K., & Carpini, M.X.D. (2006). *A new engagement?: Political participation, civic life, and the changing American citizen*. Oxford: Oxford University Press.

8
Nurturing Dissent? Community Printshops in 1970s London

Jess Baines

Introduction

Born of a particular conjunction of community activism, cultural critique, and technological possibility, self-managed 'community printshops' were set up in cities across the UK between the late 1960s and mid 1970s. The motivation to provide much-needed print resources for activists was accompanied by the aspiration that direct access to the means of print-media production could also foster social and political empowerment. They were part of an emergent phenomena of politically motivated 'alternative left' printshops that included poster collectives, printing co-operatives, and 'resource centres', and which appeared in numerous cities. This general occurrence was not particular to the UK; similar workshops were established in other parts of Europe and North America in the same period (Cushing, 2012). Although there was variation in the UK use of the term 'community printshop', it mostly referred to a printshop that was (a) 'non-commercial'; (b) had a connection to locally based activism ('community' being partially associated with geography); and (c) encouraged 'user-participation'. It is this general definition that I will be using. As will become evident, the manner and extent to which each of these three factors played out varied both between printshops and within their individual existences.

The mobilizing and 'participatory' potential of contemporary online media for the growth and sustenance of critical and creative civic engagement is, with good reason, being closely analyzed by media scholars and commentators. In these analyses there are echoes of the earlier, 'pre-internet' ambitions and practices of the community printshops – as well as some of the challenges they faced. This is not the only resonance of course; the social history of new communications technology is littered with (unrealized) hopes for their possibility to empower civil society; the telegraph, the radio, and the portable video recorder are amongst those heralded in this way (Briggs & Burke, 2005; Couldry & Curran, 2003). Recent years have witnessed a singular but notable reversal of this trend; in both the UK and the US there has been a resurrection of activist 'analogue' print media. The following quote is taken from a published celebration of this activity:

> Since the technology is easy to learn, people with little or no experience can represent themselves ... Silkscreen allows lots of people to participate in the production and distribution of a print ... With control of production in the hands of the creators, the process is also very empowering. (Moller, in MacPhee, 2009: 51)

The social(ist) construction of technology in this statement bears an uncannily close resemblance to the assertions of some of the early community printshops. It is also just such claims that in the community printshops' specific historical context would, in time, be challenged. Generally then, I want to propose that the experiments of the late twentieth century community printshops have a place in the evolving narrative of social movement media practices. Specifically I want to trace how a range of particular London-based community printshops sought to support, sustain, and initiate critical civic engagement. The instigation, aspirations, practices, and narratives of the printshops cannot be detached from their changing discursive and material contexts and as such these aspects closely inform the discussion.

The chapter draws on the Bourdieusian inspired notion of field (Bourdieu & Wacquant, 2007) to conceptualize these 'contexts'. In particular it follows Crossley's (2002) proposition that social movements, or certain constellations of politicized activity can be usefully considered as 'fields of contention'. That is, a distinct and dynamic social space (a 'field') constituted by the relations between different kinds of agents (individuals, groups, organizations, institutions), discourses, artefacts, resources, practices, and contestations specific to it. Fields are sites of 'strategic' action, organized around particular stakes and claims to distinctive value. Struggles over the definition of that value and the nature of what is at stake are also what determine and shape a particular field. Fields are only ever relatively autonomous, especially those concerned with influencing or changing another field (for example the field of institutional politics), but also because they will always be impinged upon to varying degrees by other fields. They may also be 'nested' in or overlap with other fields and as with all aspects concerning a field, this is historical and dynamic rather than fixed (Bourdieu & Wacquant, 2007). The community printshops began as one of the (many) constitutive elements or 'agents' in the emergent 'field of urban community activism'. They were also co-constituents of a growing 'field of alternative printshops'. The urban community activist field overlapped with the declining 'field of 1960s counter culture', and the emerging movement 'field of women's liberation'. By the early 1970s, it was part of a wider 'field of leftist contention' comprising various post-1968 social and protest movements and across which individuals, practices, discourses, and resources traversed. The community printshops were shaped by – and arguably contributed to the shaping of – the ethos, practices, opportunities, and culture of the field of community activism. Therefore consideration of key features of this field context assists us in mapping and making sense of their historical particularity and specific trajectories.

The structure of the chapter is as follows; firstly key elements of the community activist field in which the printshops emerged are briefly set out; I then move to explain some of the ways that particular printshops attempted to initiate and empower critical civic engagement during their early years. The remainder of the chapter is then devoted to the various directions each took within various simultaneous and interrelated field contexts, including the decline of urban community activism, a changing wider field of leftist contention, Thatcherism and the advent of 'municipal socialism' (that is, changes in the field of institutional politics), as well as developments in the field of alternative printshops. The research draws on 15 in-depth interviews with previous community printshop members, archival sources including leaflets, newspapers, newsletters, and reports issued by the printshops, along with contemporaneous publications.

The field of urban community activism

The community printshops were part of the newly expanded field of urban community activism that 'pervaded urban Britain' between the late 1960s and late 1970s.[1] It emerged after a period of increasing government intervention at the local level, from planning to the delivery of the post-war welfare state and largely in response to these operations (Smith & Jones, 1981). Its concerns, activities, and actors were diverse. By the early 1970s the field was comprised of a dynamic formation including tenants associations and squatting campaigns, anti-urban redevelopment protests, Claimants Unions, actions against racism and fascism, independent advice centres, women's centres and playspaces, community newspapers, and community arts activities. The common thread was the concern with the struggles of ordinary life outside of the workplace (the historical focus of the mainstream and revolutionary left). Key dimensions of the field particularly relevant to the instigation, practices, and early trajectories of the printshops were: the involvement of 'radicals', 'officially sponsored' community activism, and 'community arts'.

The radical interest in this 'new' political field came from various directions and was part of a wider proliferating field of contentious political and cultural activity. Much of this is well known; the anti-Vietnam war movement, student and worker protests both at home and around the world, a thriving counter culture, the growth of squatting, and so on. The late 1960s and early 1970s were also a period of widespread activism by working class tenants (Sklair, 1975). For many radicals this was more evidence of the growing ferment, the general struggle against profit, exploitation, and repression, and they joined the dots: 'Solidarity with industrial, student and tenant strikers and liberation fronts all over the world' (Poster Workshop, c.1968). The decline of the student, peace and anti-Vietnam war movements led participants from those particular protest fields into community activism, especially those that rejected the orthodoxies of the growing 'revolutionary left'. The urban neighbourhood was reconceived as a new space of mobilization, with concrete and immediate issues to be addressed, where political confidence and consciousness might be developed (Craig, 1989; Lees & Mayo, 1984). These entrants brought their political 'know-how'; tactics and organizing strategies along with a participatory ethos developed not just in protest, but also increasingly via the extension of anti-authoritarian and collectivist principles into everyday life. Community activism was collective action, a participatory 'do it yourself politics' (Radford, 2004: 1). As the above list of activities shows, 'protest' was but one part, it was also about setting up participatory 'alternatives', from playgrounds and advice centres to newspapers and printshops.

Interest in 'community participation' also came from 'top down'. Despite the growth of welfare provision, significant concentrations of both 'deprivation' and 'disaffection' in urban Britain were increasingly evident.[2] The political and social anxiety was that these combined 'inner city problems' signaled alienation from mainstream political processes, potentially bred dissent, and as such represented a threat to longer-term social stability, especially in the global context of late

1960s radical ferment (Hain, 1982). The government response was a series of policies and programmes delivered at the local level to encourage 'self-help' and 'community spirit', particularly on public housing estates. A 'community' dimension was incorporated into various state services and new jobs for 'community workers' mushroomed, along with indirect funding for semi-independent 'community development' projects. The intention was that 'difficulties' could be resolved without 'the polarisation of conflict inherent in community action' (Lees & Mayo, 1984: 22). Despite some suspicion of state sponsored 'pseudo-participation' and of community 'work' as a mean to dissipate dissent, these initiatives provided activists with both political and resource opportunities including jobs and funding (Baldock, 1977). This shared axis of interest and interaction (direct and indirect) between 'official' initiatives and 'grassroots' agents – not least through the exploitation of opportunities and the struggle to define and capture the terms, content and aims of 'community participation'– was a constitutive dimension of the dynamics of the community activist field.

Feeding into and interacting with the above developments was the emergence of the 'community arts movement', a field in its own right. The aspirations were generally similar to those of community activism; community arts were seen as a vehicle for communication and expression by marginalized groups, and as such could play a role in effecting progressive political change (Kelly, 1984). Community artists aimed to 'democratize their skills' and 'demystify' processes, in tandem with the wider 'movement for demystification' involving radical lawyers, health workers, architects, and planners that would characterize the field of 1970s community activism (Kenna et al., 1986: 8). This impetus, along with the belief that participation in community arts projects could precipitate a process of 'conscientization', fuelled the instigation of numerous community arts media projects, from radio and video to photography and printing (Nigg & Wade, 1980). Its stress on 'participation' and 'marginalized communities' meant that funding became available. The grant-giving Arts Council of Great Britain (ACGB) set up a Community Arts Panel in 1974. Applications could also be made to local authorities, the community dimension fitting into policy agendas indicated above. Another significant source was the Calouste Gulbenkian Foundation, a charity with a commitment to 'community development'.

It was as part of this varied and dynamic field of community activism, with its 'do it yourself' ethos, notions of 'empowerment' and 'participation' (both radical and ameliorative), new ideas about the role of creativity, the emergence of potential sources of economic support, and not least, community activists' need for cheap access to printing, that the first community printshops came into being. With this in mind we can now turn to see some of the particular ways in which the printshops were shaped by and co-constituted this field and how they were positioned within it.

Community printshops: 1968–c.1980

The four community printshops introduced below – Notting Hill Press, Community Press, Union Place Resource Centre, and Lenthall Road Workshop – were typical in being instigated by people engaged with community activism, but often with little, if any, experience of printing. Three of them had small offset-litho presses, two of them screen-printing. These relatively cheap and easy to learn (although to what extent will discussed later) technologies were the bedrock of community printshops across the country. The time period that these brief accounts refer to coincides with the 'dynamic' phase of urban community activism.

Notting Hill Press

Notting Hill Press (NHP) was set up in 1968 by two women (Foster and Ganes) involved in the growing community activism of Notting Hill (Foster, interview, 2013). The area was rapidly emerging as a vibrant locus of autonomous and often confrontational community action through the combined input of veteran activists from the housing and anti-racist battles of the 1950s and early 1960s, countercultural radicals, and a wide range of leftists politicized through the peace and the anti-Vietnam war movements. By the late 1960s, there was a network of community activist groups and an open weekly platform for local discontent, the Notting Hill People's Association. Like most unfunded political and community groups of the time, they mostly relied on the borrowed use of basic duplicating machines which severely limited their communicative capacity. Through peace movement connections Foster and Ganes acquired an offset-litho printing press, went on a two-week training course and set up Notting Hill Press (NHP) to resolve the issue. In order to secure the press's future, different local groups owned its assets, a safeguard for when it ran into the inevitable financial difficulties. This happened on more than one occasion (1970, c.1975), but this arrangement enabled the press to 'rise from the ashes as a phoenix for the people and the community' (Grimes, interview, 2012).

NHP was crucial to the instigation of the weekly *People's News*, which acted as a much needed means of sharing information amongst the various groups and with the local population at large, but also for 'increasing the confidence of groups in their ability to present challenges to and attacks on the authorities in a clear and forceful way' (O'Malley, 1977: 71). Although in its first incarnation Notting Hill Press did not operate a 'print it yourself' policy, (that would come later with its rebirth as Crest Press in 1970), part of this confidence came from groups learning how to do their artwork, as well as the capabilities and limitations of the printing process. NHP printed for the gamut of local housing and playspace battles, claimants unions, local strikers, radical black newspapers, and new alternative ventures. Connections with a 'detached youth worker' brought local skinheads in, who got involved for example by doing cartoons for the striking dustmen's newsletter. Foster (interview, 2013) described the press as 'very widely embedded, deliberately across a wide section of groups [...] it was seen as *their press*, part of the resource for a neighbourhood network'. News of NHP spread and community activists travelled, not just across London, but also from further afield to get their newspapers printed, so scarce was this kind of resource. It inspired and supported housing activists in Manchester, who were travelling down to print their paper, to set up Moss Side Press (MSP) in 1970. MSP soon became the printer for a growing number of community papers in the north of England including the *Rochdale Alternative Paper*, who with assistance from MSP set up another press. As Dickinson (1997: 82), has remarked, these new 'alternative printing facilities [...] provided the key' for the proliferation of local radical newspapers across the UK in the 1970s. The next incarnation of NHP was as Crest Press (1970–c.1975), whose logo of dungareed militants (one male, one female) attacking the royal crest 'if you don't hit it, it won't fall!' signaled a more explicitly radical politics for the press. Crest would incorporate printing and activists from the emergent squatting, gay liberation, and women's movements, changes indicative of the new (and shaping) influences within the community activist field. They also extended the press's participatory ethos by encouraging people to 'print it themselves' (Saunders, 1974).

Community Press

Community Press was started in Islington, north London, in 1972, and came out of the locally growing squatting scene. Their following statement about the press is indicative of the radical aspiration for community activism and the role of the printshop:

> We see the press as a weapon in a political struggle – we want it to
> be used by local groups who are pushing for more control over their

own lives and situations and who are fighting against the profit system and against bureaucracy ... we are not a Council-sponsored 'project' aimed at do-gooding and participation – which means participating in a way which the Council controls us and keeps us down! (in Zeitlyn, 1975: 50)

The press's statement is also evidence of their desire to be differentiated from the 'top-down' initiatives that were promoting community engagement. Nor did they want to be seen locally as 'radical interventionists', militants who parachuted themselves into others' struggles to impose their own 'revolutionary' agenda (Segal, 2007: 99). An early leaflet by the group, distributed in the area they were squatting, states, 'One of our main objectives is to create a situation in which people do things for themselves and when we say people we include ourselves'; the 'confidence' to do this can 'only be achieved through people living and working together on a day-to-day basis' (Open Workshop, 'Statement of ongoing activities', 10 July 1972). Community Press became established as the production hub of a wider set of activity that included the local radical paper *Islington Gutter Press*, a squatters' advice centre, an under-fives campaign and meeting space. There was a strong emphasis on people learning to 'do it for themselves' (Gwynn-Jones, interview, 2011). By the late 1970s they had set up a weekly 'print training' day for people to learn the presses, assisted by a small Arts Council grant. Until this point, their stance was that 'we don't do printing *for* people ... we expect them to learn' (in Zeitlyn, 1975). The involvement with the paper, which tried to cover every local campaign as well as instigating some, meant they were well-known, with the press becoming a point of contact for a myriad range of activism. They were also in demand from 'every left wing viewpoint under the sun' including internationally orientated left groups, 'Palestine, Chile, Iran, Ireland' (Holland, interview, 2011). This was all grist to the socialist mill and the broader agenda of building of an active local left community, as well helping to pay the bills.

Union Place

The aim of establishing a printing facility at the heart of wider remit of community activism was shared by Union Place Resource Centre in south London, set up in 1973 by a group of artists and radical ex-community and social workers, in a pair of squatted shop-fronts. By the mid 1970s they had taken advantage of the available 'community development' grants from the Calouste Gulbunkian Foundation and Lambeth Council. This facilitated their broad range of activities: running a Claimants Union, producing their own radical community papers (*Knuckle* and *Wallpaper*), supplying free meeting space and cost price printing resources, going to local estates to meet residents, and supporting local campaigns and tenants associations. They were also the 'publicity arm' of the nearby squatting scene. As Rose (interview, 2011), who joined in 1974 after involvement on a local adventure playground recalled 'It was twofold thing, in a way it was an intervention, maybe these campaigns weren't actually happening yet. If they weren't, we would instigate them or encourage them to happen'. Out of this involvement, Union Press also began to publish local stories.[3] Another ex-worker explained,

> We believed in documenting the everyday experiences of the ordinary person ... so many of them never felt able to believe that people were even going to bother to listen to what they had to say ... so we encouraged people to voice their opinions and express themselves politically, artistically ... and for quite a lot of these people there was a very distinct change in their sense of identity, in their sense of empowerment. (Williams, interview, 2011)

Union Place developed connections with the Federation of Worker Writers and Community Publishing (FWWCP). The movement that FWWCP represented was, in large part, a consequence of community politics and the community printshops. Campaigning about the present conditions of people's lives, along with new access to the means of print production, led to a realizable desire to also record their history. There was a parallel between the fact that the everyday quality of working class people's lives, outside of the workplace, had not been a subject for 'proper' politics, and the fact that their past had not been the proper subject of history.[4] The impetus to redress this was 'not out of any simple illusions about the good old days, but because the life of the past represented the investment of human energy that was to be cherished and allowed to address itself to new needs' (Morley & Worpole, 1982: 4). Publications were distributed in local alternative and community bookshops, and there was a demand for them.

Lenthall Road Workshop

Lenthall Road Workshop (LRW) was established in 1975 by three women as a community screen-printing and photography workshop in Hackney, north-east London. They did so with initial support from the nearby Centerprise, who had opened in 1971 as one of the first 'community bookshops' and where the above-mentioned FWWCP had been born. Similarly to Union Place, LRW took advantage of newly available funding to sustain the workshop, in this case from the new Community Arts Panel (ACGB). Far more so than the offset-litho community print-shops (for example NHP and Community Press), because of their focus on poster making and photography, it was the potential of visual rather than 'textual' production and representation that was central to LRW. Although the women who set up the workshop emerged from squatting and housing activism, the growing Women's Liberation Movement, for which visual representation was of central interest, came to inform its emphasis. LRW was not the only 'women's printshop'; the desire for the WLM to control the production of its own media had led to the instigation of a number of women-only printing workshops during the 1970s (Baines, 2012). For the women-only printshops and their users, 'mastering' traditionally male-identified technology was perceived as both personally empowering and a step towards dismantling limiting constructions of gender, and as such collectively empowering (Cadman et al., 1981). The politics of the Women's Liberation Movement fed into the 'mixed' community printshops, too, from the collective refusal to print sexist material, to the shared childcare arrangements of Union Place (Rose, interview, 2011) and the involvement of Community Press and Paddington Printshop in setting up women's centres (Segal, 1980; Phillips, 2005).

LRW worked with and taught screen-printing and photography to the now usual wide range of community, left, and social movement groups and cultural projects; from nursery campaigns and radical mid-wives to squatters and anti-fascists. The workshop also soon became a creative social space for feminists to make political posters together and learn to print in a women-only environment. In 1977 LRW set up the Hackney Girls Project, an alternative youth club that ran for several years. According to Moan (personal communication, 2012), 'at that time and place youth clubs were rough as guts and dominated by young men. Many parents would not let their daughters go to them at all. So we attracted a lot of young women ... and really opened their eyes'. Later LRW would collaborate with feminist social workers to set up workshops for women who were at 'crisis points in their life' (Pollard, interview, 2011). LRW saw these projects as part of their role in develop-ing a supportive resource in which people 'who did not have much of a voice' in 'public life', including themselves, could use print to create their own images and messages, and be 'empowered' through doing so.

The above 'snapshots' of these four distinct workshops reveal some of the ways in which community printshops participated in the ongoing development of the community activist and the women's liberation movement fields. Their extended activities contributed to that crucial dimension of activism, 'movement building'; from 'consciousness raising', information sharing, building networks, growing new groups and adherents to co-developing resonant symbolic forms. The necessary precondition of this activity was what Bourdieu (1996) terms 'illusio', by which he means the collective 'belief' in the worth of the field and its stakes. This belief or 'illusio' forms the ongoing basis for the existence and functioning of all social fields. The struggles (internally and with other fields), the development of discourses and practices, of symbolic forms, resources, of an internal culture and 'a history', all contribute to sustaining 'illusio'. The concrete existence of the printshops, the flow of groups that used them, of media generated, of knowledge shared, were arguably tangible, illusio-sustaining evidence *of* a movement. Significant parts of the wider field of (leftist) contention shared key aspects of the same illusio: that radical social change was possible and that it would come from 'the grassroots'. By the early 1980s, if not earlier, this 'belief' had considerably waned. Lent (2001) has characterized the broader 1980s social movement field as one whereby much of the radicalism of the 1970s gave way to 'institutionalisation and professionalisation'. However, many community printshops continued well into the 1980s, including three of those described above. I now want to turn to their survival in the related contexts of the decline of community activism and the changing wider field of leftist contention, firstly setting out those developments, then focusing on the printshops themselves.

After community activism: Changes and challenges

By the end the 1970s, the dynamic period of urban 'community action' was mostly over (Waddington, 2008). In the tenth anniversary edition of *Islington Gutter Press*, this demise is explained as follows:

> The space for grassroots activity [had disappeared], as the confidence of campaigning groups faded with successive defeats, and the ever more vicious reality of a confident Tory government under Thatcher. Many former activists who did not lapse into cynical despair, retreated into the Labour party ... to abandon former dreams of self-organisation and active campaigning politics. (*Islington Gutter Press*, 1982 no.93, 7)

Thatcher's election victory (1979) had come as a demoralizing blow to many on the left who had believed that the 'intense socialist agitation' of the preceding years was evidence of changing 'mass' consciousness (see Rowbottom et al., 1980). The always double-edged discourse of 'self-help' was also, as Stuart Hall amongst others have noted, well and truly captured by the new Conservative government's rhetoric and policies. However, although the period between the late 1970s and early 1980s can be characterized as one in which the earlier optimism about mass social change had begun to wane (Lent, 2001) it was also one of widespread left oppositional activity. For a while, Thatcher's new right economic policies and welfare and trade union dismantling boosted campaigning activity and offered the left a clear and identifiable enemy to rally against. As one of the workers at Lenthall Road Workshop said, 'Even though it was Thatcher's time, I thought we were thriving ... I also remember feeling very enabled somehow by the numbers of groups that had the same kind of desires ... somehow the backlash of movements was very strong' (Johnson, interview, 2011). New mass protest movements also emerged or revived, such as the Campaign for Nuclear Disarmament (CND) and the Anti-Apartheid Movement – both spawning groups all over the country, as did the 'era defining' 1984–1985 strike by the National Union of Mineworkers (NUM). All this activity generated print needs, many of which were served by the alternative print workshops, including the community printshops.

The survival of some of the London community printshops into the 1980s was, it might be argued, an effect of the *failure* of radical community politics. As Waddington (2008) and other have noted, 'radical' community activism began by fighting the welfare state but already, by 1974, was also put in a position of having to defend it against central government cuts. The next move was going to work *within* it; the late 1970s and early 1980s were marked by the increasing flow of ex-radicals into the Labour party and local government (Lansley et al., 1989). Various factors had facilitated this apparent change of heart towards traditional political structures. As the above *Islington Gutter Press* article states, the demise of radical community activism had led some in this direction. Lent (2001: 168) has noted a decline in 'mass' active support for other social movements by this time. The Labour party was also changing; the left of the party had become more influential and it sought to connect with the various strands of 'extra parliamentary activity' to reinvigorate its approach. Significantly, local government, once seen by the Labour left as marginal to the proper business of politics (and mostly abandoned to the right and centrist elements that community activists battled) was reconceived as a powerful base from which to conduct opposition to Thatcher's government (Egan, 2006).

The effect of this reconfigured field of local government was the revival of 'municipal socialism' in the early 1980s, and a series of policies, sub-committees, and financial support relating to some of the activity community activists, social movements, and the non-aligned left had otherwise been autonomously pursuing. The GLC (Greater London Council) under 'radical Labourite' Ken Livingstone, with its huge budget, was the flagship. The 'new left' Labour councils also used their resources to campaign against the Conservative government's policies and support other groups that were doing so. Again, this directly or indirectly generated a vast amount of print, some of which went through the community printshops. The influx of 'ex-radicals' into the Labour Party and local government brought an ideological commitment to co-operatives, which fed into the local economic strategies of some of the new left local authorities (Gyford, 1985), leading to various kinds of support, from the funding of Co-operative Development Agencies to 'community accounting' courses and 'soft' loans. The GLC, in particular, also developed cultural policies that were informed by a populist conception of the arts, including the need to use them for political purposes, aiding a thriving 'alternative' arts scene (Bianchini, 1987) and support for community arts projects.

Between the late 1970s and early 1980s there was also a growth in London of purely 'service' left printing co-operatives, some taking advantage of the newly favourable climate of 'swinging left London' created by municipal socialism (Pennington, interview, 2011; Swash, interview, 2011). They were for the most part, though, born of an increasing awareness of the need for a straightforward printing service for political and campaigning movements – along with a lowering of expectation with regard to the 'social processes' that the operations of a printshop could engender (Marshall, 1983; Williams, interview, 2011). Community Press took this road. As with other community printshops, their users and networks had always extended beyond the immediate field of community activism, providing a reason, and a bare means, to continue. Financially it was difficult, and they were in competition with the new crop of service printing co-ops. The small grant they had received from the Arts Council dried up in the early 1980s. Although they still showed people how to produce their artwork, groups no longer learnt to print. They tried to become more 'business-like'. This adjustment of ambition and practices, along with a (relatively) more formalized approach was reflected in other areas of the radical community activist field, such as the creation of housing co-operatives by squatters. Other initiatives became charities with management committees or incorporated into state services, all adding to a growing 'voluntary sector', increasingly peopled by many with 'left' sympathies (Hilton et al., 2012). To some extent this added to the 'market' that had been expanded by left-Labour council funding (Swash, interview, 2011). Those involved shared similar political backgrounds, often 'felt at home' using the community and co-operative printers, and wanted to support them (Elston et al., 1983). However they increasingly also wanted a more 'professional' service. To survive in this changing context, Community Press felt they had to 'try and smarten up a bit' (Millet, interview, 2013). One of their advertisements from the time simply states, 'Community Press: Quality Printing, Competitive Prices'. They did not succeed and in 1987 amalgamated with one of the newer generation of printing co-ops, Trojan Press.

Union Place continued until the early 1990s. This was made financially possible through a grant from the local Labour council. However, corresponding with general atrophying of the community activist field, Union Place's 'interventionist' involvement in this area had ceased by the early 1980s. Local connections diminished, too, as the last of the '70s-style community activists' moved on (Tompsett, interview 2011). The appraisal of community activism by the mid-1980s collective is telling:

> Community politics has proved to be inadequate for its role of mediating between grassroots groups and the abstract but no less effective social forces set in motion by the capitalist system. [It] has proved to be useless in defending various communities from these forces. (in Kenna et al., 1986: 22)

Despite this loss of 'illusio', throughout the 1980s the press provided a resource for non-contentious, council-funded community groups, along with an ongoing range of left activity, from industrial action to 'troops out of Ireland' and local squatting advice groups. They remained committed to showing groups how to do their artwork but no longer considered it viable for them to learn printing, and found people uninterested in doing so (Tompsett, interview, 2011). They had 'a sort of renaissance' in the late 1980s by introducing desktop publishing facilities. This brought a new wave of local people in, although it served more as free training for potential employment than something to be mobilized in the service of political empowerment (Swingler, interview, 2011). By the mid 1990s, although they still received a small amount of funding from the local council, the dwindling user base, lack of new people willing to get involved, along with a series of break-ins, led to a decision to finally close.

Lenthall Road Workshop (LRW) also survived the 1980s; supported through continuing, albeit diminishing, grant aid. Their ongoing participation in the field of feminist activity signaled a rather different trajectory to the other presses. They continued to print with a mixture of women's, community, and campaigning groups, run the Girls Project, and participate in local festivals at least until the late 1980s. In the first half of the decade they also became a resource for the emergent Black Women's Movement in London. Connections with *Outwrite* women's newspaper, and new black women's centres, projects, and conferences, as well as the black arts scene (some of which was benefitting from the newly available funding), meant that LRW continued to be a space for women to get together, make posters, teach other how to print, and do photography. This all began to fade for a variety of reasons. New workers with different interests and commitments were one. The curtailment of the municipal socialist experiment and its funding for projects like LRW and many of those that used them was another. A final and fairly crucial factor was that the demand by groups for screen-printed posters had vanished (Bruce, interview, 2011). LRW eventually closed around the same time as Union Place.

The decline of community activism and changes in the wider field of leftist contention in 1980s London through transformations in the field of local government; developments in the field of feminist activity; the funding, institutionalization, and professionalization of areas of movement activity; the hostile political climate of Thatcherism; and a general waning of the 'collective effervescence' that had generated the field of community activism and its printshops in the late 1960s and early 1970s, as we can see, reshaped them in different ways. The amateur, anti-professional, 'DIY spirit' that had characterized the fields of urban community activism and the women's liberation movement of the 1970s did not necessarily resonate with some of these changes. It is to this once-pervasive aspect of the community printshops' aspirations and practices that I finally turn.

As the 1986 exhibition catalogue *Printing is Easy ...? Community Printshops 1970–1986* makes apparent, the notion that 'printing it yourself' could be empowering had been dispelled in many workshops. In their survey of over 30 community printshops across Britain, the authors found that 'several of the longest-established and best-known printshops had abandoned the open-access DIY philosophy ... that they themselves had done so much to popularise' (Kenna et al., 1986: 7). Contributions from individual workshops described the 'DIY' system as 'punitive', 'discriminatory', 'patronizing', ' a subtle form of oppression', where people were coerced into doing things 'for their own good', and suggested that it denied the process of skill acquisition and devalued skills per se. For some, this latter point had always been a tension, given that printing was conventionally a working class trade (Worpole, 1978; Green, interview, 2011). The notion that 'printing was easy' and therefore we could do it for ourselves had been part of a broader discourse and set of practices that informed both the community activist field and the 1970s Women's Liberation Movement field. It was related to the desire to de-bunk and share 'specialized' knowledge in order that we might start, collectively, to 'take control of our lives'. The twin repressive forces preventing this were the ever-encroaching tentacles of capital and state. Doing it ourselves, from pregnancy testing to squatting, was often expressed as the concrete everyday application of the principle of 'taking control' of one's life and of bypassing *the* system where necessary/possible. In 1974, Zeitlyn, who joined Inter-Action, a community arts project in London, issued the first of several *Print: How You Can Do It* manuals. These manuals were initially heavily supplemented with the case for *why* we should be 'doing it ourselves', specifically pitting the 'active producer' against the 'passive consumer'. Printing it yourself allowed you to move from one position to the other. As an LRW worker explained, 'once you start seeing yourself as someone who can *do things*, then you are in a position to take control of your life' (Somewhere in Hackney, 1980).

However, printing was not that easy, especially small offset-litho. Neither was screen-printing, if you wanted to do it well. The left in Britain, with the exception of a resistance to 'slickness', had not taken design and aesthetics particularly seriously, and poorly designed and printed media was common. This attitude would start changing in the 1980s, not just as an effect of institutionalization and 'professionalization', but also through the influence of new entrants into left and social movement fields, for whom the amateurish aesthetics of the 1970s spoke of a political generation who had had their day, and failed (Robinson, interview, 2011). Tied into the expanding field of consumer and promotional culture, there was also a growth of 'design consciousness' in the 1980s (Crowley, 2004). Even parts of the 'old left' began to recognize that a new generation 'could be reached through their pleasure in consumption' (Phillips, 2007: 56). Magazines such as *Marxism Today*, *New Socialist*, and *New Statesman* began to overhaul their design (some with the help of Neville Brody, one of the gurus of the 'designer decade'), contributing to the phenomenon of 'designer socialism'.

The 'DIY' ethos had by no means disappeared in this period; it found particular form in the various peace camps of the 1980s, the post-punk 'zine explosion', and the anarcho-squatting scene. However, the prime tool for its application to media practices was now the photocopier; an eminently more accessible technology, in terms of operation, than both small offset-litho and screen-printing. Photocopying gradually became more widely available in the 1980s, especially with the rise of commercial 'instant print' shops. Some of the small-scale leaflets and newsletters that had once been the province of places like Community Press began to go through these shops (Millet, interview, 2013). In 1983, with financial support from the Greater London Council, Community CopyArt, a collectively run, open access 'instant printshop' appeared in London. They provided a resource for both campaigning groups and artists for whom the photocopier had emerged as creative tool, the two often coming together. They were a one-off, there was no spread of similar resources in London, and despite their lone status CopyArt found it 'hard work getting people to find out about us' (in Kenna et al., 1986: 65). By the early 1990s, they had also become a casualty of the Conservative government's clampdown on municipal socialist spending.

Conclusion

The community printshops were conceived as 'resources' for the cultivation of urban community activism. The cases discussed have shown how this could far exceed the provision of amenable print services for local activists. The media output they made possible, from protest placards, to corruption-exposing community newspapers, 'DIY' welfare rights and squatting manuals, working class autobiographies, anti-deportation, feminist, and festival posters – to give but a few examples – were also part of creating the culture of the diverse field of community activism. This was not just in terms of useful and salient symbolic forms, but also the practices that co-generated them: practices consistent with the 'DIY' and collectivist values of the field. As Calhoun explains, '[h]istorically fields represent successful claims to distinctive kinds of value and to distinctive capacity to provide that value' (Calhoun, 2013: 50). These particular values were not just those of the community activist field; for a period they suffused a wider field of leftist contention. As discussed earlier in the chapter, those values were gradually undermined as the 1980s wore on and although the support occasioned by the movement of ex-radicals into the field of institutional politics may have prolonged the printshops' survival it also partially served to undermine their distinctive value. In the context of institutional approval, 'doing it ourselves' somewhat loses its political meaning. The radical ambitions for urban community activism may have been voluntaristic, yet it was that larger sense of political possibility (illusio) that fuelled the instigation of the printshops and as such laid the foundations for the ongoing provision of valuable resources, not just for that diverse constellation of activity that comprised the field of community activism, but for numerous simultaneous and successive protest, social movement, and cultural groups well into the Thatcher years.

Notes

1. There has been no published historical overview of community activism in the UK. At the time of writing, David Ellis (York University) is working to address this with his doctoral thesis, 'Pavement Politics: Community Action in Urban Britain, 1968–1987'.
2. These reports included: Abel-Smith, B. & Townsend, P (1965) *The Poorest and The Poor.* London: Bell; Lynes, A (1963) *National Assistance and National Prosperity*, Occasional papers in Social Administration, No.5, Welwyn: Codicote Press; Milner Holland (1965) *Report of the Committee on Housing in Greater London*, London: HMSO; Central Advisory Committee for Education Plowden Report (1967) *Children and their Primary Schools* London: HMSO.
3. Examples of Union Place's local publishing included: Nelson, J (1978) *No More Walls*. London: Union Place Community Resource Centre; (1976) *Nine Days 1926: the General Strike in Southwark*. London: Dustbin Press; (1976) *As Things Are: Women, Work and Family in South London*. London: Bonfire Press.
4. Although there were important forerunners to the worker writers movement, such as the History Workshop, founded in the late 1960s by Raphael Samuel. See http://www.historyworkshop.org.uk.

References

Baines, J. (2012). Experiments in democratic participation: Feminist printshop collectives. *Cultural Policy, Criticism and Management Research*, 6: 29–51.

Baldock, P. (1977). Why community action? The historical origins of the radical trend in British community work. *Community Development Journal*, 12(2): 68–74.

Bianchini, F. (1987). GLC R.I.P. Cultural Policies in London 1981–1986. *New Formations*, (1)Spring: 103–117.

Bourdieu, P. & Wacquant, L. (2007). *An Invitation to Reflexive Sociology* Cambridge, MA: Polity Press.

Bourdieu, P. (1996). *The Rules of Art*. Cambridge: Polity Press.

Briggs, A. & Burke, P. (2005). *A Social History of the Media* Cambridge, MA: Polity Press.

Bruce, J. (2011). Interview with author.

Cadman, E., Chester, G., Pivot, A. (1981). *Rolling Our Own: Women as Printers, Publishers and Distributors*. London: Minority Press Group.

Calhoun, C. (2013). For a social history of the present. In P. Gorski (ed.), *Bourdieu and Historical Analysis*. Durham and London: Duke University Press.

Couldry, N. & Curran, J. (eds) (2003). *Contesting Media Power: Alternative Media in a Networked World*. Oxford: Rowman & Littlefield Publishers, Inc.

Craig, G. (1989). Community work and the State. *Community Development Journal*, 24(1).

Crossley, N. (2002). *Making Sense of Social Movements*. Maidenhead: Open University Press.

Crowley, D. (2004). Design magazines and design culture. In R. Poyner (ed.), *Communicate! British Independent Graphic Design*. London: Lawrence King and Barbican Art Gallery.

Cushing, L. (2012). *All of Us or None: Social Justice Posters of the San Francisco Bay Area*. Berkeley: Heyday.

Dickinson, R. (1997). *Imprinting the Sticks: The Alternative Press Beyond*. London Aldershot: Ashgate.

Egan, D. (2006). Bureaucracy and radical politics: The case of the Greater London Council. *New Political Science*, 28(3): 377–400.

Elston, F., Harrison, K. & Whitbread, C. (1983). *Report on Printing Co-operatives in London for GLEB*. Greater London Enterprise Board.

Foster, B. (2011). Interview with author.

Green, P. (2011). Interview with author.

Grimes, S. (2012). Interview with author.

Gwynn-Jones, D. (2011). Interview with author.

Gyford, J. (1985). *The Politics of Local Socialism*. London: George Allen & Unwin.

Hain, P. (1982). The nationalisation of public participation. *Community Development Journal*, 17(1): 36–40.

Hilton, M., Crowson, N., Mouhot, J. F. & McKay, J. (2012). *A Historical Guide to NGOs in Britain: Charities, Civil Society and the Voluntary Sector Since 1945*. London: Palgrave Macmillan.

Holland, G. (2011). Interview with author.

Johnson, C. (2011). Interview with author.

Kenna, C., Medcalf, L. & Walker, R. (1986). *Printing is Easy ...? Community Printshops 1970–1986*. London: Greenwich Mural Workshop.

Kelly, O. (1984). *Community, Art and the State*. London: Comedia.

Lansley, S., Goss, S. & Wolmar, C. (1989). *Councils in Conflict: The Rise and Fall of the Municipal Left*. Basingstoke and London: Macmillan.

Lees, R. & Mayo, M. (1984). *Community Action for Change*. London: Routledge & Kegan Paul.

Lent, A. (2001). *British Social Movements Since 1945: Sex, Colour, Peace and Power*. Basingstoke and New York: Palgrave.

MacPhee, J. (ed.) (2009). *Paper Politics: Socially Engaged Printmaking Today*. Oakland: PM Press.

Marshall, A. (1983). *Changing the Word: The Printing Industry in Transition*. London: Comedia.

Millett, S. (2013). Interview with author.

Moan, C. (2012). Personal correspondence with author.

Morley, D. & Worpole, K. (eds) (1982). *The Republic of Letters: Working Class Writing and Local Publishing.* London: Comedia.

Nigg, H. & Wade, G. (1980). *Community Media.* Zürich: Regenbogen-Verlag.

O' Malley, J. (1977). *The Politics of Community Action.* Nottingham: Spokesman.

Pennington, J. (2011). Interview with author.

Phillips, J. (2005). *Transforming Print: Key Issues Affecting the Development of londonprintstudio.* University of Brighton. PhD thesis.

Phillips, A. (2007). The alternative press. In K. Coyer, T. Dowmunt & A. Fountain (eds), *The Alternative Media Handbook.* Abingdon: Routledge.

Pollard, I. (2011). Interview with author.

Radford, J. (2004). The point of the battle is to win it. In H. Curtis & M. Sanderson (eds), *The Unsung Sixties: Memoirs of Social Innovation.* London: Whiting and Birch.

Robinson, A. (2011). Interview with author.

Rose, C. (2011). Interview with author.

Rowbottom, S., Segal, L. & Wainwright, H. (1980). *Beyond the Fragments: Feminism and the Making of Socialism.* London: Merlin Press.

Saunders, N. (1974). *Alternative London/5: A Guide to How, When and Where.* Wildwood House.

Segal, L. (1980). A Local Experience. In S. Rowbotham, L. Segal & H. Wainwright (eds), *Beyond the Fragments: Feminism and the Making of Socialism.* London: Merlin Press.

Segal, L. (2007). *Making Trouble: Life and Politics.* London: Serpents Tail.

Sklair, L. (1975). The struggle against the Housing Finance Act. *Socialist Register,* 12: 250–292.

Smith, L. & Jones, D. (eds) (1981). *Deprivation, Participation and Community Action.* London. Boston. Henley: Routledge.

Somewhere in Hackney (1980). Director: Ron Orders

Swash, T. (2011). Interview with author.

Swingler, R. (2011). Interview with author.

Tompsett, F. (2013). Interview with author.

Waddington, P. (2008). Looking ahead: Community work in the 1980s. In G. Craig, K. Popple & M. Shaw (eds), *Community Development in Theory and Practice: An International Reader.* Nottingham: Spokesman.

Williams, P. (2011). Interview with author.

Worpole, K. (1978) Afterword in *Worker Writers & Community Publishers, Writing* London: Federation of Worker Writers and Community Publishers.

Zeitlyn, J. (1974, 1975, 1980). *Print: How You Can Do It Yourself.* London: Inter-Action.

Index

GPSR Compliance
The European Union's (EU) General Product Safety Regulation (GPSR) is a set
of rules that requires consumer products to be safe and our obligations to
ensure this.

If you have any concerns about our products, you can contact us on

ProductSafety@springernature.com

In case Publisher is established outside the EU, the EU authorized
representative is:

Springer Nature Customer Service Center GmbH
Europaplatz 3
69115 Heidelberg, Germany